THE FIRST OF HEARTS

Selected Letters of Mrs. Henry Adams

1865 - 1883

INTRODUCTION BY

COKIE ROBERTS

EDITED BY

WARD THORON

Willowbank Books

San Francisco Los Angeles

Originally Published
December 1936
by

THE ATLANTIC MONTHLY PRESS BOOKS
LITTLE BROWN AND COMPANY IN ASSOCIATION
WITH THE ATLANTIC MONTHLY COMPANY

Reprinted by permission
Massachusetts Historical Society

Willowbank Books edition
September 2011

ISBN: 978-1-4634-2452-7 (sc)
ISBN: 978-1-4634-2451-0 (hc)
ISBN: 978-1-4634-2453-4 (e)

Printed in the United States of America
This book is printed on acid-free paper

Produced by

authorHOUSE®

AuthorHouse™
1663 Liberty Drive
Bloomington, IN 47403
www.authorhouse.com
Phone: 1-800-839-8640

"Is it any consolation to remember her as she was? that bright intrepid spirit, that keen fine intellect, that lofty scorn of all that was mean, that social charm which made your house such a one as Washington never knew before, and made hundreds of people love her as much as they admired her."
    — John Hay to Henry Adams, December 9, 1885

"Tea often stretched into dinner, and dinner into a party lasting till midnight. Delighted with their delight in each other, the friends sealed their bond with a name: 'The Five of Hearts.'"
    — Patricia O'Toole, "The Five of Hearts"

CONTENTS

INTRODUCTION

by

Cokie Roberts

"Congress bumbles on. Everyone laughs at its assumed spasms of virtue, no one is deceived by any reform pretenses." Clover Adams's political commentary in 1883 could serve as the lead of a legislative story today—that's one reason why it's so much fun to read her mail. First published in 1936, *The Letters of Mrs. Henry Adams* were edited and annotated by Ward Thoron, who was married to her niece. Though Thoron expunged some of Mrs. Adams's most derogatory descriptions of political players, he left many wonderfully wicked observations of the Washington scene, where Henry Adams and his wife played prominent roles in the early 1880s. Clover Adams's caustic commentary on the place and its people came in the form of weekly letters to her father in Massachusetts; those are the letters reprinted here.

Marian Hooper was born in Boston on September 13, 1843. The nickname Clover came from her mother, who died when Clover was only five years old. After that she and her older sister and brother were raised by their father, Dr. Robert William Hooper, a physician and graduate of Harvard college. Her mother's distinguished Massachusetts Sturgis clan (before they married, Henry Adams wrote to a friend that his intended "belongs to a sort of clan, as all Bostonians do") was marked by mental illness. That family history was so well known, including the gossip that Clover witnessed her aunt's suicide, that when Henry announced their engagement he probably anticipated his brother Charles's reaction: "Heavens!—no!—they're all crazy as coots. She'll kill herself just like her Aunt." In fact Henry begged his younger brother Brooks to stick up for him because he knew his choice would "make a row, and people will discuss it to please themselves."

But Henry Adams, son of a statesman, grandson and great-grandson of presidents, was smitten with the young woman's "intelligence and sympathy." Those qualities plus Clover's "very active and quick mind," and the fact that "she decidedly has humor and will appreciate *our* wit" attracted the 34 year-old Henry to the 28 year-old "young female," but he was, to put it mildly, clear-eyed about her. "She certainly is not handsome...she knows her mind uncommon well...she dresses badly...she has enough money to be quite independent," he said by way of introduction. Then, after he had spent a month living with the Hoopers before the tiny private wedding on June 23, 1872, Henry explained that having had no mother, Clover "has grown up to look after herself and has a certain vein of personality which approaches eccentricity. This is very attractive to me, but then I am absurdly in love." Confessing that he found it "rather droll to examine women's minds," he added, "They are a queer mixture of odds and ends, poorly mastered and utterly unconnected." He did acknowledge that his wife-to-be "reads German—also Latin—also, I fear, a little Greek, but very little."

Reading that along with Clover's joke on their honeymoon that Henry had insisted she buy new gowns in Paris because "People who study Greek must take pains in their dress," I was reminded of a letter written almost 100 years before from Henry's great-grandfather John Adams to his wife Abigail. Adams was off in Philadelphia helping draft the Declaration of Independence when he discovered his daughter was studying classical languages. Grumbling that "it is scarcely reputable for young ladies to understand Latin and Greek," the absent father decided it would be all right for her to continue what was considered a masculine pursuit as long as no one knew about it.

Henry, despite his denigrating comments about women's minds, was following an Adams tradition, taking on an educated woman of strong intellect with definite views of her own. He picked a mate from a family where women were encouraged in expressing those views, achieving the education to back them up and advocating for women's education in general. Clover's sister Ellen was working to create the "Harvard annex," the institution for women that became Radcliffe College, something Henry's great grandmother Abigail would have championed. At one point Ellen asked Clover to see if she could get some members of Washington society to contribute to her "Annex." The response: "It's no use to expect anything from 'Washington nabobs,' bless her innocent heart! No one here cares for higher education—for women or men either; they'd laugh in one's face."

But not many people in Washington dared laugh in the face of Mrs. Henry Adams. Soon after she and her husband moved to town in 1877 they became the social arbiters. He had quit his job at Harvard to work on a book about Albert Gallatin, Thomas Jefferson's Treasury Secretary and his grandfather John Quincy Adams's co-negotiator of the Treaty of Ghent and then ambassador to Britain. Twelve years earlier, Clover had been to Washington to witness the grand review of the Union Army at the end of the Civil War and her letter describing that exciting scene starts this volume. But the years after the war brought chaos and corruption to Washington as the "gilded age" dawned. In 1877 Republican Rutherford Hayes had recently won a bitterly contested election, keeping the city in a partisan uproar after the impeachment of Andrew Johnson and the tawdriness of the Grant administration. Having a new well-connected couple on the scene must have been welcome. Perfect strangers clamored to be received at the house Clover and Henry rented on Lafayette Square. Even so, Adams's book on Gallatin landed with a thud. But the research had kindled the author's interest in the era, so the couple decamped for Europe for Henry to start work on his massive histories of the presidencies between Adams and Adams. The pair returned to Washington in the fall of 1880, with yet another president, James A. Garfield, newly elected and that's where the letters here begin.

For all her worldly sophistication, Clover Adams was probably glad to get back home. "The more we travel," she had written to her father from London, "The more profoundly impressed we are with the surpassing-solid comfort of the average American household and its freedom from sham." Of course her household was far from average. Her letters from Europe go on and on about all the expensive things they bought, which they proceeded to install in their Washington home. But home decor didn't long occupy Clover's interests. "The air is thick with political flakes," she reported soon after they arrived, as she joined in the speculation about who might be in Garfield's Cabinet. Then six months later, after Garfield was assassinated, the speculation started all over again about Chester A. Arthur's Cabinet, but the city was distracted by the trial of Garfield's murderer, which Clover found "intensely interesting."

What's striking here is how open the political scene was to women. Historians tend either to insist that women occupied no political space before suffrage or, more commonly, they ignore women altogether. Reading their letters always gives the lie to that omission. Women might not have had a great deal of power (though some, like Dolley Madison, definitely did) but they did exercise considerable influence over powerful men. And Mrs. Henry Adams quickly assumed influential womanhood in Washington. As he was leaving his post as Secretary of the Interior, the Adams's old friend Carl Shurz brought *her* his report on Indian affairs, which she deemed "worth reading." At a dinner seated next to Secretary of State Frederick Frelinghuysen, "we had a good deal of talk about politics," where she advised on how the Republicans could carry Massachusetts.

Women's letters tend to be far more interesting than those of their male contemporaries because they cover so much more of life. In them we read not only about politics, though Clover's epistles are full of that permanent preoccupation of Washington, but also about how people look and how their houses are furnished and what they're wearing and serving at their dinners. Like many women, Clover also includes a few recipes for her father to pass on to his cook, highlighting her dish of oysters stewed with curry powder. Oddly, though she tells us about her time spent on horseback, Clover doesn't write about her photography, an unusual avocation at that time and one in which she excelled. We also learn about local customs, both interesting and onerous.

It amused me, for example, that Henry Adams's wife so despised the Washington institution of "calling," where people in government and society were expected to present themselves and their "calling card" at another person's home, signaling respect. "The 'calling' nuisance requires a cool head and imperturbable nerves to meet it squarely," she complained. Clover probably didn't know that Henry's grandmother, Louisa Catherine Adams, had caused a Cabinet crisis when as the wife of Secretary of State John Quincy Adams she refused to call on the wife of every member of Congress who came to town. That decision earned her a summons to the White House and dressing down for her stubbornness. Louisa only relented when it became clear that her perceived rudeness might harm her husband's presidential aspirations.

But Clover had no political campaign to worry about and there were certain people she simply refused to acknowledge. At the top of that list: "the rat Blaine," James G. Blaine, the perpetual candidate for president and former Senator from Maine. "For us it will be most awkward," Clover admitted when Garfield named Blaine Secretary of State, "never having called on them before, it will simply be impossible to make up to them now." When Blaine was implicated in scandal and ousted from State, Clover gloated, "I am glad indeed that we never broke the man's bread nor so much as pulled his doorbell."

But Clover and Henry Adams broke bread with so many others, either entertaining or being entertained nightly. Many of the best-known names of the era sat at their table; many others wanted to but weren't invited. Henry James was an old friend (though Clover told him not to bring Oscar Wilde when he came to visit) and the Turkish Ambassador Aristarchi Bey practically lived at the Adams house. With their close friends John and Clara Hay and Clarence King they formed a tight group called the Five of Hearts, and the Hays and Adamses built huge houses adjoining each other on Lafayette Square. (The houses are now gone, replaced by the venerable Hay-Adams Hotel.) Reading Clover's mail, the names echo from the early Republic—Frelinghuysen, Fish, Clymer, Schuyler, Van Rensselaer, Bayard, all families who provided public servants generation after generation, just as the Adamses had. But one newcomer started showing up with great frequency at the house on H Street: the beautiful Elizabeth Cameron, wife of Senator Donald J. Cameron of Pennsylvania. She was a friend of both Clover and Henry, but Washington is a gossipy town and there was plenty of gossip about just what the relationship might be between Adams and the unhappily married Lizzie Cameron.

Henry had been working on his histories for years, publishing sections here and there. But he also penned two anonymous novels. One, *Democracy*, so accurately skewered the Washington establishment that a parlor game to guess the author went on for years. Some friends were convinced that the tart-tongued Clover had written the book, and she certainly must have contributed to it, but it was Henry's sly doing. His second novel, *Esther*, was published under a pseudonym, but if Clover read it she would have certainly known her husband's style. The book was vicious to the character who was clearly Clover, rapturous toward the Lizzie Cameron clone. It would have been devastating for any wife to read. A little more than a year after *Esther* was published, Clover Adams's beloved father became deathly ill. With her sister, Clover sat vigil at Dr. Hooper's bedside until he died on April 13, 1885. She herself never recovered. Adams tried to cheer her up and she wrote that he was tender and dear. What then was the portrayal of her in *Esther* all about?

On December 6, a Sunday, the day Clover Adams had set aside to write to her father over the years, Henry went to the couple's bedroom in the big pile of a house they had built on H Street. He found his wife lying on the floor, having swallowed some of the potassium cyanide she used in her photography. She was forty-two years old. When the obituary writers learned that Henry Adams's wife had committed suicide, they turned her tongue against her, claiming she was known for saying "bitter things." But the Boston *Transcript* hailed Marian Hooper Adams as a "brilliant and accomplished woman." And when her letters were published in 1936 the review in *Time* magazine judged their "spontaneous liveliness" revealed "a vital, vivid, unexpected character."

Here then are those letters.

Cokie Roberts is a political commentator for ABC News and a senior news analyst for NPR News, where she was the Congressional Correspondent for more than 10 years. From 1996 – 2002 she and Sam Donaldson co-anchored the weekly ABC interview program *This Week*. She is the winner of three Emmys and the author of *Founding Mothers: The Women Who Raised Our Nation* and *The New York Times* number one bestseller *We Are Our Mothers' Daughters* among other books.

PART I

AN EARLY LETTER

May 1865

Marian Hooper to Mary Louisa Shaw

HISTORICAL NOTE

The Grand Review of Grant's and Sherman's Armies was the culminating event of perhaps the most dramatic six weeks in American history.

On April 9, 1865 Robert E. Lee surrendered the Army of Northern Virginia to Ulysses S. Grant in Appomattox, Virginia. Four days later, on April 13, John Wilkes Booth shot Abraham Lincoln as the President watched a performance of "Our American Cousin" in Ford's Theater in Washington, D.C. On April 26, Joseph E. Johnston surrendered the last remaining important Confederate army to William Tecumseh Sherman and the Army of Tennessee. On the night of the same day the assassin Booth was shot and killed by a Union solider at Richard H. Garrett's farm in southern Maryland.

And finally in late May the nation's eyes turned to the Grand Review of the Armies, which took place in Washington over two days, May 23 and 24, 1865. It had been conceived as a purely military spectacle, a passing of troops in front of their commanders before dismissal and disbanding. But all the emotions of the past four horrific years somehow converged on the moment and released an overpowering burst of feeling. The Grand Review became not simply a massive military parade, but a tribute to the victorious soldiers, an act of national rebirth, a farewell to war. In the words of historian Charles Braceleen Flood, it "turned out to be something so vast, so moving, that its effect overwhelmed even the generals who organized it."

There are many long, fascinating accounts of the Grand Review in the standard histories of the Civil War, but for freshness of detail and charm of voice, few can match the letter that young 22-year-old Marian Hooper wrote to her cousin Mary Louise Shaw describing her own personal experience of it. The letter, an important American document in its own right, makes a perfect introduction to the remarkable character and vitality of Clover Adams.

The notes in this and all subsequent letters are by Ward Thoron. Some have been shortened for this edition. Thoron's sources are cited in the notes or in the Bibliography.

THE GRAND REVIEW OF GRANT'S AND SHERMAN'S ARMIES

MAY 23 & 24, 1865

Marian Hooper to Mary Louisa Shaw

114 BEACON STREET,
Sunday, May 28, 1865.[1]

DEAREST LOU: I can think of no better way of showing the deep sympathy I feel for you, in being away from this victorious country in these past two months, than by writing you a long letter telling you what I have seen. To begin at the end instead of the beginning, I got home from Washington last week, having had one week of intense excitement and enjoyment—for one week I have had my eyes wide open and my ears and my mouth, and my pulse and heart going like race horses.

A week ago Thursday, Ellen, Pater, and I were coming home from Greenfield, where we had been making a visit at the Davises'. Reading the newspaper in the cars, I found there was to be a grand review of Grant's and Sherman's armies the next week. Then and there I vowed to myself that go I would. I begged Father to take me, but he hooted at the idea of such a thing. I lay in wait for John Reed,[2] to attack him as he went down town. He came, and I seized him and begged him to take me. He scoffed and jeered, manlike, and left me momentarily quenched. I then stamped for an hour or two; said all the naughty words I could think of—then put on my most festive bonnet and went forth to seek a man. I went to Uncle Henry's.[3] He wanted to go but could not possibly. I came home, and found Ellen had "tuke" the fever since morning and found Mollie Felton[4] also infected. Well, the

---

[1] Dated from her father's house at Boston; to her cousin Mary Louisa Shaw, then in Europe.
[2] John Reed, only child of her aunt, Elizabeth Trevett Hooper, wife of Benjamin T. Reed of Boston.
[3] Dr. Henry Jacob Bigelow, husband of her aunt, Susan Sturgis.
[4] Mary Felton, daughter of President Felton of Harvard College.

3

day wore on, and never a man in the horizon. Ellen said, "Despair is a free man, hope a slave," and folded her hands. I said, "Ellen, you're craven-hearted, I *shall* go." I drove to Brookline in the rain, to find Alice Mason.[1] She was out. I came home to find Annette Rogers,[2] who, hearing at the Sanitary how we felt, had attacked her father—and he, heaven bless him, said that he would take her and Mollie and Ellen and me. He telegraphed for rooms. We waited. At noon Saturday came the answer, "I cannot engage you any rooms." We held a council of war, and decided to go.

We left Boston Saturday evening, and travelled all night and all the next night—got to Washington—no rooms—no place to see the review from, and no chance apparently. Ellen and I looked at each other blankly—then said that we would go to Uncle Sam's.[3] He was just home from the West. We came to his house, where President Johnson has been living since the assassination; soldiers pacing up and down, we passed in; guards at the entry, we asked for Uncle Sam. He fairly staggered at seeing us. His house was filled with the President's guests—he, himself, in that position. We told him we only wanted a corner to lie in; so up we went to the attic, and agreed to pass as the housekeeper's nieces—to take our meals with her. It was all he could do, not cheerful, but a little better than sleeping in the streets, which we thought might be our fate. Looking out of the attic window, whom should I spy plough-ing through the mud but James Higginson[4] with an orderly riding behind. I called, "Jim, Jim!" at the top of my voice. A sentry ran after him, and he came booted and spurred. We told him we did not want to stay where we were if he could get us a room anywhere else. We then went to the Sanitary Headquarters, found our party, and that there was an attic room in a house near Willard's;[5] we

---

[1] Alice Mason Hooper, widow of her cousin, William Sturgis Hooper (1833-1863); he was an aide on the staff of General Banks and died in the service; she was a daughter of Jonathan Mason and Isabella Weyman.

[2] Annette Rogers (1841-1920), daughter of Henry Bromfield Rogers (1802-1887) and Anna Powell Mason Perkins; Mr. Rogers had taken an active part in the work of the Sanitary Commission, a body charged with the distribution of relief to the soldiers.

[3] Samuel Hooper's house was at the northwest corner of 15th and H Streets.

[4] James Higginson, brother of Henry L. Higginson.

[5] Willard's Hotel, at 15th and F Streets.

could sleep there and take our meals at the hotel. So we decided on that; wrote a note to Uncle Sam, and all four of us turned in to our welcome attic room. I only tell you all this to show you what fun we had in meeting one obstacle after another, and knocking them over as fast as they came up. Even the horse-cars were engaged to sleep in, and many people, it was said, passed the night in the street. Mollie and Annette and I drove to Georgetown to find an officer in a hospital, for whom I had some money. A lovely summer afternoon—blue sky overhead—roses everywhere all over the houses—regiment after regiment came marching past, bands playing—squads of contrabands looking on. We sang out as each regiment passed, "What regiment are you?" "Michigan!" "Wisconsin!" "Iowa!" And so on! It was so jolly, and they all looked at us as we passed, in a pleased sort of a way—then home to dinner. Before night we had tickets to the Congressional platform—the best place from which to see the review—Uncle Sam got them for us. In the evening Uncle Sam brought a Major Knox to see us, a young fellow—officer of the guard—who knew a thing or two, having been through Sherman's campaign—Vicksburg and all. Ellen and I drove with them to the Forbeses' to make a call.

Tuesday A.M., up at five-thirty, the most perfect day I ever saw; a bad breakfast—so bad! and then off to our seats. Mr. Wolcott, Ellen, and I to the Congressional platform; the others, opposite us at Mr. Forbes's,[1] which he put up by permission of General Augur

---

[1] John Murray Forbes (1813-1898), successful merchant, ardent patriot, pioneer in the development of the Western railroads; his own description of the incident mentioned is to be found in Vol. II (p. 140) of Mrs. Hughes's *Letters and Recollections of John Murray Forbes:*—

"The great event of our last days in Washington was the grand review of the armies of Sherman and Grant, which must have taken place early in May, and in which I had the chance to take a hand. When the preparations for it were going on, I found that it was planned to have only a very small grandstand for the President and the government officers, right in front of the White House; and it occurred to me that, with plenty of room on each side, it would be a good thing to have seats for the convalescents of the army who were well enough to be out, there being at that time a very large number in the hospitals around Washington. So I went to General Augur and proposed it, he being then in command of the city. There were all sorts of difficulties; no money; no time; no orders for anything more. It was Saturday afternoon and the review was to begin Monday morning, but I would not 'take no for an answer,' and proposed to the general to

to seat wounded soldiers from hospitals, who came, some in ambulances, some hobbling on crutches—and wasn't it just like Mr. Forbes with his kind heart. We were early and got nice seats, roofed over to keep off the sun; and eighty feet from us across the street sat the President, Generals Grant, Sherman, Howard, Hancock, Meade, and many others—Secretaries of War and Navy—diplomatic corps and ladies. The platform covered with Stars and Stripes, gay flags; between the pillars pots of flowers—azaleas, cactus, and all in full bloom; then Grant's victories in great letters laid over the flags between the pillars—Vicksburg, Shiloh, Richmond, Wilderness, Antietam, Gettysburg. Up drove Uncle Sam's carriage—Martin stately on the box—out got the President. He sat in the middle of the box, Stanton on his right—Grant on Stanton's right—Sherman in the corner on the left, opposite Grant; and then after each crack general had passed out of sight with his division, he came on foot and into the box, shaking hands all around, and then looked on with the rest.

About nine-thirty the band struck up "John Brown," and by came Meade with his staff, splendidly mounted. Almost all the officers in the army had their hands filled with roses, and many had wreaths around their horses' necks. After Meade passed there was a pause. Suddenly a horse dashed by with a hatless rider, whose long golden curls were streaming in the wind; his arms hung with a wreath, and his horse's neck with one, too. It was General Custer, who stands as a cavalry officer next to Sheridan. He soon got control of his horse and came back at a more sober pace, put himself at the head of his division, and they came riding by, 10,000 men. Sheridan's cavalry, Custer's Division, are called cutthroats, and each officer and man wears a scarlet scarf around

---

give me an order for the ground on each side of the grandstand, to which he with much promptness acceded, and I at once got hold of the carpenter who had made the changes in my hired house, and before Monday morning he had platforms and benches for about 1500 sitters. Only a part of these could be filled by the convalescents, but they proved very useful, for no provision had been made for navy officers and many others who ought to have been thought of. I had what tickets I wanted for myself and friends, and had the opportunity to oblige a great many who crowded into Washington for the spectacle, among whom I remember Professor Benjamin Peirce of Cambridge. My seats were next to the grandstand, so that we saw everything to great advantage."

his neck with ends hanging half a yard long. Among the cavalry came the dear old Second, Caspar Crowninshield looking splendidly on his war horse—then came artillery, pontoon bridges, ambulances, army wagons, negro and white pioneers with axes and spaces, Zouave regiments, some so picturesque with red bag trousers, pale sea-green sashes, and dark blue jackets braided with red, red fezzes on their heads with yellow tassels. Other Zouave regiments came with entirely different uniforms, gay and Arablike. And so it came, this glorious old army of the Potomac, for six hours marching past, eighteen or twenty miles long, their colours telling their sad history. Some regiments with nothing but a bare pole, a little bit of rag only, hanging a few inches, to show where their flag had been. Others that had been Stars and Stripes, with one or two stripes hanging, all the rest shot away. It was a strange feeling to be so intensely happy and triumphant, and yet to feel like crying. As each corps commander and division general rode by, the President and secretaries and generals stood up, and down went the swords as salute, and the colours dipped. Between the different corps there was often a delay of five minutes or so. Then the crowd rushed to the front of the stand, cheering the different generals, who had to stand and acknowledge it. Grant looked so bashful and modest with his little boy sitting on his lap—it was touching to see him. Sherman was nervous and looked bored—talked fast all the time, his hands gesticulating. I like the President's face—it looked strong and manly.

About half past three the procession ended. We got separated from our party; met Jim and we [went] to the Forbeses'; found about thirty people there having luncheon-dinner, and fell in with them—General Barlow, Hallowell girls, stray officers, etc. About seven P.M. Annette Rogers and I went off to see Ford's Theatre. It is closed, but we went round to the back—saw the stable where Booth's horse was kept, and the back door by which he escaped— found a coloured woman who saw him lead his horse up to the theatre door (she lives in the alley, and said she went to the door, hearing a noise—saw, as he stood in the lighted doorway, that it was "Mr. Booth," as she called him. About an hour after, she heard a noise as of a rushing horse—ran to the door, but the horse and rider were out of sight). She had been one of the witnesses, as she heard Booth call "Ned" three or four times to a man in the theater to come and hold his horse. From that we went to the house, where the President was carried and where he died. The room is a small one in an ell on the ground floor; the pillow is soaked with blood, and the pillow case; it is left just as it was on that night—a painful sight, and yet we wanted to see it, as it is an historical fact and it makes it so vivid to be in the place where such a tragedy has been enacted.

Wednesday, another glorious day—bright and cool, and we sit in the same place as before and see Sherman ride by at the head of 70,000 men, who, in physique and marching, surpass decidedly the Potomac Army. Regiments where the average height is six foot two or three—real Americans all, intelligent and brave-looking. Very little cavalry in this army—squads of negroes, picked up upon the march, with picks and shovels on their shoulders. At the end of one army corps come two very small white donkeys, each ridden by a small black boy; a black boy marching by the donkey lifts his cap and salutes the President's box, which is only done by generals in the procession, and the fun makes us all laugh. Sherman has come into the box, and today looks eager and happy, talking to his wife, whom he met yesterday for the first time for two years. They all shake hands with Sherman as he comes in—but when Stanton holds out his hand, Sherman looks at him as if he were a dog, and hardly vouchsafes a cool bow. It's a breach of military etiquette, if not worse, as the Secretary of War is his superior officer. Sherman is undoubtedly a genius, but not a man of half the character of Grant; he is furious at the way in which his disgraceful treaty with Joe Johnston has been received, and cannot control his temper. I make the acquaintance of a reporter of the *New York Herald*, who sits next to me. He's been through Sherman's campaign and tells me the names of the generals as they ride by. Howard looks finely with his one arm; and General Logan, with Indian blood in his veins—very little of anything else, I should think. By and by comes the dear old 2d Massachusetts Infantry,[1] not an officer in it now that we know. General William Dwight from the sidewalk calls out, "Three cheers for the 2d Mas-

---

[1] The 2d Massachusetts Infantry Regiment took part in the battles of Winchester, Cedar Mountain, Antietam, Chancellorsville, Gettysburg, Atlanta, the March to the Sea, Savannah, and Sherman's Carolina campaign.

sachusetts!" and they come with a will. By four o'clock it is all over, leaving one stunned, almost, with all this excitement—then a hasty dinner; after which Ellen and Jim and I go to walk—come home starved. Jim is sent to buy us crackers and fruit, and we sit and eat and talk on the doorstep till bedtime, different people dropping in. Then we four girls hie to our loft, and chatter and laugh till Morpheus becomes inexorable.

Thursday morning, up early, and off to the trial of the conspirators—a long way off. Ellen and I stay about half an hour, and then come away, having an engagement to drive with Uncle Sam and Major Knox. We drive through a lovely wooded road, Sherman's army lying on each side of the road and under the trees; mules and horses tied to fences; army wagons in long succession filing by; batteries, etc. We go to General Logan's headquarters on a grassy hill. Major Knox introduces us to him and some of his staff. We stay there some time; then we drive off to find General Sherman's headquarters, which seems to be well-nigh impossible. When we find it, to our disgust the General has gone in town. So we drive back to Washington, get a dinner, and then we four girls go to Armory [Square] Hospital to tea. Ellen has written you about it, so I won't, except that I never had such an interesting evening in my life. Before tea I talked to some men in the ward—one bright little fellow, wounded at Cedar Creek, who was standing by Charley Lowell when he was shot. Another young fellow, sitting up near him, said he was in that fight, and after it was over he saw General Sheridan come up, throw his arms round Custer's neck, and kiss him, saying, "Well, old fellow, you've done a good work today."

Friday, a pouring rain, so we can't go over the river to Arlington and the camps, as we meant to—Jim and Ellen go to the hospital—Annette and I drag poor Mr. Rogers to the court again. It's crowded; but we squeeze in and get some reporters' chairs. Mr. Rogers waits outside and reads the paper. Being a woman has its advantages on this occasion. The evidence is not very interesting, but it is to see the prisoners. Mrs. Surratt[1] only shows her eyes, keeping her fan to her face. All the men except Paine have weak,

---

[1] The conspirators had their ordinary rendezvous at the house of Mrs. Mary E. Surratt. She and the other conspirators were tried by a military commission, and she was hanged on July 7, 1865.

low faces. Paine is handsome but utterly brutal, and sits there a head higher than all the others, his great gray eyes rolling about restlessly, not fixing on anything, looking like a wild animal at bay. It is a sad impressive sight.

Friday night we leave Washington and get home in twenty-four hours. I am very tired. It's taken me three hours to write this letter and I haven't written it carefully at all. It is absurd to try and describe such a week—I know that you will like it better than nothing and so send it, hoping that some words will be legible.

PART II

LETTERS TO HER FATHER
FROM WASHINGTON

1880-1883

HISTORICAL NOTE

After their marriage in June, 1872, Henry and Clover Adams went on an extended trip abroad. They visited London, Paris, and various cities in Italy and then spent three months in Egypt traveling along the Nile, a not completely satisfactory experience. Indeed, Clover may have suffered a brief form of nervous breakdown during this part of the trip, though biographers differ on that question. The couple returned to Boston finally in November, 1873. There Henry resumed his editorship of *The North American Review* and also took up a new post as assistant professor of history at Harvard.

In the summer of 1879 they made a second long trip abroad and toured in England, France, Spain, and Morocco. They returned in early October, 1880, not to Boston, but to Washington, where Henry intended to pursue his career as an independent historian.

In Washington they rented a house from William Corcoran on President's Square, better known now as Lafayette Square. Clover's first letter to her father describes the house. As Henry wrote to a friend, "I fear there is a great deal to be done to it before we can get in . . . I look forward placidly to recurring winters and summers in Washington and Beverly, until a cheery tomb shall provide us with a permanent abode for all seasons."

Despite Henry's characteristic if "cheery" gloom, it was an exciting time to begin their Washington residence. The Presidential campaign of 1880 was at its height, and the results of the state elections in Ohio and Indiana, which had just taken place, were a source of encouragement to the Republicans—the Adamses were firm Republicans—after an earlier disappointment in Maine. In the Republican Party more generally the situation was somewhat mixed. The small group of New York and Pennsylvania politicians who had long dominated the party had failed to have General Ulysses S. Grant renominated for an unprecedented third term. In the course of a memorable convention in Chicago the party had chosen instead General James Garfield as their standard bearer.

Once installed in Washington, the Adamses began to show considerable interest in Garfield's campaign. Politics and politicians will figure prominently in these letters. But like the great letter describing the Grand Review, they will gradually disclose Clover's vivid and memorable personality. At the same time they present an unrivaled portrait of life in the nation's capital twenty years after the Civil War. This is the period that Henry's biographer Ernest Samuels called "The Golden Age of Lafayette Square."

It should be noted that "Wormley's" refers to Wormley's Hotel, located at 1500 H St. in Washington. "Boojum" is the Adams's Skye terrier.

CHAPTER I

WASHINGTON

OCTOBER 1880-MAY 1881

WASHINGTON,
Sunday, 10th October, 1880.

DEAR PATER: Thanks for your note of the 7th. It seems unnatural to be seeing old friends here before all of you. We left New York Thursday; Misses Schurz[1] waited a day to come on with us, and Wayne MacVeagh[2] was on the train,—Cameron's brother-in-law,—full of politics and most interesting to our long-famished souls. He is an Independent, and the clan Cameron is not in sympathy with him.

Lovely weather here—cool and crisp, a fire every evening. Up to our eyes in work, hardly time to eat and sleep; Corcoran sweet as barley candy, and the house bids fair to suit us well. All plumbing is to be in new brick addition on east side, separated from main house by double brick wall; laundry in brick building in yard, which has five rooms and will hold coachman and any servants we may wish. We ought to stay and oversee everything, but of course shall not. We find a cabinet-maker who will make wooden man-

---

[1] The daughters of Carl Schurz, the Secretary of the Interior.
[2] Wayne MacVeagh (1853-1917) married, after the death of his first wife, Virginia Cameron; he was an able lawyer and devoted to the cause of good government, was one of the leaders in a movement to reform the Republican Party in Pennsylvania, long dominated by his father-in-law, Simon Cameron, and his brother-in-law, James Donald Cameron. At the Chicago Convention, he and his colleague, Wharton Barker, had succeeded in bringing about a defection in the Pennsylvania delegation from the "unit rule," and this action of theirs, helping as it did to confirm the Independents in the New York delegation in a similar stand, was largely responsible for the adoption by the Convention of an anti-unit rule which ended the chance of renominating Grant. After more than thirty-three ballots, the supporters of James G. Blaine and John Sherman finally agreed on General Garfield, who was then nominated. As a peace offering to the Stalwarts who had remained faithful to Grant, Chester A. Arthur was nominated for the Vice Presidency.

13

telpieces and library bookcases; his work in two of our friends' new houses is quite as good as Leach's. This saves us much bother and expense. Have taken six years' lease with right to renew, pay two hundred dollars a month; Corcoran spends twenty-five hundred dollars in repairs and pays all taxes. On the second floor we get six bedrooms, two bathrooms, and new servants' staircase—verandas behind all three stories.

Miss Clymer and her brother[1] here this A.M.; he sailed in White Star three days before us and had nasty voyage—head winds and gale. What a scratch we had! We go to New York Wednesday and hope to head for Boston Friday; will write or telegraph from there. *Adiós.* Affectionately

M. A.

WASHINGTON,
Sunday, October 31st, 1880.

DEAR PATER: Just a few lines to tell you of our being here. We had a very busy day in New York on Thursday—on our feet from breakfast time to dusk, Boojum knowing himself a champion shopper and enjoying it, especially the feminine blandishments which fell on his ears: "That sweet little dog!" We bagged our library paper at Herter's, four vases at Vantine's for gas lamps. Tell Ned the last importation of which he sent word to Bil Bigelow was Chinese. Got five cheap bedroom rugs at Sloane's; said "How do you do" and "Good-bye" in the same breath to Mrs. Lawrence and Miss Chapman[2] at the Brevoort, and fled South into a warm storm. After heroic struggles we got some south rooms out of Wormley,—squalid and dear,—but we shall do very well and it will be an incentive to driving workmen as hard as we can. We find the house progressing and no mistakes are made in our absence. It is a solid old pile, outside all round fourteen inches of brick; no laths, but plastered on to the brick; such stout chimneys that we can have four-foot openings in the ground-floor rooms.

Yesterday was such a driving storm that we saw no one except those in the house, a cup of tea at Miss Schurz's off my own table

---

[1] Miss Mary Clymer and her brother, Shubrick Clymer. She later married, in 1889, Thomas F. Bayard.

[2] Mrs. Bigelow Lawrence and her sister, Miss Fanny Chapman.

being the only outing. Today is warm and windy; Mrs. Loring and Harriet[1] have just been to see me; the former is to celebrate her golden wedding in the winter. We hear nothing of politics—have seen only diplomats, who never talk of them. I hope you too are warm and sunny today; Boojum sends his love and thanks to Betsy; mine to Fanny and the magpies[2]—I send them three pairs India rubbers tomorrow. Ever affectionately

M. A.

P.S. I forgot to say that on Thursday evening Henry met at the Brevoort my partner in the emerald mine scheme. He took the Spanish papers from me in March on his way home; has since then consulted the superintendent of mines of New Granada, finds from him that the mine I found in the British Museum manuscript has been reopened from local tradition, but they find the quartz too hard to work the emeralds profitably in that mine. But it shows that my trail was not a false one, though fruitless, and blows his theory to atoms. So, like your oft-quoted friend, we have split on that rock called quartz's.

WASHINGTON,
Sunday, November 7th, 1880.

DEAR PATER: Thanks for yours of Sunday last. Doll's[3] death is indeed a real loss to Boston—his partner will scarcely fill his place. We've had a quiet, restful week here, our work at the house not yet begun—several days of rain, alternating with summer heat, making even a wood fire impossible. Wednesday we took a lovely drive; the leaves hang on bravely here. Our stable is painting, and so much epizoöty raging that we shall let our horses stay in Virginia for a week yet. The election news[4] gave quiet satisfaction here, except to our Southern friends. I'm told Mr. Corcoran[5] gave

---

[1] Mrs. Loring (Harriet Boott), wife of Edward G. Loring, at one time one of the judges of the Court of Claims; her daughter, Miss Harriett Loring.
[2] The five young Hooper nieces and their mother.
[3] Doll of Doll & Richards, the picture dealers in Boston.
[4] The elections were held Tuesday, November 2, and resulted in General Garfield receiving 219 electoral votes, while General Hancock received 150.
[5] William Wilson Corcoran, their landlord, a public-spirited and philanthropic resident of Washington, who had accumulated a substantial fortune as a banker.

ten thousand dollars toward the Democratic campaign fund. Miss Eustis,[1] who lives with him, says our red outbuildings throw a "cheerful glow" into their dining room, and though he gasped at first, I am amused to find that he has ordered the sides of that and stable which abut on his yard painted red too, at his expense; I had ordered them left brown, as they were on his side. The addition was plastered yesterday, and today a high northwest wind will dry it bravely. I took my ebony cook to see her new quarters the other day and when she entered the kitchen her lips parted like a black walnut piano suddenly opening, and she exclaimed: "Oh, it's powerful large!"—twenty-seven by twenty-two is pretty ample.

Sunday evening we divided between the Bancrofts'[2] and Judge Loring's; the former seemed younger and fresher even than when we left, Mr. Bancroft chuckling over Evarts's[3] *mot* in saying that he was "overeighted." Judge and Mrs. Loring are to have a golden wedding this winter. Dined Thursday with the Hopkinses[4] in their pretty new house. Miss Beale[5] sends you many kind messages; wants you to bring Kitty[6] when you come. Why can't you in your spring visit anyway—and scour the country when the dogwood is in bloom? Have a vile cold in my head, so *adiós*.
Affectionately

CLOVER

WORMLEY'S,
November 9th, 10 A.M.

DEAR PATER: Yours of the 7th came last night. I want you to do something for me. Can't get any tea here fit to drink; as you know where "Heard Mixture" can be got, will you kindly order me a small chest—about fifteen pounds or so—and tell the man to send

---

He endowed and established the Corcoran Art Gallery, and the Louise Home for aged gentlewomen.
[1] Miss Clementina Eustis, whose brother had married a daughter of Mr. Corcoran.
[2] Mr. and Mrs. George Bancroft.
[3] William Maxwell Evarts was then Secretary of State.
[4] Mr. and Mrs. Archibald Hopkins; she was Charlotte Everett Wise, a cousin of Henry Adams.
[5] Miss Emily Beale.
[6] Dr. Hooper's mare.

it on at once by Adams Express to this hotel. And will you ask Betsy or William to pay this for me; it is so small to pay by cheque. I will pay tea and this in one cheque to you or Ned. Will do as much for you if you want anything in the lobbying line. Weather here like seventh heaven, a pleasure to breathe even with a cold. Have finished M'Carthy.[1] Do read it! Charles writes me about it in enthusiasm, wants us to read it—it's like looking through old newspaper files. Ned would like it. The raking down of Vernon Harcourt in Volume III is delicious to those who don't fancy him.

Mr. Woolner writes me from London, October 28th; says he has sent my Bonington—that "if you don't say it's one of the 'largest' small pictures you ever saw, I shall say that the Atlantic winds have swept out much of your power of appreciating." Isn't he good, with a small purse and large family, to send me such a present. I must send him an Aztec vase or some bit of Tiffany silver. He says they are having "horrible drizzling weather." Love to all the folks. Yours affectionately

M. A.

WORMLEY'S,
Sunday, November 14, 1880.

DEAR PATER: The tea-chest came safely yesterday A.M., and we used it for five o'clock and find it most delicious. I've been trying teas here at a dollar twenty-five and a dollar, and found them not at all nice. Many thanks to you for your trouble. Another week of hard work is behind us and the chaos is settling. The process of scraping off papers brought to light so much cracked plaster that the work of pointing it has brought despair to the soul of Corcoran's contractor. He didn't realize when he undertook to put the house in perfect order that he would have two driving New Englanders at his heels. Our cabinet-maker—late officer in the rebel army—has kept us dancing, but bookcases and mantelpiece are finally in Henry's den, and room half papered—will be finished tomorrow. We stuck in Turkey rug, chairs, and table last evening, and have agreed to give Schurz[2] his tea there this P.M. to silence his

---

[1] Justin M'Carthy's *History of Our Own Times* was published in 1878-1880.
[2] Carl Schurz (1929-1906), born in Germany, became involved in the Revolution of 1848, and took refuge in Switzerland, France, and England, where, for

derisive doubts. "Few! Few! The bird builds her nest," says my Portuguese grammar.

We are much amused by our work and, though most anxious to get in, very comfortable here. The daily dinner is quite amusing; we've so many friends and acquaintances that we can talk across, and Boojum wanders alternately from Spanish counts to army offi-

---

the next four years he supported himself by teaching. He married in 1852 and came to the United States. Here he took an active interest in politics and supported Lincoln, who sent him to Spain in 1861 as United States Minister. The year following, he returned to the United States and entered the army, and saw active service first as a Brigadier General of Volunteers and later as a Major General, at times in command of a division. At the close of the war he resigned, and in 1866 became chief editor of the *Detroit Post*, and a year later editor and joint proprietor of the *Westliche Post* of St. Louis. In 1869 he was elected to the United States Senate, where he served one term. From 1870 to 1872 he organized a liberal Republican movement in Missouri—which, however, came to naught—and opposed President Grant's San Domingo policy. He was selected by Henry Adams and his friends to lead the Independent Party they endeavored to form, but he abandoned them and supported Hayes for the Presidency. He entered President Hayes's Cabinet in 1877 as Secretary of the Interior. His efforts to reform the abuses in the Indian Bureau and to conduct his department in a businesslike way subjected him to much abuse from "machine" and patronage politicians who had flourished under the Grant régime.

Apropos of Schurz's abandonment of the Independents at the time of Hayes's nomination, Henry Adams says, in a letter to Lodge, dated September 4, 1876 (*Letters*, p. 299): "I cannot help laughing to think how, after all our labor and after we had by main force created a party for Schurz to lead, he himself, without a word or a single effort to keep his party together, kicked us over in his haste to jump back to the Republicans. If he had taken the least pains to hold his friends together, I feel sure we would have spoken with effect. I, for one, would have been glad to join in any combined action, whichever way the majority decided. And in that case, Schurz's voice would not now be isolated and shrill. Well! We knew what he was! I am not angry with him, but of course his leadership is at an end. The leader who treats his followers in that way, is a mere will-o'-the-wisp. I hope he will get his Cabinet office, and I hope he will forget that we ever worked to make him our leader, independent of party. He can hereafter buy power only by devotion to party, and further connection with us would not help us and would be fatal to him."

Nevertheless, his relations with the Adamses continued friendly and socially intimate. He and his daughter Agatha were constantly at their house, and Henry and Marian Adams actively espoused his side in the various attacks that his political enemies organized against him. In 1881, after President Garfield's inauguration, Schurz became one of the proprietors and the editor-in-chief of the New York *Evening Post*.

cers and is well treated. Today we are to eat roast beef with the Beales. The fair Emily has been quite ill, but is convalescing. She wishes me to tell Bil Bigelow[1] to come here and practice; says: "Tell him I'll make it worth his while, I'm ill so much." Will you give him the message.

Weather until yesterday lovely, then and today raw and cold. Our friend Mr. Hewitt has got into an awful mess. Have you seen Judge Noah Davis's charge against him and Mr. Hewitt's lame and impotent defense?[2] We have been so much thrown with him that it will be awkward to go on just the same. It is utterly indefensible on his part. Give Ellen the enclosed about her friends the Crosses;[3] it may amuse her. Let me know, please, when the Peabodys get into No. 91[4]—the 16th was their aim. If you were as near as New

---

[1] William Sturgis Bigelow had studied and been graduated in medicine, although he never practiced.

[2] The reference is to the forged "Morey Letter," circulated during the last week of the presidential campaign, in which General Garfield was made to express views on Chinese immigration which it was feared might injure his chances in the Pacific States. Notwithstanding General Garfield's denial, Mr. Hewitt and the National Democratic Committee were inclined to believe in its authenticity, and so publicly expressed themselves. Criminal proceedings were instituted against the original publisher, and at the preliminary hearing Judge Davis, who presided, indulged in a violent attack on Mr. Hewitt, and presently the Grand Jury found true bills against the proprietor and editors of *Truth* for the publication of the Morey Letter and articles upon it.

[3] John W. Cross married George Eliot, May 6, 1880; she died December 22, 1880. At the time of this marriage Henry Adams comments (*Letters*, p. 322): "We were more startled by George Eliot's marriage to John Cross than by the elections themselves. As Cross is semi-American by his business connection, she is half way to emigration. I suppose her American admirers will howl over the fall of their idol, but I can't say that I care much for the idol business, and I am clear that if she found her isolation intolerable, she was quite right to marry Cross if she could get him. It is not quite so easy to explain why Cross should have been willing to marry her, for most men of thirty or forty prefer youth, beauty, children and such things, to intellect and gray hairs. Some people say it was a pure marriage of convenience on both sides, but I know that the Cross family have a sort of superstitious adoration of her."

[4] Their Boston house, No. 91 Marlborough Street, had been leased to Mr. and Mrs. John Endicott Peabody.

York, we should run on to Thanksgiving. Any news from Ellen Dixey?[1] Please answer all my questions. Affectionately yours

M. A.

1607 H Street, Washington,
Sunday P.M., November 21, 1880.

Dear Pater: You see by my new paper that we are partly in our new quarters. If you were sitting by this blazing wood fire in Henry's den looking out on "bare ruined choirs" and evergreens you would think us very cosy. At five I'd make you some tea—"A.H. mixture" from Boston; before that we've some calls to make, which we can find no time for on week days: Jerome Bonapartes,[2] who very civilly called first; your friend Madame Lewenhaupt,[3] etc., etc. The town is filling fast and we expect an interesting winter. Sunday we had a quiet pleasant dinner with the Beales and an hour in the evening with the Bancroft Davises.[4] Wednesday, dined with the Schurzes, he playing deliciously to us after dinner. Last evening, dined with the John Hays;[5] only Schurz and his daugh-

---

[1] Mrs. Richard C. Dixey's (Ellen Sturgis Tappan) son, Arthur, was born November 21.

[2] Jerome Napoleon Bonaparte-Patterson (1832-1893), a grandson of Jerome Bonaparte and Elizabeth Patterson. He entered the French service in 1854 and served with distinction in the Crimean and Italian campaigns. After the fall of the Second Empire he married Caroline Appleton Edgar, a widow.

[3] Madame Lewenhaupt, wife of Count Carl Lewenhaupt, Minister from Norway and Sweden at Washington, 1876-1884.

[4] Mrs. J. C. Bancroft Davis (Frederica Gore King).

[5] John Hay (1838-1905), in later years the most intimate of Henry Adams's friends. Their acquaintance dated back to 1861, when Adams passed a few months in Washington as private secretary to his father, who was then in Congress; their intimacy began in 1879 and continued for the rest of Hay's life. John Hay's public career began in 1861 when he came to Washington as one of President Lincoln's private secretaries. After Lincoln's death he entered the diplomatic service and served as Secretary of Legation in Paris and Madrid and as Chargé d'Affaires at Vienna. Returning to America in September 1870, he joined the staff of the *New York Tribune*, and continued there until his marriage in the winter of 1874 to Clara L. Stone, the daughter of Amasa and Julia Gleason Stone of Cleveland, to which city he then transferred his residence. In 1879, Mr. Evarts invited him to be Assistant Secretary of State, a position which after some hesitation he was induced to accept; with the change of administrations in

ter—it was lively and amusing. When we got home at ten, no Boojum could be found. At three in the morning he gave a tap on our bedroom door, one which is never used, but he seemed to have thought that if he knocked at the parlour door—which is an out-room to mine—we should not hear him. He crept to his bed like a guilty rat-catcher. Usually, when we go out, he flops on a young woman from Troy and passes his time in her room.

The air is thick with political flakes.[1] One, that Fish[2] is to be next Secretary of State as a sop to the Conkling wing of the party—the latter wouldn't be able to rule him anyway. No one seems to put much faith in the future strength of Garfield's spine; he is

---

1881, he retired. After declining the position of secretary to President Garfield, he returned to the *Tribune* and acted as its editor for the next six months, during the absence of Whitelaw Reid in Europe. The next few years he devoted to literary and historical work—the first installment of his novel, *The Breadwinners*, appeared in August 1883, and that of the Lincoln history in November 1886. In 1884, he and Henry Adams bought adjoining lots at the corner of H and 16th Streets in Washington, and employed H. H. Richardson to design their houses, which were completed in the fall of 1885.

[1] The *Nation*, November 11, 1889: "The newspapers are busily at work making up General Garfield's Cabinet for him. Foremost among them, and with a certain air of authority, is the Cincinnati *Commercial*. It gives Mr. Blaine the filling of the Navy Department, for the comical reason that 'there is a great depressed shipbuilding interest in Maine'; to Mr. Conkling the Post-office for his friend Platt; to Cameron the War Department; and to General Logan the Department of the Interior. No Cabinet could be made to contain more of such elements of corruption as exist in American politics, and the suggestion has therefore a bouffe sound which makes it a possible joke. The same prophet declares that General Grant will probably have the English mission, 'owing to the flattering estimation in which he is held by the English people' and to the fact that 'his daughter is the wife of an English gentleman.' The scandals of his administration, too, against which the *Commercial* used to bellow so lustily, are, it appears, all forgotten and forgiven in consideration of his 'admirable conduct since the Chicago Convention.'"

The *Nation*, November 25, 1880: "At this moment we read in the speculations about the Cabinet, and without either surprise or indignation, that Mr. Conkling does not want a seat in the Cabinet for himself, but will insist on 'Tom' Platt getting the Post-office, and that Mr. Blaine, too, would sooner stay in the Senate, but will expect Mr. Eugene Hale to get the Navy Department, and so on."

[2] Hamilton Fish (1808-1893) had been Secretary of State under President Grant, and was probably acceptable to Senator Conkling.

thought to be too much inclined to conciliate. Miles[1] is talked of for General Myer's[2] place, but he has no scientific training and is so successful as a fighting general that he seems hardly the man for the place.

Mrs. Evarts has very kindly asked us to join their Thanksgiving dinner, so we shall have a Vermont turkey, if not a Massachusetts one. You ask in your last if I've found the wagon you offered me yet. We had no time as we came through, but as I hardly could enjoy it before February or March, we shall hunt for one in our next trip there. The saddle horses we expect to be ready for in about a week. We are doing our best to get in, but plastering the addition has been a tiresome business. Did Mrs. Walter Cabot's child get well? I'm anxious to hear. Love to Fanny. Take good care of yourself and Aunty. Affectionately yours

MARIAN ADAMS

1607 H STREET,
Wednesday, November 24, 1880.

DEAR PATER: As you take an interest in our daily incidents, read the enclosed. This gentle Teuton has been doing our cornices and on Saturday P.M. lost his temper with Henry, saying he "couldn't please him." Henry tried to soothe him and I went in and mollified him in such execrable German that he came round and was very polite. He went from here to his own house, and from there seemed to have no alternative but the grave or the gallows.[3] He is a fine-looking six-foot man, and if he had chosen to stick his putty

---

[1] General Nelson Appleton Miles (1839-1925) entered the army as a volunteer in 1861 and served with great distinction. At the close of the Civil War he continued his military career in the regular army and was particularly successful in dealing with Indian outbreaks at various times between 1869 and 1886. He rose to the rank of major-general and in 1895 succeeded General Schofield as commanding general of the United States army. Mrs. Miles was a sister of Mrs. James Donald Cameron and a niece of General W. T. Sherman as well as of John Sherman, who was Secretary of the Treasury in the administration of President Hayes.

[2] General Albert J. Myer (1827-1880), the chief signal officer in the War Department, died in August.

[3] According to her letter of December 5, this plasterer stole the painter's putty knife and cut his wife's throat. The clipping she enclosed is missing.

knife into us a few hours earlier, it would have been uncomfortable all round.

Cold and still, here; plastering retarded in drying; furniture left last Friday, Leach writes. Woolner's Bonington has come—is an oil painting about eight by ten inches, and is very delicious, we think. As Bonington ranks with Turner in England, and higher in Paris, I'm rather staggered at so valuable a gift. Custom House charged two dollars, as I, thinking it was a water colour, told Mr. Sturgis to rate it at four pounds! Many thanks for your tea. You are like Hepzibah Pyncheon,[1] who gave away all her gingerbread camels. I have a score to send Ned as soon as I get time, which will fill your purse nicely. *Vale.* Affectionately

M. A.

1607 H STREET, WASHINGTON,
Sunday, November 28, 1880.

DEAR PATER: Thanks for your last. I wish you gave better news of Fanny, and that we could be of any use to her in any way.

We are working very hard, but it is all for ourselves. We have sworn spherical oaths to Corcoran's contractor that we will eat and sleep in this house Saturday next. His nasty plaster has kept us waiting—the weather being dead against it—and all plumbing in ell, so we can't go in till that does. Our furniture got here Tuesday, but they waited three days before they sent us word! Yesterday Henry and our groom John Brent went to Potomac depot and I received at this end fifteen wagonloads in three hours. The car was so full that a mosquito who tried to go as a stowaway got his ribs broken. Leach is a trump and his mantelpieces very nice; the one we designed for the library you must say you like even at the risk of perjury. But a truce to our affairs.

Had a quiet dinner at the Evartses' Thursday; met only the John Hays and a twenty-six pound turkey of Senator Anthony's raising. Evarts and John Hay were both witty and full of talk. Next Wednesday we are to dine with the Jerome Bonapartes; I've not seen her since we were infants. I must inaugurate your red

---

[1] In Hawthorne's *House of the Seven Gables.*

velvet gown. Clarence King[1] has been very ill; has now gone on six weeks' leave to Mexico, will turn up here about January 1st. Why did Harshaw decline to get up when that blooming telegram came? We are happy in thinking we were economizing on Turner, etc., in Queen Anne's Gate, for if we'd been in Boston we should inevitably have sold Calumet as being too high and gone as the other "publicans" did.

[1] Clarence King (1842-1902), the fifth of the band of intimate friends known among themselves as "The Five of Hearts," the other four being Mr. and Mrs. Henry Adams and Mr. and Mrs. John Hay. Henry Adams's acquaintance and friendship with King was of the summer of 1871, when they accidentally met one evening at the door of a cabin in Estes Park, Larimer County, Colorado; King was chief of the United States geological exploration of the 40th parallel and Adams had gone out to join one of the field parties at the invitation of his classmate, Frank Emmons, one of King's assistants, and at the moment was traveling with Arnold Hague, another of them. The meeting is fully described in the *Education* (p. 309). King was engaged on this work for ten years, and his final summary of his work was published in his *Systematic Geology* in 1878; it was through his efforts that Congress was induced to undertake the surveys of the country under the direction of the Department of the Interior, and he was appointed by Secretary Schurz in 1879 to organize it into the United States Geological Survey and was its first director. By 1881 it was well established, and he resigned in order to devote himself to some of the deeper problems of geology. Of him Adams says: "King had everything to interest and delight Adams. He knew more than Adams did of art and poetry; he knew America, especially west of the hundredth meridian, better than any one; he knew the professor by heart, and knew the Congressman better than he did the professor. He even knew women; even the American woman; even the New York woman, which is saying much. Incidentally he knew more practical geology than was good for him, and saw ahead at least one generation further than the textbooks. That he saw right was a different matter. Since the beginning of time no man has lived who has known to have seen right; the charm of King was that he saw what others did and a great deal more. His wit and humor; his bubbling energy which swept every one into the current of his interest; his personal charm of youth and manners; his faculty of giving and taking, profusely, lavishly, whether in thought or money as though he were Nature herself, marked him almost alone among Americans. He had in him something of the Greek—a touch of Alcibiades or Alexander. One Clarence King only existed in the world." At the time of King's last illness Hay wrote (*Education*, p. 416): "The best and brightest man of his generation, with talents immeasurably beyond any of his contemporaries; with industry that has often sickened me to witness it; with everything in his favor but blind luck; hounded by disaster from his cradle, with none of the joy of life to which he was entitled, dying at last, with nameless suffering, alone and uncared-for, in a California tavern."

Think of us tomorrow at the christening of a brat whose mama rejoices in the pen-name of "Bessie Beech,"—so the *Star* says,— just because I had a colic in October and called in her husband to see me writhe. If I had not disgraced myself by convulsive laughter at her literary party I would not go this time. It's so nice that the Bernhardt[1] is being socially tabooed on this side, our English cousins made such asses of themselves. See to it that Boston snubs her off the stage anyway. Miss Beale always speaks of Henry J. Bigelow as *old* Dr. Bigelow, and when I laughed she said: "I assure you I should never say 'old Dr. Hooper.' He's very different!" Henry Jacob would be pleased!

Tomorrow, weather permitting, our horses come. Miss Randolph had them ridden from Virginia to Ellicott City; will send them to a place eighteen miles from here, and our groom ride and lead them down. She says they are "splendid animals and much admired," though Prince nearly ended the days of one of her pupils by buck-jumping. She and her school revel in my old phaeton. Your tea fills our soul and cups bi-daily—is as good as some we gave fifteen francs for in Paris. Weather here beneath contempt— snow, rain, slush,—but we too busy to care. Much love to Auntie and Cambridge folks one and all, large and small. Tell Betsy Boojum and I miss her good care of us. *Adiós.* Affectionately

CLOVER

1607 H STREET, WASHINGTON,
Sunday, December 5th, 1880.

DEAR PATER: We are really in, though the courage born of despair alone brought us; but the tocsin has sounded for painter and plumber, and by Christmas we hope to be in good shape. Papers run short and have to be sent for, and I'd rather have a house to fit up in Morocco qua workmen; but it's great fun and we are well and jolly, and our African adjutants have fewer nerves than those of the Emerald Isle, and the boss painter thinks the library "perfectly elegant." It cheers him for the loss of his putty knife, which he says the German stole to cut his wife's throat with.

---

[1] Sarah Bernhardt (1845-1923) made a tour through the United States in 1880.

We have had a stream of friendly calls today: first the Miss Thorntons,[1] waiving ceremony, as I have been too driven to welcome them home; then Mr. Lowndes,[2] who shared our eccentric luncheon; then Miss Beale, who gave a convulsing account of the return from Chicago of herself and her party—Logans, Conkling, Camerons, and Mortons; then Schurz, with his new report for me. Yesterday came a charming book, *Pretty Peggy*,[3] from Mr. Sam Barlow,[4] for which I was pining but resisted in New York; and at noon a quantity of cut flowers with Mrs. Hayes's[5] compliments—a nice little attention from our new opposite neighbor. We made our annual call on her Friday evening and sat in big Hadley rocking chairs in front of a wood fire, and it looked almost pleasant in that upholstered barrack. I stoutly defended Henry James and Daisy Miller[6] to stout Mrs. Smith of Chicago, and protested that the latter was charming and that the author adored her. We had a simple quiet dinner of eight at the Bonapartes' on Wednesday, which the Sunday papers with their Midas touch have transformed into a "superb banquet." Aristarchi Bey[7] was very jolly and we had a great deal of fun. The horses came safely on Thursday and are in fine figure; we hope to try them tomorrow, but time is what we have least of just now. Stylographic is faint and feeble tonight and broke down, as you see. Much love to Fanny and Aunt Eunice. How is Nanny Warton's[8] dog? *Adiós.*

MARIAN ADAMS

[1] Sir Edward Thornton (1817-1906), the British Minister at Washington from February 7, 1868, to June 30, 1881.

[2] James Lowndes, a charming South Carolinian, who, after serving in the Confederate Army with the rank of colonel during the Civil War, settled in Washington and there practised law. He was supposed to be portrayed as "Carrington" in *Democracy*. Some years later he married Miss Laura Tuckerman.

[3] *Pretty Peggy and Other Ballads* by S. Low, illustrated by Rosina Emmet and published in 1880.

[4] Samuel Latham Mitchell Barlow (1826-1889).

[5] Mrs. Rutherford Birchard Hayes (Lucy Ware Webb of Chillicothe, Ohio), wife of the President; they were married in 1852.

[6] Henry James's novel, *Daisy Miller*, was published in 1878.

[7] Grégoire Aristarchi Bey, the Turkish Minister at Washington from 1873 to 1883. He was a great social favorite.

[8] Miss Nancy Craig Wharton.

1607 H STREET, WASHINGTON,
Sunday, December 12th, 1880.

DEAR PATER: It's hard to find even half an hour to write a letter in, but the scrap I send is my mite. We had a week of cold weather, high wind, and hard work, but the sepulcher is getting whited externally and comfort will come by and by. It's an old shell of a house and can't be kept smart as new; Mr. Corcoran amiably says: "We've made a silk purse out of a sow's ear." For strain and labor, building would be easier.

Public news not exciting yet. Mr. Schurz brought me his report Sunday and it's worth reading.[1] He is much pleased with the experiment to be made at Hampton of educating young Indians.[2] Wednesday, dined again with the John Hays; only eight in all and very nice—Aristarchi Bey, Japanese Minister[3] and his wife. He has given Henry two water colours he brought him from Japan: one about four feet by two, by the best artist there, he says, Run Lin, a winter snow scene framed with brocade—it covers six feet of our bare wall in front entry; the other is narrower and not so original, though very nice. We are going to send him in return my Théodore Frère,[4] as he much affects pictures; and, little as we care for that, it's far away better than any he has. We are mere public pensioners in receipt of daily alms. Friday came a letter from Mr.

---

[1] The *Nation*, December 9, 1880: "Secretary Shurz's report is mainly devoted to Indian affairs, and inspires regret that its author is not to continue for another four years to control the experiments begun during his administration, and so full of promise and encouragement."

[2] The Hampton Normal and Agricultural Institute, at Hampton, Virginia, was founded by General Samuel Chapman Armstrong with the aid of the American Missionary Association, in 1868, as an industrial school for negroes. After 1878, Indians were also admitted.

[3] Jushie Yoshida Kiyonari, the Japanese Minister at Washington from 1874 to 1881. Henry Adams writes of him, November 28, 1878: "Ten days ago I went uninvited to Yoshida's, the Japanese Minister's, and played whist with him and his Japanese wife till midnight, after which I beat him at Go-Bang and he showed me how to play Go; after which we closed with oysters and champagne and *such* a headache the next day. . . . Yoshida, who has since departed for Japan, has already sent me a little blue-and-white Japanese teapot to console me for his absence." (*Letters*, p. 309)

[4] Charles Théodore Frère (1815-1888), a French landscape and genre painter.

Hewitt[1] begging me to accept a box of some very good tea he has just got over. He is a tea maniac and says it's "an adroit way" of founding a claim for a cup of tea every P.M. next winter. He encloses a copy of his defensive letter in the *Nation*—I fancy he finds his position just now most uncomfortable. He has many good traits, of which judgment and tact are not two. When the tea comes I shall only write of that and not touch on his "Morey" scrape, for which we think him much to be blamed. Called Thursday on Madame Lewenhaupt, who was most cordial and sweet; spoke of her visit to you with evident satisfaction. After lunch I am going to try my beloved Daisy for an hour; it's milder today. Do write me that Fanny wants me to do something for her or send her something. Much love to all Cambridge family. *Adiós*. Affectionately

M. A.

General Miles was here Thursday; has sent me a pair of white Sioux moccasins. Mr. Woolner sends me by mail a charming little engraving of my Bonington,—an artist's proof,—adding much to the value of the picture. Nice letter

---

[1] Abram Stevens Hewitt (1822-1903), manufacturer, political leader, and philanthropist. After graduating from Columbia College in 1842, he taught mathematics there. As an iron manufacturer he conducted his enterprise with unusual consideration for his employees, and during the Civil War his conception of his patriotic duty was such that he refused any profit on the gun-barrel iron he made for the government. After the fall of the Tweed Ring in 1871, he took a prominent part in the reorganization of Tammany Hall; he served in Congress from 1875 to 1879, and also from 1881 to 1886, when he was elected Mayor of New York. In *The Education* (p. 294) there is the following reference to him: "Henry Adams . . . knew, more or less, all the men in any way prominent at Washington, or knew all about them. Among them, in his opinion, the best equipped, the most active-minded, and most industrious was Abram Hewitt, who sat in Congress for a dozen years, between 1874 and 1886, sometimes leading the House and always wielding influence second to none. With nobody did Adams form closer or longer relations than with Mr. Hewitt, whom he regarded as the most useful public man in Washington; and he was the more struck by Hewitt's saying, at the end of his laborious career as legislator, that he left behind him no permanent result except the Act consolidating the Surveys."

from Lady Clark;[1] much pleased with her maple-leaf letter, tell Betsy; is going to winter in Cornwall in a lent house.

1607 H STREET, WASHINGTON,
Sunday, December 19th, 1880.

DEAR PATER: Another busy week has rolled over us and we begin to see daylight. Plumbers and carpenters driven out and painters soon will be, so if before the next cold wave we can manage to heat our addition we shall do nicely. The plan of pipes in the middle is better for warmth, but for health, I think, especially here, it's safer to have them well away from the sleeping rooms. There's a deal of tinkering, as letting a house is not conducive to keeping things smart; everything is dirty and worn, but when you see them they'll be better, I hope.

Weather enchanting, and we've ridden nearly every day, finding our old haunts very glad to see us. Dined last Sunday at the Schurzes'—only General Miles, a curious "Missourah" army woman, and G. A. James. Does Governor Long know better than Schurz about Ponca affairs? The latter has made it a matter of deep study for nearly four years, and is not hard-hearted, and in intelligence can hardly be behind Governor Long, whoever he may be. Nothing known, little guessed as to Garfield's new Cabinet, and a good deal of curiosity felt as to whether he'll try to conciliate Conkling. The Grants came to stay with our oblique neighbors the Beales on Monday and the "boys in blue" made our corner lively, but Mrs. and Miss Beale both broke down and took to their beds, so that their royal guests beat a retreat on Friday. No news from Mr. King; he has been dangerously ill in Arizona, but got well and went on six weeks' leave to Mexico. We hope to see him here very soon.

Now that the front door is dry, a few people drop in at dusk; yesterday General Mackensie,[2] on his way to Arkansas, Schurz,

---

[1] Charlotte, only daughter of Mr. Justice Coltman, married, in 1851, Sir John Forbes Clark, Bart., of Tillypronie.
[2] General Ronald Slidell Mackensie, graduated at West Point in 1862, in the Engineer Corps; he was brevetted a Major General in 1865, and died in 1889.

and Lord Lymington,[1] a brother of Lady Catherine Gaskell, a harmless youth and not a swindler like Lord Marcus Beresford, whom Miss Schurz saw much of coming back from Utah in September and found charming—he was Mr. Winthrop's Lord Pelham Clinton, too! Tomorrow I shall try and send by express a small package in which will be four small Spanish offerings for Christmas. One for you, which I bought especially for you in Seville; it was packed there and I don't dare open it for fear in its long wanderings it may have suffered; it's very national and you'll not see any others. Ned will tell you how they mount or hang them; I don't know. Also, there will be three small bits of Seville pottery for Ellen, Loulie, and Polly to use for flowers. I can get nothing nice here and am too busy to hunt, so these duds must do for their stockings. We must get a few waifs and strays for Christmas dinner. In a day or two I hope to get my pantry and unpack glass and china.

A letter from London yesterday from a friend who says, "The fogs have begun to eat into the membrane of our lives." When I remember what Paris was a year ago today, and then look out on this sky and sit soaked in sunshine, I think gratefully of Plymouth Rock and Christopher Columbus, 1492 to 1620. What a long time to wait it was, though! Mrs. Chardon Brooks[2] writes Henry that she has chosen out a picture by Teniers to send to us as a memorial of Uncle Chardon. He had some nice pictures, and on our gaunt library walls thirteen feet high this will be very welcome. Much love to Fanny and all "Fayerweather" friends. Ever affectionately

CLOVER

1607 H STREET,
Tuesday, 21st.

DEAR PATER: Yours of the 19th and 20th came today fast on each other's heels. I wish much that I could drop down on you for Christmas in your Jacqueminot velvet dress and "rest and scream among my fellows," but it's impossible. Workmen still about, ser-

---

[1] Newton Wallop, Viscount Lymington (1856-1917), succeeded his father as sixth Earl of Portsmouth in 1891.
[2] Peter Chardon Brooks (1798-1880), an uncle of Henry Adams, married Susan Oliver.

vants new and not used to our ways, and Henry at last with his nose to the grindstone after so much time lost or stolen. So with much regret I must put it out of my mind.

Saw in last night's *Star* that Lamar[1] is back and have written to him to come and dine Christmas. Hope to get our china closet by that. The Salamanca embroidery you gave me last Christmas is up today, and thrilling; your cabinet is much admired; Mrs. Peter C. Brooks's Teniers came yesterday—we like it much, and, having seen many in Madrid Gallery, it seems like an old friend.

I am much amused but not surprised at your suspecting me of having written *Democracy*,[2] as I find myself on the "black list" here with Miss Loring,[3] Arthur Sedgwick,[4] Manton Marble, Clarence King, and John Hay! We hear that King has been cut by

---

[1] Lucius Quintus Cincinnatus Lamar (1825-1893), "the most genial and sympathetic of all Senators and universally respected and admired." (*Letters*, p. 310) The following reference to him in *The Education* (p. 185) is of interest: "Some twenty years later . . . Adams became closely intimate at Washington with Lamar, then Senator from Mississippi, who had grown to be one of the calmest, most reasonable and most amiable Union men in the United States, and quite unusual in social charm. In 1860 he passed for the worst of Southern fire-eaters, but he was an eccentric by environment, not by nature; above all his Southern eccentricities, he had tact and humor; and perhaps this was a reason why Mr. Davis sent him abroad with the others, on a futile mission to St. Petersburg. He would have done better in London, in place of Mason. London society would have delighted in him; his stories would have won success; his manners would have made him loved; his oratory would have swept every audience; even Monckton Milnes could never have resisted the temptation of having him to breakfast between Lord Shaftesbury and the Bishop of Oxford." Mr. Lamar entered Congress in 1873; the Senate in 1877; the Cabinet, as Secretary of the Interior, in 1885; and the Supreme Court of the United States, as an Associate Justice, in 1888.

[2] Henry Adams's novel, *Democracy*, was turned over to the publisher in the spring of 1879, and published anonymously in 1880, when it ranked as the "best seller" of the year. The secret of its authorship was probably known only to his wife, Hay, and King, and was well kept. Very late in his lifetime he admitted his authorship to his nieces, Mrs. Thoron and Miss E. O. Adams. The fact that some of the principal characters in it were thought to resemble Mrs. Bigelow Lawrence, her sister Miss Fanny Chapman, Miss Emily Beale, James Lowndes, and James G. Blaine, excited such curiosity in Washington as to the author, and the various surmises of the public were a subject of jest and merriment to those in the secret.

[3] Miss Harriet Loring.

[4] Arthur George Sedgwick (1844-1915).

Blaine and Gail Hamilton[1] for his supposed authorship. John Hay says *he* has "given up denying it"; that "it will be known after the 4th of March." Miss Loring has still the inside track, but Arthur Sedgwick is running her hard. All I *know* is that *I* did not write it. Deny it from me if anyone defames me absent, and say to them, as Pickering Dodge of his parrot: "If she couldn't *write* better than that I'd cut her——head off."

A high old-fashioned snowstorm here; the attempts at sleighing numerous and humorous. "If the red sleigher thinks he sleighs," Ralph Waldo Emerson would point him to the Brighton Road for the genuine article. Shall be glad to hear if your señorita reaches you whole. Much love. Affectionately

CLOVER

1607 H STREET, WASHINGTON,
Sunday, December 26th, 1880.

DEAR PATER: Your most welcome Christmas present came on Friday. I protest—feebly—against being pampered to such an extent, but shall enjoy it none the less. If the horseleech's[2] daughters had called you father their importunity would have had no *raison d'être*; probably the horseleech kept them very short. I shall buy a nice little wagon when winter is over, and a harness. For though you gave me one in 1874, when I went to Europe I turned that, with my phaeton, over to our friend Miss Randolph—the only way I could repay her for taking care of our two horses. She is passing Christmas with Mr. Corcoran and coming to lunch quietly today; is very sad at the deaths last week of a favorite niece and nephew in Virginia. She has a household of eight persons to run and looks nearly worn out; clear grit is all her stock in trade.

We had a quiet Christmas, which was sleety and cold, and the luxury of a day's rest in the house very great. Lamar did not come to dine; only General Walker[3] of the Census, who was too busy to

---

[1] Gail Hamilton (Mary Abigail Dodge—1833-1896) was then Mr. Blaine's secretary.

[2] "The horseleech hath two daughters, crying, Give, give."—Proverbs xxx, 15.

[3] Francis Anna Walker (1840-1897) graduated at Amherst in 1860; fought all through the Civil War and reached the rank of a brigadier general; after the war, for a while, he was an editorial writer on the staff of the *Springfield Republican*, and presently drifted to Washington, where, in 1869, he was made chief of the

go to New Haven with his wife and seven children. He was full of talk and most interesting. Garfield would be wise to offer him Schurz's place. Mr. Tibbles[1] and his squaw, "Bright Eyes," are doing their best to bother Poncas and Schurz. What a tempest Governor Long has stirred up! Mr. Walker gave a very sad account of King. As far as anyone can learn his movements, he went some weeks since on leave of absence to Mexico to look into some mine,—Prietas, I believe,—ill, shaken with fever, and heavily out of pocket. We hope daily to see him here, but he is so reckless of life and strength that his friends feel uneasy about him. Mr. Walker utterly disbelieves in Eastern capitalists going into mines; says men in the West pocket all the gains when there are any.

We are buried in snow today. The Square is beautiful with its snow-laden trees, but this is not the weather we contracted for in coming South. It's not Washington at all and our horizon is dark today, for a new ceiling came down in the night, owing to the new roof not being tight, and the main sewer is blocked. So with an empty reservoir at the top of the house, which has had no water for a week and no exit below, we are in a tight place. We have sent in cold haste for the miserable contractor whom Corcoran employed, and his Sunday is likely to be as uncomfortable as ours. The patience and amiability of my better half never fail in these crises. Job had his little worries, but he never had to deal with Washington workmen. After this experience I will contract to run the Solar System and make something handsome out of it, too. In Tetuan we lived in a charming house with no roof. I asked what they did when it rained, and they said: "We draw a canvas cover over the top of the house." That same evening a deluge came; the curtain

---

government bureau of statistics. It was at this time he and Adams met and their friendship began. He superintended the 9th Census in 1870, and the 10th in 1889; was professor of political economy and history at the Sheffield Scientific School from 1873 to 1881, and eventually president of the Massachusetts Institute of Technology.

[1] Thomas H. Tibbles (1838-1928) during the Civil War was a newspaper correspondent and also in the secret service; later he went to Nebraska and founded a paper, became interested in the rights and wrongs of the Ponca Indians, and was very active in that controversy. He married an Indian maiden on the Omaha reservation, called "Bright Eyes"—her other name was Susette La Flesche (Inshtateamba).

kept out some water and the rest went into jars and tubs. Drainage there was none; soil pipes leading into the streets; no fires, no nothing, and they liked it very much.

I took the *Jolly Huntsmen* to Miss Beale. She has been ill for some time and I did not see her; she will, of course, write and thank you herself, as I did for mine. They are charming, as all Caldecott's are. Mr. Nordhoff[1] sent me a book of his early life as a cabin boy which he promised me three years ago. Edward Atkinson[2] told me of it and rated it with *Two Years Before the Mast*, or even higher. Miss Schurz sent me a nice holder for my teakettle with a dainty motto, and Mrs. Campbell[3] a pot of gumbo and a pincushion. Friendly candy and Christmas cards filled in gaps. Tell me, did the terra-cotta plaque reach you whole or broken? I fear from your note that it was not all right. It was pleasant to see Thornton[4] here and get various items from him; his and your account of Aunt Anne is very sad. Tell Ned, as our present demands for money are numerous, I shall deposit this cheque of yours and pay bills, but it's not really going for papers and such; but of bric-à-brac, pictures, and all such we have more than enough. I wish you were here with your sleigh today, but no guest shall share our discomfort for yet a while. Many thanks for your daily bulletins. Affectionately

M. ADAMS

1607 H STREET, WASHINGTON,
Sunday evening, January 2d, 1881.

DEAR PATER: Every minute of the day has been so taken up that I've had to wait for a quiet after-dinner hour in which to send you your weekly screed. You will have seen from day to day in your papers how we have been freezing—14° below zero Thursday night. This means in this latitude great discomfort. When one's water supply is clean gone, it's not easy to "wash one's soiled li-

---

[1] Charles Nordhoff (1830-1901), then Washington correspondent of the *New York Herald.*
[2] Edward Atkinson (1827-1905).
[3] Mrs. Archibald (Harrod) Campbell; her daughter Mary married Oswald Charlton of the British Legation in 1877.
[4] Thornton Kirkland Lothrop (1830-1913).

nen at home," but you can fancy us basking in sun and peace. The voice of wailing is heard in the land. One Ethiop has succumbed under the burden and leaves tonight; he grinned gaily when rebuked and said he "reckoned he could keep things cleaner."

Society has been chilled—or rather thrown out—and we denied ourselves a party at the British Legation and two dinners this week, I in obedience to my dentist, and Henry who has had a most uncomfortable pull of rheumatism. We have never seen so few people, but the January thaw will make a change. Four snowstorms in ten days makes getting about a serious matter. If we had a nice sleigh we might get some fun out of it; as it is, we've not seen Prince and Daisy[1] for two weeks. "Patience and shuffle the cards," as the old proverb has it.

No news in politics; the administration are gently winding up their affairs. Mrs. Hayes longs for her quiet home in Ohio; Schurz longing to make money in St. Louis at his paper; and John Hay pining for the fleshpots of Cleveland. He told me today, to my great amusement, that a lad who came here with Lord Lymington to tea thought I did not show him enough deference. Mrs. Hay, who was here at the time, denies the charge. As Pepys said: "Lord! Lord! what fools some men be!"—and women too, I fear.

Thanks for the ruby pin which Mrs. Lodge[2] brought me. By the way, there is some hitch as to the sending of our vases lent to the Art Museum—two most precious Greek and one Aztec (white and silver) from King. Charles Loring[3] promised to send them long ago. We fear he is ill. Will you, if it comes your way, make some gentle inquiry? I'm curious to know how the Peabodys find our late house; and has Mrs. Peabody a new baby? Miss Beale has been very ill and suffered greatly; says you are an angel to send her a picture book; will write as soon as she can. Madame Outrey[4] and children laid up with whooping cough—have not seen them even once; Outrey the picture of calm despair. *Adiós.* Keep well. Affectionately

CLOVER

---

[1] Their saddle horses.
[2] Mrs. Henry Cabot Lodge (Anna Cabot Mills Davis).
[3] Charles G. Loring, director of the Boston Museum of Fine Arts.
[4] Maxime Outrey was the French Minister at Washington from February 1877 to June 1882.

1607 H STREET, WASHINGTON,
Sunday, January 9th, 1881.

DEAR PATER: From our Siberian clime I send a cold greeting. Yes, we still live, and if Henry and I cannot get our exercise with our saddle horses, he has quite enough on the roof, cleaning out ice-bound gutters, while I toil sadly and ineffectually within with a pathetic gentleman just fresh from Denmark, who followed the African brother in quick succession. When I gently shouted to him, on the second day of his career, that his sudden deafness would make his success in this capacity almost impossible, "Lady," he said with a sad smile, "I do always before hear like one rabbit." And when I said he was to say "Not at home" to visitors, he suggested that he had better vary it by saying "She is ondressed." It's a horrid bore, on top of all hard work, to scuffle with raw servants untrained to my ways.

I fancy Garfield is going to find his indoor man a thorn in his side. It's a strong measure to make Blaine Secretary of State, with his stained record.[1] No one doubts his ability and that Mrs. Blaine is well suited to the place, but it's a gross insult to the moral sense of the community, and a beginning which makes even friends and supporters of Garfield shake their heads and say, "Who next?"

---

[1] James Gillespie Blaine (1830-1893) was married, in 1850, to Harriet Stanwood; was first elected to Congress in 1862 and served there until his election to the Senate in 1876. From 1869 to 1875 he was Speaker of the House of Representatives. In 1876 and again in 1880 he was the leading, though unsuccessful, candidate for the Republican nomination for the Presidency, and his defeat, in one case by Hayes and in the other by Garfield, was largely due to the charges brought by his political opponents, that as Speaker he had obtained a personal profit through the sale of bonds of the Little Rock and Fort Smith Railway; and it was thought that confirmation of this charge of corruption was to be found in a series of business letters written to him by Warren Fisher of Boston which fell into the hands of Fisher's secretary, Mulligan. Upon Garfield's inauguration, Blaine resigned from the Senate and was appointed Secretary of State. He retired from that office in December 1881, after Garfield's death. In 1884 he was nominated for the Presidency, but was defeated at the election the following November by Grover Cleveland. In 1888 he again held office as Secretary of State under President Harrison. Notwithstanding Mr. Blaine's great ability and unusual personal charm, he was anathema to the reform and independent group to which the Adamses belonged and whose mouthpiece was the *Nation*, and the bitterness of their feelings is amply reflected in Mrs. Adams's letters whenever she has occasion to allude to him or to Mrs. Blaine.

Blaine represents the corruption element as thoroughly as any man can,—even Robeson has never been found out,—but the famous Mulligan letters branded Blaine. For us it will be most awkward; never having called on them before, it will simply be impossible to make up to them now, and as we are on terms of great intimacy with several of the head officials in the State Department the position is not easy. Henry will hurry up his work there so as to finish by March 4th, not wishing to be a protégé of a man that he does not recognise socially.[1]

We hoped that General Walker would succeed Schurz, but New England won't get two cabinet places. Garfield may have made this offer on the same principle by which the railroad president explained the appointment of a flashy conductor: "He already has his diamond pin and gold watch." Fernando Wood[2] may go into the Treasury—it would conciliate the Democrats, and his being an ex-forger would make him up to dodges. Here is Emily Beale's last. She tells me that a few weeks ago she came back from Philadelphia under ex-Secretary Robeson's[3] care, of whom she is very fond. She says that Allison[4] sat with them in the car. Speaking of the lost chance of the New Jersey senatorship, Robeson said: "Miss Emily, I want a permanent place. Don't you know of one for me?" and Miss Beale says without forethought or after-

---

[1] Adams to Gaskell, January 29, 1882: "Among others our pet enmity is Mr. Blaine, whose conduct towards your government has perhaps not endeared him to you. His overthrow has been a matter of deep concern to us, both politically and personally, for we have always refused him even social recognition on account of his previous scandals, and I assure you that to stand alone in a small society like this, and to cut the Secretary of State for Foreign Affairs, without doing it offensively or with ill-breeding, requires not only some courage but some skill. We have gone through this ordeal for many months until at length there has come relief, and I trust that Mr. Blaine is blown up forever, although it is costing us the worst scandal we ever had in our foreign politics. Today there are plenty of people who would like very well to have made as strong a protest."

[2] Fernando Wood (1812-1881), a Democratic politician from New York City, who had been mayor of that city from 1854 to 1861 and was then serving his tenth term in the House of Representatives.

[3] George Maxwell Robeson (1829-1897), Secretary of the Navy during both administrations of President Grant (1869-1877); then a member of Congress from New Jersey. He married Mary I. Ogston, widow of Richmond Aulick of the United States Navy.

[4] William Boyd Allison (1828-1902), then a senator from Iowa.

thought she answered: "Why, you know the penitentiary has been yawning for you for years." Robeson said never a word, but she said: "Allison gave me the most vulgar wink I ever received from a Western senator." For goodness sake don't tell Ellen Gurney this; she will blush for our surroundings. Godkin[1] might enjoy it.

Thursday we went to a very pleasant reception at John Hay's. A Spanish diplomate was introduced who was for three years under our friend Don Leopoldo at the University of Granada—Don Luis Polo,[2] an Andalusian; puts himself at my feet, which he kisses, and I in return put my house at his disposition, which is all the Spanish I can remember. Had a nice chat with Bayard, etc. Miss Bayard to tea Thursday—very pretty, just from a lunch of fifty girls at the White House, full of go and very jolly; asked tenderly for you. Yesterday tea at Mr. Lowndes's; dinner at the Clymers'[3]; reception at the Evartses', very pleasant, shoals of pretty women and charming gowns. It soothes one's irritated nerves after two successive London seasons to see women who are worth looking at. A young girl from Cleveland in pale blue velvet was a "sight for sair 'een." Tuesday Mrs. Bancroft has a musical party. Thursday Mrs. John Hay wants me to pour out tea for her, and we may as well keep about until March 4th—we are not likely to train much in the coming circus. We long for the sun; it's nearly as bad as Paris here. Professor Marsh[4] is coming to dine today in spite of my wiggledy-piggledy household. Much love to Cambridge folks.

---

[1] Edwin Lawrence Godkin (1831-1902) founded the *Nation* in 1865, and it rapidly became the foremost weekly review in the country "because of the ability, information and unflinching integrity of the editor." In 1881 he sold the *Nation* to the owner of the New York *Evening Post*, of which it then became the weekly edition. Godkin joined the editorial staff of the *Post* and from 1883 to 1899 was its editor-in-chief, succeeding Carl Schurz in that post. When Henry Adams, on his return from Europe in 1868, was preparing to go to Washington to take up the occupation of a political correspondent, he asked Edward Atkinson for an introduction to Godkin, and this seems to have been the beginning of their acquaintance.

[2] Don Luis Polo de Barnabe, the Third Secretary of the Spanish Legion.

[3] Mrs. George Clymer was a daughter of Commodore Shubrick; her husband had been a surgeon in the United States Navy.

[4] Othniel Charles Marsh (1831-1899), professor of vertebrate palæontology and anatomy at Yale and in charge of the division of vertebrate palæontology in the United States Geological Survey.

Your red velvet gown of Christmas 1879 had many compliments yesterday. *Adiós*

CLOVER

1607 H STREET, WASHINGTON,
Sunday A.M., January 16th, 1881.

DEAR PATER: This gray sad-looking morning promises a quiet hour in which to chat with you. Henry is at his dentist and Boojum and I are purring by the fire. We've escaped your late cold snaps but pay for it in dull, leaden skies, so unlike Washington that we can hardly believe we are so far south. Captain Dewey[1] seems to be the only man brave enough to wade in slush and slip on half-buried ice for love of the saddle; we have fairly abandoned it.

No exciting news for you; air full of rumors of the coming Cabinet. It is believed by the hopeful that Garfield's going over to Blaine means a hand-to-hand fight with Grant and Conkling.[2] If the new President has any backbone it will be well tested before the year is out. Tuesday a very pleasant musical party at the Bancrofts'; Miss Read, Mrs. Paran Stevens's sister, sang and a pretty Miss Harlan of Kentucky. Wednesday a quiet dinner at Mrs Wadsworth's; only Miss Beale and we—and she was most amusing. Thursday P.M. a golden wedding reception at Judge Loring's;

[1] Admiral George Dewey, U.S.N. (1837-1917), then a Commander in the United States Navy, stationed at Washington as naval secretary to the Lighthouse Board.

[2] James Abram Garfield (1831-1881), the President-elect, had served with gallantry during the Civil War and reached the rank of a Major General of Volunteers in 1863. On being elected to Congress that same year, he resigned from the army, and from then on he served continuously in the House until 1880, when he was elected to the Senate. A hard worker and good speaker, he succeeded Blaine in 1877 in the leadership of the Republicans in the House of Representatives. At the Chicago convention in 1880, Garfield was Chairman of the Rules Committee—which reported the anti-unit rule, so fatal to the "Stalwarts"—and led the Sherman adherents. The two principal factions, however, were those supporting General Grant, for a third term, and James G. Blaine. On the 36th ballot almost the entire vote hitherto cast for Blaine and Sherman united on Garfield and he was declared nominated. Henry Adams appears to have seen quite a little of Garfield at Washington in 1869, and their relations then appear to have been friendly. In the epidemic of scandals of 1874, Garfield did not escape being accused, although the charges were never proved.

the flowers were exquisite and the lively old people touchingly happy. I dined at the Beales' to fill a sudden gap, as Madame Lewenhaupt, your pretty friend, was ill. General Sherman was my left-hand neighbor; beyond him the great Conkling,[1] looking more asinine and offensive than ever. After dinner, he being the only man in the parlour, a pile of telegrams were handed to him and he read out the easy triumph of the "machine" and the nomination of his man Platt.[2] He read out, "Evarts[3] one vote," and added patronisingly: "A tear for the departing administration." Mrs. Don Cameron regretted Morton's failure.[4] Now New York is all in his hands and he can make it hot for Garfield.

[1] Roscoe Conkling (1829-1888), Senator from New York from 1867 to 1881, when he and his colleague, T. C. Platt, resigned in consequence of a dispute with President Garfield over federal patronage in the State of New York, and offered themselves for reëlection, but without success. During President Grant's administration, Conkling's influence at the White House was very great, and until his defeat in 1881 he controlled the Republican Party in the State of New York. He opposed President Hayes's efforts at reform, and particularly the purge of the Custom House, in 1878, that resulted in General Arthur's removal from the collectorship. He was one of the principal leaders in the "Stalwart group" organized by the New York, Pennsylvania, and Illinois politicians of the old school, in the interest of Grant's renomination for a third term. With James G. Blaine his relations were never cordial.

[2] Thomas Collier Platt (1833-1910), president of Adams Express Company, had served two terms in Congress from 1873 to 1877. He was elected to the United States Senate at Conkling's dictation to succeed Francis Kernan, whose term was to have expired March 4, but who had resigned the previous May at Conkling's request.

[3] Evarts would retire from the State Department on the fourth of March.

[4] Levi Parsons Morton (1824-1920) was a partner in the banking house of Morton, Bliss and Co., the London branch of which acted, from 1873 to 1884, as the fiscal agent of the United States Government. Early in the '70s, Mr. Morton became interested in New York politics and was credited with having given financial assistance to the regular organization of the Republican Party in that state in its campaigns. He was elected to Congress in 1879, and during its sessions he and Mrs. Morton entertained with a touch of metropolitan splendor that provincial Washington was not then accustomed to. However, they were much liked by Washington society. In the summer of 1880, Mr. Morton was persuaded to become the treasurer of the Republican National Committee, and as such he managed the finances of General Garfield's campaign. The French Mission was his reward for these services. His political intimacies with the machine politicians who were opposed to reform discredited him in the estimation of the group of Independents who frequented the Adamses' circle, and his firm's

From there went on to Mrs. John Hay's reception, which was very lively; Miss Bayard in a charming pink dress and full of fun. Mrs. Don Cameron[1] asked if she might come to tea and declined to wait till I called first. She is very young, pretty, and, I fear, bored, and her middle-aged Senator fighting a boss fight in Harrisburg; so she came on Friday, wailed about Harrisburg, and was quite frank in her remarks about men and things. Poor "Don"[2] will think she's

---

connection with the Chile-Peru case confirmed this prejudice. Mr. Morton's subsequent career was distinguished; he was elected Vice President of the United States in 1889 and Governor of the State of New York in 1895.

[1] Mrs. Cameron (Elizabeth Sherman), a niece of Senator John Sherman and of General W. T. Sherman, married, in 1878, Senator James Donald Cameron, a widower of at least twice her age.

[2] James Donald Cameron (1833-1918), a Senator from Pennsylvania from 1877 (when he succeeded his father, Simon Cameron) to 1897, when he retired from politics altogether. He had been president of the Northern Central Railway of Pennsylvania (1863-1874), and Secretary of War under Grant from May 1876 to March 1877; he was Chairman of the Republican National Committee during Hayes's campaign and during his term as President. He married twice; his first wife, Mary McCormick, died in 1874.

In the *Education* (pp. 333-334), Henry Adams refers to the "Cameron type" in part as follows: "Months of close contact teach character, if character has interest; and to Adams the Cameron type had keen interest, ever since it had shipwrecked his career in the person of President Grant. Perhaps it owed life to Scotch blood; perhaps to the blood of Adam and Eve, the primitive strain of man; perhaps only to the blood of the cottager working against the blood of the townsman; but whatever it was one liked it for its simplicity. The Pennsylvania mind, as minds go, was not complex; it reasoned little and never talked; but in practical matters it was the steadiest of all American types; perhaps the most efficient; certainly the safest. . . . Practically the Pennsylvanian forgot his prejudices when he allied his interests. He then became supple in action and large in motive, whatever he thought of his colleagues. When he happened to be right— which was, of course, whenever one agreed with him—he was the strongest American in America. As an ally he was worth all the rest, because he understood his own class, who were always a majority; and he knew how to deal with them as no New Englander could. If one wanted work done in Congress, one did wisely to avoid asking a New Englander to do it. A Pennsylvanian not only could do it, but did it willingly, practically, and intelligently. Never in the range of human possibilities had a Cameron believed in an Adams—or an Adams in a Cameron—but they had curiously enough, almost always worked together. The Camerons had what the Adamses thought the political vice of reaching their objects without much regard to their methods. The loftiest virtue of the Pennsylvania machine had never been its scrupulous purity or sparkling professions. The machine worked by coarse means on coarse interests; but its practical suc-

fallen among thieves when he comes back. She is a sister of General Miles's wife, a niece of Sherman.

Last night a reception at the Evartses'; I backed out and sent Henry, while Mr. Lowndes, who dropped in to dinner, kept me company by the library fire. We can't have any dinners, being still in search of a man; the poor Dane was quite unequal to the task, so we shoved him into a French hotel. When I told him I had no fault to find, that I knew he had done his best, he answered with a tragic earnestness worth of his compatriot Hamlet: "I have done like a fool." We are slowly getting right side up, and in a few days I hope to get my spare rooms finished, but it would be no pleasure to any guest to be here in this dismal weather. As soon as we get a good man and fill the place of a maid who is not well, then we hope to be more hospitable.

I've been interrupted for an hour in this by a call from Mrs. Evarts and her daughter on their way home from church; she was curious to see our restorations, of which she had heard. Anything more like an old scrap-bag than our furnishings you never saw, but a few pretty duds go a long way in this town. I wish the days were longer and sunnier; I don't have time to breathe and yet do nothing. Much love to Fanny and all Cambridge folks on the hill. Vases came at last from Art Museum; also lace and Persian embroidery—all in good order. *Adiós.* Very affectionately

CLOVER

1607 H STREET, WASHINGTON,
Sunday, January 23rd, 1881.

DEAR PATER: This is the weekly "record of a quiet life." Social instincts are certainly modified by climate, and until we get more sun we shall hug our fireside, but you are mistaken in thinking we got your cold snaps. Yesterday I goaded Henry into a ride, the thermometer saying 40°—and such a ride! The horses are not sharpened, and the roads proved solid ice under the mud. The beasties balanced themselves on their tails, and when Georgetown

---

cess had been the most curious subject of study in American history. . . . Following up the same line, in his studies of American character, Adams reached the result—to him altogether paradoxical—that Cameron's qualities and defects united in equal share to make him the most useful member of the Senate."

Cemetery was reached it seemed wiser and more economical to dismount and save future transport, but curiosity led us on to see if we could get home. We slid gaily down a long hill and crawled over horsecar tracks, frozen and penitent, to our stable. It's very disgusting to waste horses and exercise in this way.

Of politics, next to nothing. Blaine will go into Evarts's shoes, you may depend, though Nordhoff affects to know nothing of it in his daily letter to the *Herald*. It's a hard nut for the reformers to crack, but they'll do it. Robeson has ratted and is swinging over to Blaine, it is thought. By the way, do you remember in my last I told you of a dinner at the Beales' where Conkling read out telegrams announcing Platt's election? And how Mrs. Cameron made a remark about Morton? I did not say that I, by way of sticking in a pin, expressed regret that Depew[1] was not chosen, and that Conkling sniffingly observed,—not looking at me, for we don't bow,— "Mr. Depew had one vote, and that is one more than I thought he would have." In the Sunday *Herald* from Boston the political correspondent, Edmund Hudson, gave a paragraph to the story, only luckily my name did not figure, but a "hostess of liberal proclivities." Such a trifle shows one what a whispering gallery Washington is, and how one must always be on their guard. Newspapermen and women are everywhere, and petty items are their bread and butter.

Today the *Capitol* says: "Mrs. Sallie Ward Armstrong[2] is coming here with a superb wardrobe and is expected to make a sensation." A curious juxtaposition for Mrs. Bigelow Lawrence. Perhaps the Kentucky lady will put up at Wormley's. Mrs. Lawrence and Miss Chapman are jolly and handsome as ever and drop in a good deal at tea time. We all miss General Taylor[3] sadly and no

---

[1] Chauncey Mitchell Depew (1834-1928), then general counsel for the Vanderbilt system of railways. In 1872 he had joined the Liberal Republican movement and was nominated and defeated for the office of lieutenant governor of New York.

[2] Mrs. Sallie Ward Armstrong was the first wife of Bigelow Lawrence, from whom she was divorced.

[3] Richard Taylor (1826-1879): "Gen. Dick Taylor of Louisiana, brother-in-law of Jefferson Davis, himself one of the best of the rebel Major Generals, a great friend of the Prince of Wales, a first-rate raconteur and whist player, a son of a former President of the United States." (*Letters*, p. 310)

one takes his place. We look for Mr. King daily; he is overdue and ought to be working hard for his appropriations, so his friends say, but he bloweth where he listeth and official traces cannot keep him in the shafts. Congress is wasting time and doing nothing important to the public.

Mrs. Hayes was at the Evartses' reception last night, smiling as a basket of chips. I told her how we wished they would stay for another four years, as we should have no friends at the new court. She has enjoyed the White House as no President's wife ever did before, but is not sorry to go back to her own quiet town in Ohio. She's a kind, simple-minded woman; a touch of the country schoolmistress about her, but not a bit of nonsense or vulgarity. I had a little chat with General Sherman last night. His daughter is married to a Lieutenant Thackara[1] stationed in Boston now. Why don't you call on her some day? I doubt if she has received any attention and it would, I know, please her papa, and Ohio people are sensitive about "stuck-up Boston folks." They sniff at Beacon Street, but I believe even Howells underestimates the "South End."

Mrs. N. has come to Wormley's for the winter. *Il ne fallait que ça!* I do hate cats! She is so loving to me; she hears I am at "home at five o'clock." I can evade resident bores tolerably by having no day, by never suggesting that they should come to tea, and by omitting almost all receptions. But cordial Bostonians, who never came near us there, are so cordial here that it's quite touching.

Henry pegs away at his work and thinks his house charming. It is far more attractive than Uncle Sam's, and in spring will be most comfortable when the piazza and garden come into play. We have two spare rooms now ready. When will you come? The sooner the better—and again in April; and tell the Gurneys we depend on their visit. Don't let them back out. Any day now we are ready. Much love to Auntie and to Fanny. Affectionately

M. A.

1607 H STREET, WASHINGTON,
Sunday, January 30th, 1881.

---

[1] Lieutenant A. M. Thackara graduated from the United States Naval Academy in 1869 and married, in 1880, Eleanor Sherman, daughter of General W. T. Sherman. He was later United States Consul at Havre and Consul-General at Berlin and at Paris.

DEAR PATER: Another gray sky with no promise of spring in it, and yet three years ago Henry brought me home wild flowers from the woods outside of the town on February 15th. Now we trot our Siberian wastes of snow and ice and the horses walk on top of snow without breaking through. But Pennsylvania Avenue is bare as in summer. Still, for all this, we've had some nice rides this last week and feel all the better for it. Sturgis Bigelow appeared at midnight on Thursday; we found him coming back from a mild carouse. He seems happy and not eager to go back to his work and his native town. Last night we had the Bonapartes to dine, Miss Chapman, and the Randolph Tuckers[1] of Virginia, and it was quite pleasant. We went later to a reception at the Evartses'—many people who were worth talking to—and much enjoyed an hour or more. Evarts and Schurz are evidently gay at the sight of the end of their tether with no scandal to blush for and no newspapers to "make them afraid." Someone quoted Evarts as saying that he was now so near the end that he wasn't "even afraid to insult a Senator."

Your friend Mrs. N. came flying in to tea the other day, and after caracolling round for an hour and trying to find from Henry the amount of our income, she came to me, held my hand lovingly, and with great tact—two Ohio people and two Spaniards standing by—said: "Such a charming house! What I call a refined *Boston* house." That kind of thing is what makes Bostonians so generally popular! But she is very happy; and with an Italian prince, an English lord, and no end of counts in the diplomatic corps, the future has possible germs of hope which "make the widow's heart sing for joy." If you had brought me up properly I should not indulge in petty, spiteful gossip!

We had a delicious opera to go to last Tuesday, and for it cut the Japanese Minister's party. Tuesday next, dinner with Schurzes and concert in the evening. Friday, dinner at the Lewenhaupts'. Saturday, dinner at Mrs. Wadsworth's for the Nat Thayers. Miss Beale and Miss Devens[2] dine here tomorrow for Bil's amusement.

---

[1] John Randolph Tucker (1823-1897), Democratic Member of Congress from Virginia, 1875 to 1887; in 1894 he was elected president of the American Bar Association.

[2] Miss Devens, daughter of the Attorney General.

Clarence King expected daily; heard from after a thousand miles on mule-back in Mexico. When are you coming on? And when are the Gurneys coming? April is nicer for weather, but now for society. Love to Fanny and babies and to Betsy—am glad to hear she is all right again. Affectionately

M. A.

1607 H STREET, WASHINGTON,
Sunday, February 6th, 1881.

DEAR PATER: *De profundis* of a miserable cold I clamour to you. Monday last was a snare and a pitfall to the hopeful, and we cooled off the house and warmed up by a sharp trot, hence these sniffles. Tuesday a dinner at the Schurzes' and a charming concert in the evening at a far-off hall—the German Minister[1] taking Schurz's place, the latter dining out; he was, as usual, very lively and very uproarious. Friday a dinner of fourteen at the Lewenhaupts'—a handsome and dainty feast; the host took me in, inquired especially for you. Bayard and his two daughters there, Miss Chapman, Marquis de Podesta,[2] a new Hungary count,[3] and lesser lights; broke up at ten for a party at Mrs. Berry's for the Thayers. I went home and to bed and made Henry take my excuses.

Last night, dinner of twenty or more at Mrs. Wadsworth's, also for the Thayers. General Beale took me in and he is always easy to talk to; De Bildt,[4] Swedish secretary, on my right, and quondam editor, is intelligent and chatty, so that only physical disability spoiled my feast. All went off to party at the Evartses', but I to bed; Henry said it was gay and amusing. Someone who was at tea here yesterday quoted Mrs. ex-Secretary Robeson as saying to

[1] Kurt von Schlözer (1882-1894), the German Minister at Washington from 1871 to 1882: "Among my set of friends this winter has been our old Roman acquaintance Schlözer, who is great fun, eccentric as an Englishman and riotous as a wild Highlander. We lament together over our Roman hostess and her *boudins Richelieu*. But you should try Schlözer's *Gansenbrust* if you want to experience sudden death." (*Letters*, p. 306)
[2] Marquis de Potestad Fornari, arbiter on the part of Spain on the American and Spanish Joint Claims Commission then in session at Washington.
[3] Count Lippe-Weissenfeld, counselor of the Austria-Hungary Legation.
[4] C. de Bildt, secretary of the Sweden and Norway Legation.

Edmunds[1] at a dinner the day before: "We can't produce a gentleman in America. Delfosse is a gentleman." "Yes," said Edmunds, "a gentleman, but he can't count codfish." Mrs. Robeson is fat and saucy, and if her manners get into ill-repute she may find her path thorny.

You charge me with being uncosmopolitan in refusing to recognise that beast Conkling. Few people here think him fit to associate with, except the Beales, who swallow the Grant crowd and all their pals. I think if you knew the man well you would rebuke me if I bowed to him. It is thought here that his day of reckoning is not far off. There is mud enough in every path, but one needn't choose miry places.

This coming week is pretty full; a dinner at L. P. Morton's Wednesday, at the Bancrofts' Thursday, at the Schurzes' Saturday, besides evening toots if one is energetic. Lunches I despise and lie myself out of. Fine sleighing, brilliant sun, clear, cold. History goes on quietly. We barricade our doors till near sunset and are envied by our harnessed friends. Madame Outrey improving, though not in "society" yet. Ask Aunt Eunice if she got my pæan of gratitude for the lovely hood. *Adiós.* Affectionately

M. A.

1607 H Street, Washington,
Sunday, February 13th, 1881.

Dear Pater: We've been thawing like mad all the week and the snow has fled. The lower part of the city under water yesterday; Baltimore and Potomac Depot submerged several feet—boats carrying passengers. Friday P.M. Henry and I rode some way up the river to see if the ice had broken, but not a sign of moving could we see; but at midnight it gave way with a rush and the Long Bridge—or four hundred feet of it—went last evening. This sudden thaw is hard on sewers. Our new ones we ventilated with a pipe to the level of roof and had to send in hot haste yesterday to have the old one in kitchen tapped and a ventilating shaft put in.

---

[1] George Franklin Edmunds (1828-1919), Republican Senator from Vermont from 1866 to 1891, when he resigned. He was the author of the Edmunds Act for the suppression of polygamy, and of the antitrust act of 1890 (the Sherman Act).

This is a well-managed city, though; one of the new street commissioners is Lieutenant Greene,[1] who has published some much praised books on Russia; he keeps the streets in fine order—as clean as a Dutch town.

We have had several dinners since I wrote you, which my persistent cold makes a burden instead of a pleasure. When one can neither taste nor smell, two hours of a ponderous Senator break the bruised reed. Sunday Lamar dined here alone, and was chatty and in good spirits. Wednesday a large dinner at the Mortons'; Aristarchi Bey took me in, Morton was on my other side. He is a lightweight and very ordinary; if he can be a successful public man, none need despair. He asked my political opinions. I told him I was a boss-Stalwart, believed in the machine, and the chaff spread; but he is too dull to catch chaff. Conkling has gone back on him—got money out of him—and he is supposed to feel sore. His wife is frank and sensible and worth ten of him. The old house is quite furbished with old things and new added—not in good taste, but looks filled and comfortable. No good pictures, but plenty of cheap stuff which in the charitable evening light looks well enough. An English butler and liveried flunkies add a glamour of magnificence calculated to dazzle and charm the simple Congressional guests, and the newspaper correspondents think it "magnificent."

Thursday a dinner at the Bancrofts', the hostess ill in her room so that Mrs. Bancroft Davis had to receive for her; the President and Mrs. Hayes, Bonapartes, Evartses, Allison, Senator Hoar,[2] Robesons, etc. I sat between Hoar and Bonaparte and it was not intoxicating—the latter is heavy and gentlemanly. Poor Henry had to sit next to Robeson, to whom he has not bowed for years; he knew him well in old times. They met as if no swindling chasm had intervened, and that end of the table was not quiet or subdued, to say the least. Robeson, having wriggled back to Congress on teetotal support, "treats his resolution" freely and gaily. We had to

[1] Lieutenant Francis Vinton Greene, United States Army (1850-1921), the assistant engineer for the District of Columbia.

[2] George Frisbie Hoar (1826-1904), Member of Congress from Massachusetts, 1869-1877; United States Senator, 1877-1904; presided at the Chicago convention in 1880.

go to a reception at the Schurzes' afterwards. Yesterday a dinner of twelve there; sat between Austrian Minister and Senator Pendleton,[1] "Gentleman George," who is a solemn prig, as Mrs. Lawrence says, who is much disconcerted at the German Minister's buffoonery.

Did you read Schurz's reply to Dawes?[2] Mr. Nordhoff says the Western men believe that at the bottom of all the Tibbles-Bright-Eyes movement is a land-grabbing scheme of speculators who want to get hold of the rich Dakota lands themselves and are much disgruntled that the Poncas refuse to go. Dawes has not added to his slender reputation for sagacity in these parts.

Today Lamar and Mr. Lowndes and Miss Martin[3] of Auburn, N.Y., are coming to dine. We have had much less company than usual this winter; when Lent brings large dinners and receptions to an end we shall try and be more energetic. The more I go to large dinners, the more I feel they defeat their own end; in nine cases out of ten the majority are bored, there is no good round talk, and it's an effort to both host and guest. William Bliss[4] is coming to make his mother a visit; was expected last Friday—the great snowstorm may have delayed him. Mr. King is expected daily; I hope he will stay with us. Wormley's is running over and every cranny will be filled by Inauguration. We are to dine at the White House Thursday—a State dinner—don't you pity us? The beams of the setting sun are falling on us. Also a conditional dinner at Burnside's[5] this week to meet the Hayeses—the day not fixed; were asked there yesterday, but pre-engaged. He is a nice old fellow and his dinners very funny and informal; music-box, six rocking chairs, much Apollinaris; everyone stretches across the table and all talk at once.

---

[1] George Hunt Pendleton (1825-1889), Senator from Ohio from 1879 to 1885 and author of the Civil Service Reform Act of 1883. After retiring from the Senate he was appointed Minister to Germany, 1885-1888.
[2] Henry Laurens Dawes (1816-1903), Senator from Massachusetts, was first elected to the House of Representatives in 1857 and served continuously until 1875, when he was elected to the Senate. Neither of the Massachusetts Senators was in favor with the Adamses.
[3] Miss Mary Martin, a sister of Dan Martin, one of the editors of *Life*.
[4] William Bliss, a son of Mrs. George Bancroft.
[5] Ambrose Everett Burnside (1824-1881) had an active military career during the Civil War, unfortunately not always crowned with success; he was elected to the Senate in 1877 from Rhode Island.

You are wise to postpone your visit. You complain of feeling old. I too find thirty-seven years a burden and washing and eating a heavy task. Affectionately

M. A.

1607 H STREET,
February 17th, 1881.

DEAR PATER: Heaven forbid! What does that young catamount mean? There was some chaff about it[1] and she begged and entreated me to take her to Boston; said "Billy says he'll give me a dinner every day." I said she'd not be a success in Boston, and said I didn't see it. Think of me and that young "hoodlum" in the classic haunts of my native city! I think Ellen's face would be almost "wuth it." Bless your dear hospitable heart for all its kind offers, but I chaperon no one but Henry. I am tied by both legs here. A young woman of New York wailed so often and so sadly at having to leave the Schurzes and go home that I offered to take her in for this week on condition that no "night work" would be expected. She's a nice intelligent girl and seems to find wherewith to amuse herself.

Mr. King turned up on Sunday after a fearful fourteen hundred miles on mule-back from Mexico; drowned in a flood and lost all his money and papers; is very well and jolly; is coming to us in spite of modest disclaimers, as Wormley cannot keep him unless he and Eugene Hale[2]—Senator-elect—can share one room. Inauguration will be a horrid bore; you are wise to prefer spring flowers. Dinners rage; to meet Lucy[3] and Rutherford B. three times in one week is enough! Mr. King says if he held Horshaw at 16 or 17, as it is now, *he* should get out; says it's all dark in gold and silver mines. Some of his California bonanza friends have in a few years bought in twenty-two mines; eighteen gone up; from the remaining four they've cleared seven millions. Faro or rouge-et-noir

[1] The reference is to a suggestion of Dr. Hooper's that Mrs. Adams should bring Miss Emily Beale to Boston for a visit.
[2] Eugene Hale (1836-1918), just elected to the United States Senate from Maine; he married a daughter of Zachariah Chandler (1813-1879), Senator from Michigan 1857-1875; when (for two years) Secretary of the Interior under Grant, responsible for the objectionable Ponca legislation.
[3] Mrs. Hayes (Lucy Ware Webb).

is safer. Thanks for your note. "What a risk you ran"—we might have come! Affectionately

M.A.

18th. DEAR PATER: Mr. King does not wish to be quoted as to Horshaw, so don't let what I wrote yesterday go beyond Ned, please. Pleasant dinner last night at palace. Betsy may like the invitation. Yours affectionately

M. A.

1607 H STREET, WASHINGTON,
Sunday, February 20th, 1881.

DEAR PATER: This makes note No. 3 since Sunday last; my pot-hooks and O's will weary you. We've had a week of fine bright weather, no snow, only a heavy rain on Friday night which gave way to a soft blue sky yesterday.

Tuesday a dinner at Burnside's for Mr. and Mrs. Hayes— informal and pleasant. The General clings to the old-fashioned way of having his food on the table and carving for his guests. Schurz took me down; Mrs. Hayes and I flanked the host. Senator and Mrs. Hoar were there, Anthony,[1] a Mrs. Carter of Ohio, a guest of Mrs. Hayes, who looked like a powder-puff—fortunately flour is cheap west of the Alleghanies, or the husbands and fathers would be beggars. Mrs. Hayes and I talked a little bit about Mrs. Blaine and she confided to me a story which Mrs. Blaine spread broadcast three years ago, that she accepted an official invitation to a State dinner at the White House, but, in order to show her disap-proval of the host and hostess, declined to swallow a morsel of food while under their roof. From all accounts she has lost no op-portunity of insulting Mrs. Hayes in the most marked manner. Gail Hamilton, who lives with her, calls her a "leper" in society and Miss Blaine calls those who do associate with them "that nasty Hayes set." It's a pity such bitter females should succeed the Evartses, whom everybody likes. Garfield will reap the whirlwind if he doesn't look sharp.

Wednesday Mr. King dined here quietly and we chatted over the fire till midnight. Thursday, dinner at the White House—

---

[1] Henry Bowen Anthony (1815-1884), Senator from Rhode Island, 1859-1884.

thirty-six "covers." Our old friend President Gilman[1] of Johns Hopkins took me in; and the new "bonanza" Senator from California, Miller,[2] was my left-hand neighbour; he seemed sensible and manly, was a general in the Army of the Cumberland in the war. Henry took in a simple-hearted old lady from Michigan, wife of Senator Conger;[3] neither she nor a Kentucky lady on his left had answered their dinner invitations, not thinking it a thing to do. Schumacher of Ohio is more punctilious; he said to the German Minister that he thought it was always best to accept a dinner, and then when the time came you could do as you liked about going! After dinner Mr. John Hay introduced Robert Lincoln[4] to me and we pranced through the greenhouse together. He's a quiet, gentlemanly, attractive man; tell Anne Lothrop he asked tenderly for her. The new dinner set, which is said to have cost fifteen thousand dollars, is fearful. To eat one's soup calmly with a coyote springing at you from a pine tree is intimidating, and ice cream plates disguised as Indian snowshoes would be æsthetic, but make one yearn for Mongolian simplicity. But, as Mrs. Cimabue Brown[5] says: "Let us try to live up to it." Went on to a party at British Legation for half an hour afterward; then to Schurz's reception to pick up Miss Palmer.

Friday, Gilmans to breakfast; I was ill and had to leave the table—gorging on Potomac[6] the night before has upset both Henry and me. Miss Doane, her fiancé Gardiner, and Mr. King dined here; I reappeared in the character of Mother H's dog. Yesterday, dinner for Doanes at Senator Edmunds's—very nice; on to Evartses' where Mrs. Bell and Mrs. Pratt[7] made hay. I wanted them to dine here this week, but they are off tomorrow. Spring is coming

---

[1] Daniel Coit Gilman (1831-1908).

[2] John Franklin Miller (1831-1886), Senator-elect from California.

[3] Omar Dwight Conger (1818-1898), Senator from Michigan.

[4] Robert Todd Lincoln (1843-1926), son of President Lincoln, about to be appointed Secretary of War; he had known Mrs. Lothrop before her marriage, when her father, Samuel Hooper, was in Congress and his house was one of the principal social and political centres in Washington.

[5] One of Du Maurier's characters in *Punch*.

[6] A reference to Potomac water, as no wine was served at the White House during the Hayes Administration.

[7] Mrs. Joseph Bell (Helen Choate) and Mrs. Ellerton Pratt (Miriam Foster Choate), daughters of Rufus Choate and noted for their wit and charm.

and I must go to New York for a day to get your Christmas wagon and harness. Yours lovingly

M. A.

1607 H STREET,
February 23rd.

DEAR PATER: Your Sunday letter makes us feel very sad with its account of Fanny's increased suffering.[1] Write or telegraph me if we can be of any earthly use either to Fanny, Ned, or the children, or to help lighten Ellen's care. I will be nurse or read story books all day long or play games or anything to fill any gaps. Henry and Mr. King would do nicely together and I can leave at two hours' notice. If we were in trouble Ned would find fifty ways of helping us and we feel like two brutes to keep five hundred miles off and do nothing.

I hope you join in the "amende honorable" to Schurz; the feeling here is that Boston showed great injustice in condemning a faithful servant unheard. Even Senator Logan[2] went to his office more than three weeks ago and said the attack was a "damned outrage." Dawes inspires mild contempt here; I fancy he feels uncomfortable by reason of the non-indorsement of his own State. He and his wife introduced themselves to Henry and me last Saturday at the Evartses' reception. We were not gushing to their unsought advances.

Send me word if I should go to you or to Ellen's. Yours affectionately

M. A.

1607 H STREET, WASHINGTON,
Sunday, February 27th, 1881.

---

[1] Mrs. Edward Hooper was desperately ill, and died two days later, on February 25.

[2] John Alexander Logan (1826-1886), an unusually able officer during the Civil War who rose to the rank of major-general of volunteers. Resuming an interrupted political career after the war, he was elected to the House of Representatives in 1867 and in 1871 to the Senate, where he continued to serve (with the exception of two years) until his death. A violent partisan, he was identified with the radical wing of the Republican Party.

DEAR PATER: I've been half expecting a summons from you by mail or telegraph in answer to my note of Tuesday. I should think Ellen needed a reinforcement by this time; the continued strain of responsibility and sympathy must be very wearing.

We are slowly creeping into spring; blessed Lent comes in on Wednesday and our good church friends at the British Legation have a big party to "dance it in"! We decline all dances and so shall escape that too. Tuesday Sandy Bliss had a pleasant party where I met our old friend William,[1] whom I've not seen for twenty years. Wednesday a big dinner at the British Legation—I had a nasty time; sat between a *ci-devant* blacksmith from Albany district[2] and a Spanish marquis. The former took me in, and a most "inharmonious blacksmith" he was; from the anvil he took to making machines and then the "machine" made him Member of Congress; he wears High Church garments and has social aspirations; is a donkey of the first water. If he and Levi P. Morton are self-made men I can only say they have made a mess of their work and would have done better to leave it to more competent hands. Mr. King, speaking of the banking firm of Morton & Bliss, says with a happy turn: "If ignorance is Bliss, what the devil is Morton?"

Washington is not pleasant with Mrs. N. and Miss B. on the rampage. The former is more pushing and offensive than you can imagine. Friday we had eight people to dine here. I didn't think it pleasant, but Outrey went and told his wife *"le diner pétillait d'esprit."* Ohio predominated last night at the Evartses' last reception. Schurz told me with great amusement that he was yesterday on the floor of the Senate talking to Logan on a sofa when Dawes got up from his desk and, going up to him, held out his hand. Schurz says he responded by holding out his and that Logan burst into loud laughter. That Dawes should be willing to recognise publicly a "murderer and assassin" shows either a degraded moral standard or that he thinks the vanes in Massachusetts point another

---

[1] Alexander and William Bliss, both sons of Mrs. George Bancroft.
[2] Michael Nicholas Nolan, ex-Mayor of Albany, was elected to Congress in the fall of 1880; so too was Walter A. Wood, a very successful manufacturer of harvesting machinery, but from the adjoining Congressional district across the river.

way. Dawes denounced Mr. King in the Senate last winter opening as an "extravagant humbug," Schurz says the real reason being
that Mr. King did not go to a reception to which Dawes had invited
him. The petty jealousy felt and shown here by people who have
not a deep confidence in their own social status is most annoying,
and the "calling" nuisance requires a cool head and imperturbable
nerves to meet it squarely. A man's house is not his castle here but
the public's bear garden.

Mr. King has just come in and though I've entreated him to
take a book till I've finished this letter he will keep babbling. We
are still busy with Cabinet rumours—Blaine is sure and has been
for six weeks, the rest dark horses. L. P. Morton is a good deal
laughed at; the papers book him for the English mission.

It was charming to see Mrs. Bell and Mrs. Pratt here and everyone who saw them regretted that they wouldn't stay. Mrs. N. is
understood by this time and it's well that folks here should see that
Bostonians can be decent and well-bred. Much love to Fanny and
babies.

CLOVER

1607 H STREET, WASHINGTON,
Sunday, 27th, 11:30 A.M.

DEAR PATER: Your notes and one from Ned came an hour ago.[1]
We knew from your last Sunday letter that the end was near; that it
was so peaceful after the long struggle is some comfort. How
strange it seems that those whose life is so full to the very brim
should have to give it up, and others who long to throw it away,
like Aunt Anne, must stay on and on. No one can be both father
and mother better than Ned, and those dear little mites won't want
for sunshine. I want to go on and see all of you, but after turning it
over and over have decided to wait at least a few days. Henry
flatly refuses to let me go alone and I am not willing to pull him up
from his work. If you had sent us a telegram Friday night we
should have gone on, now we think we should be a bore.

---

[1] Her sister-in-law's death was not telegraphed to her, and the letter announcing
it reached her later that morning, the day of the funeral. A stoical custom, inher-
ited from their grandfather William Sturgis and followed by several of his children and grandchildren, discouraged conventional outward signs of mourning.

It is warm and muggy here and on Friday when you were so cold the sun was almost oppressive as we rode along the river. That and quinine have carried off my feverish cold and I can sympathise with my friends who are still struggling. I've not even seen Madame Outrey yet. Today's warm rain will bring out your dogwood not much later than usual, I hope. William Bliss dined with us last night and sat chatting over the fire till late with only Mr. King and us; the former he has never met and long wanted to. He seems delicate and much as he wants to go to Boston is afraid to risk the change of climate. Tell Ned he has now Mr. King's heart in some way. Write me again. Is there no chance of Ellen's bringing Whitman and little Ellen on here for a change of air and scene? It would be so nice to see them. Ever affectionately

CLOVER

1607 H STREET, WASHINGTON,
Sunday, March 6th.

DEAR PATER: Since I wrote to you on Monday nothing has come into our days which would be of interest to you. We are told that the British Legation ball and the Inauguration went off finely and we know by the papers that Hayes is out and Garfield in. We sat by our firesides on March 4th and heard distant drums and fifes. I went in the afternoon to see Mrs. Bancroft, who is confined to her room, and William Bliss came in with a protracted account of all he had seen at the Capitol. Now the much discussed Cabinet is a fact and will soon get in running order. The only members whom we know are Wayne MacVeagh and Lincoln, whom we met only at Mrs. Hayes's dinner. The former is a square out-and-out Independent, clever, lively, a great talker and laugher. We have seen him from time to time unmuzzled; how he will appear as an official I am curious to see. But society is practically over for the season and the chances are ten to one that we shall see nothing of the new administration. In this ever-shifting panorama of course we shall find new combinations, but we shall hardly have the same intimate cosy set that we did.

The Schurzes will not break up till the end of March; we hope he will not bury himself in St. Louis, where he is editor of a German paper. New York is the second largest German city in the world, they say, and no leader is there to make opposition to Conkling. Schurz might be a most valuable element for anti-corruption and anti-machine men to rally round. Some effort will probably be made to induce Schurz to settle there. He says his Cabinet place has cost him so much that he must turn to money-making now for his children's sake.

You will see by your paper today what a narrow escape the outgoing President had with his party on his way to Baltimore yesterday.

Mr. and Mrs. Brimmer came in yesterday for a talk and a cup of tea; she tells me Ellen has had a bronchial attack. I should think she must be tired out in body and mind and she'd better take Whitman by the hand and come on here. We must get spring soon, though for the last few days it's been cold and raw. Henry's brother Brooks is coming on Thursday, he writes; he is lame and has had a hard winter and Henry Bigelow advises a change. Mr. King, who is our prop and stay, went to New York Thursday but comes back tomorrow; he takes half his meals here but keeps a room at Wormley's to see business men in. He is trying to resign and go out of office with Schurz, in whose Department he is. Garfield is much opposed to it—his resigning, that is—but I fancy he'll get out and name his successor. The loss to us will be very great. Then John Hay goes back to Ohio in spite of much entreating to stay; he and Blaine are on most friendly terms. This is the last about Roscoe. Someone asked why he was on the Committee of Foreign Relations and the answer was: "Because he is so unfitted for domestic."

Write me how Ned's babies get on and who is to take charge. Tell Ellen Gurney to let me divide with her any spring clothing, either by coming on, or I will have dresses made here if they'll send measures. I wish Henry would let me go on without him but he is "sot" and I have not the heart to drag him off from his work, in which he is much absorbed. Bil Bigelow wrote me a kind note on Tuesday; if you see him thank him and say I am going to answer soon. Mr. and Mrs. Barlow[1] were to come to Wormley's yesterday, the latter in wretched health, her friends say; I must go and

---

[1] Mr. and Mrs. S. L. M. Barlow.

ask for her this P.M. Goodbye. Take good care of yourself. Ever lovingly

M. A.

1607 H STREET,
Friday, 11th, 1 P.M.

DEAR PATER: Yours of 8th came yesterday. Unless I am really needed I don't fancy the idea of going north in March and I shouldn't pull well in single harness after so many years' practice in double. We will, if you like, go to New York on Tuesday the 15th or 16th and meet you at the Brevoort as we much need a wagon of some sort now that spring is coming on, and here can find nothing worth buying. More than one day in New York we do not want and shall bring you back with us. Brooks says he leaves on Monday probably. I'm going to write to Ellen to see if I can do anything here about the children's spring clothes; ask her to drop me a line if she wants me to do anything. We had two hours in the saddle before breakfast this morning and found it most enchanting. When you come here order your *Daily* sent here if you like that ribald sheet; you might miss even that feeble dose. If this reaches you too late for writing, send a telegram. Love to Ned and children. Yours affectionately

M. A.

1607 H STREET, WASHINGTON,
Sunday, March 13th, 1881.

DEAR PATER: I half expect a telegram from you tomorrow saying you will meet us in New York on Wednesday in answer to mine of Friday last. It's a hideous effort even to go to New York, but we much need some kind of a vehicle and this place is not good for any shopping. As we go to Boston-wards anyway in May, the long journey twice in two months is more than I can venture unless Ned needs me. He writes me that Whitman's throat troubles him. Why don't you pack him off here or further south?

Lent has set in vigorously here though a mild form of society goes on for the less strict. The Thorntons had a party last night for Lord and Lady Campbell, Lorne's brother; we declined as not going out anywhere now. Thursday John Hay and his wife came in as we were finishing dinner to get us to go with them and make our bow to Mrs. Garfield, and, as we wanted to have it over, we went. Many people there; we had a few words only with the new mistress. She made a very pleasant impression on us—quiet, ladylike, dignified, and far more at her ease than Mrs. Hayes. By the way, there is a curious fact not generally known, which is that Mrs. Hayes was the head and front of the anti-wine movement in the White House. The matter became so wearisome and annoying to Mrs. Hayes at last that she used to get up and leave the room when it was mentioned, saying: "This old lady has heard too much of that." This comes from a source which is beyond gossip. The new administration ought to have a quiet time as nothing of importance is on the stocks.

Alex Agassiz[1] and Mr. King dined with us on Wednesday, the former off Thursday to the tropics, the latter has resigned his office—a great blow to us—but can do more valuable work as a geologist out of harness and his successor will carry out his wishes. Love to folks in Cambridge. Ever affectionately

M. A.

---

[1] Alexander Emanuel Agassiz (1835-1910) as a scientist specialized in marine ichthyology, but earlier applied his scientific training to the development of the Calumet and Hecla copper mines, with substantial profit to himself, relations, and friends who had invested in that venture. He donated to Harvard College a museum of comparative zoölogy and important sums of money for furthering the study of biology there. He was a son of Jean Louis Rondolphe Agassiz (1807-1873), the naturalist, geologist, and teacher. Mrs. Henry L. Higginson (Ida Agassiz), an intimate friend of Mrs. Henry Adams, was his sister.

DEAR PATER: I didn't quite take it in that our informal parting on Thursday was really the good-bye. I hope you found temptations at Vantine's—some "vital" vase or rug. We had a somewhat weary six hours in an overheated car which left a legacy of cold and uncomfortable throat; got home to a welcome of crackling logs in four rooms and a joyful dog.

Miss Schurz came in to tea in spite of the drizzling rain, and Mr. King and Mr. John Hay to dine and chat over the fire until midnight. Miss Schurz is going to Boston on Tuesday to Hotel Vendome on Commonwealth Avenue; do ask Ellen Gurney if she has an extra ten minutes in town to leave a card on her, and you'll go, won't you? She's a dear little woman and has toiled bravely for four years in the public service. I hope she'll have much attention in Boston; she is tired out and blue and goes for a change. Tell Mrs. Jack Gardner,[1] if you see her, and Nannie Wharton, who received hospitality from her when she stayed with me.

I hope you escaped the Chicago blizzard as we have by a warm rain. Today warm and clearing. Poor Boojum is suffering from conjunctivitis; is in Dr. Loring's[2] hands with daily applications of nitrate of silver and belladonna, etc. Mr. Hay on Thursday pronounced it cataract, but Mr. King vowed it a case of "tom-cataract," which Loring also thinks. We had the best ride of the year on Friday and shall get another today. The buds on the maples in our garden are very red and the air is full of promises. This small town is a haven of peace as compared with New York. Friday Nick Anderson[3] of Cincinnati turned up at five o'clock and stayed to dine; came for four days and to his own amazement bought a charming house.

Last long letter of twelve pages, tell Ellen, came yesterday from Mrs. Baird Smith, who asks tenderly for her and Whitman; is

[1] Mrs. John L. Gardner.
[2] Dr. Francis Boot Loring, an oculist, a son of Judge Edward G. Loring of the Court of Claims; married Lillie Latrobe of Baltimore.
[3] Nicholas Anderson (1838-1892), son of Larz Anderson of Cincinnati, and a classmate of Henry Adams at Harvard. He had a distinguished Civil War record.

delighted with two books of Howells which I had sent her—
Foregone Conclusion and *Undiscovered Country*.   Am reading
Carlyle's last trash; such driveling egotism is sickening and yet
there is a sickly fascination to it.   Love to Aunt Eunice.   Affectionately

M. A.

1607 H STREET, WASHINGTON,
Sunday, March 27th, 1881.

DEAR PATER: A blustering raw March day without, a blazing log
within and a convalescing dog; a week's record of the quietest.
Sunday last, Mr. John Hay, Clarence King, and the new Secretary
of War, Robert Lincoln, to dine; a good deal of good talk.   Tuesday, Hay and Lincoln again, General Burnside, General Francis A.
Walker of the Census, and de Bildt, Secretary of the Swedish Legation, to dine; a very pleasant and successful dinner.

King went away for good on Monday, to our extreme regret,
having got out of office, named and seen confirmed his successor,
Powell of Illinois,[1] in whom he has great confidence. He did it so
noiselessly that Professor Hayden,[2] who would have done his best
to upset it, knew nothing of it till it was done. Mr. Hay insisted on
being relieved too, and Blaine had to give way and appoint the
only available man, Hitt,[3] late Secretary of Legation in Paris. He is
rich, but socially of little use, from what one hears. Hay went to
Fortress Monroe Thursday to join his wife, so that one by one our
intimates are gone. This is Washington all over, nothing ever the
same for a week running.

---

[1] John Wesley Powell (1834-1902), a geologist and ethnologist, was appointed
director of the Geological Survey in 1881 in succession to Clarence King, a post
which he occupied until 1894.
[2] Ferdinand Vandeveer Hayden (1829-1887) had been in charge, from 1867 to
1879, of the geology of the United States Geological and Geographical Survey
of the territories. On the reorganization of the Geological Survey in 1879, he
became for seven years one of its geologists.
[3] Robert Roberts Hitt of Mt. Morris, Illinois, married Sallie Reynolds of Indiana.
He was appointed Secretary of the Legation at Paris in 1877, and, after a short
stage in the State Department as Assistant Secretary, was elected to Congress in
1882 and served there until 1892.

Yesterday Henry dined *en famille* at the Bancrofts'; I backed out on account of a cold. Gerald Walker and the new Attorney-General came in, though, to cheer my solitude, and Henry came back early. Wayne MacVeagh is an old friend of ours, a most outspoken man, who is not muzzled by being in the Cabinet, which seems to be framed on the genuine "happy family" principle well known in aquaria. If he and Blaine lie down together the lamb will have to be inside the lion. Conkling is mad as a hornet with Garfield—all the world knows and vows he has been sold out. As long as the politicians wrangle among themselves as to spoils the country can go on its prosperous way rejoicing. Blaine's health is very shaky.

We were asked to dine today at the Evartses', but asked to be allowed to go in after dinner instead, and so MacVeagh is coming to dine here and we shall adjourn there for a cup of tea later. Wednesday, invited to three dinners—Outreys', Bayards' and Hopkinses'—declined them all; even Lent does not stop society in this social town. Mr. Lodge sent us a Boston paper in which we read most of the speeches at the Schurz dinner.[1] Charles Eliot was too dry to get through, Schurz's own we thought very good. I hope you were there.

Village cart not yet come, expect it daily; new harness promised for tomorrow is to be very jarring—straw collar, russet reins, silver-nickel; consulted both de Bildt and Colonel Bonaparte, who are very horsey. Have just begun Gibbon's *History*, a bone which will take months to gnaw. Henry hard at work, gloating hourly over his comfortable quarters. Eugene Hale has taken Morton's house. Love to Auntie and all the Cambridge households. Very affectionately

M. A.

1607 H STREET, WASHINGTON,
Sunday, April 3rd, 1881.

DEAR PATER: You wrote howling about your dry March winds last Sunday and we too have had a bad week; chilly, windy, dusty, no

---

[1] "A number of Boston gentlemen of the best standing, both socially and politically, have asked Mr. Schurz to a dinner on the 22d, as an expression of their high opinion of the administration of his office during the last four years."

peach blossoms or any real sign of spring. I fancy we shall catch it soon and be up in the eighties.

Sunday last McVeagh, the Attorney-General, dined here and we adjourned for a cup of tea at the Evartses', having excused ourselves from dining with them. Mr. Hay dines with us every day now, his wife lingering on at Fortress Monroe, where peach blossoms have come. Until the Senate stops this disgraceful wrangle and goes into executive session to confirm appointments, Mr. Hay must act as assistant secretary and Mr. Hitt possess his soul in patience. The latter dined with us on Thursday; he was civil in Paris about Henry's papers. He is a child of the West—Indiana,—has a rich wife; his attempts at social ease and elegance are a little trying. He'll do well enough; Blaine could get no one else to take it.

Garfield's housekeeping is not a success so far and he is said by his friends to be much worried. Blaine is far from well; if he could be got rid of—sent as Minister to England for instance—it might smooth matters a bit. He's a jealous intriguer and will do the administration no credit. John Hay is a warm friend of his and stands up for him on all occasions, but he is a stout Stalwart and shuts his eyes and opens his mouth. His detestation of Conkling is most whole-souled. Everyone of whatever party admits that the democratic Senators are quite right in standing where they do; the Republicans have made a vile bargain and can't get out.

Miss Bayard came to dine Thursday to offset Hitt and was pretty and gay. Yesterday Miss Welling, a handsome girl who lives here, Hay, and Robert Lincoln. We made Mr. Hay read us "Blue Jay" after dinner. At ten he and the Secretary of War went off to Blaine's first official reception. How glad I am that we have never called and are saved from all social contact with them. Miss Beale tumbles in to tea two or three times a week—looks very ill. Schurz was in on Tuesday and Friday; he and Miss Schurz much enjoyed their visit to Boston; the latter was touched and pleased by your attention to her. Schurz himself went to St. Louis Friday night to look after his private affairs. It is said here that Kirkwood,[1] his successor, is smashing round like a bull in a china shop, making removals, appointments, etc. We shall see. Outreys sail

---

[1] Samuel J. Kirkwood (1813-1894), one of the Senators from Iowa, resigned from the Senate to enter Garfield's cabinet as Secretary of the Interior.

for France 27th of this month for spring and summer; she is much pulled down with a long illness. Love to Cambridge families and to Aunty. Yours affectionately

M. A.

1607 H STREET, WASHINGTON,
Sunday, April 10th, 1881.

DEAR PATER: We've a week of rough weather behind us, disgraceful for this latitude—wet, windy, cloudy, nasty. Thursday charming, Friday and yesterday rain, which, if our daily map from the weather bureau tells the truth, you have quite escaped.

We've had a guest since Monday, Charles F. Adams 3rd,— John's boy,—who came for his Easter vacation; leaves this P.M. on through express. Henry has worked heroically putting him through his sights. Mr. Hay has been laid up so that we've not had him as a pleasant daily guest at dinner. He's off this week, though the Senate has not confirmed his successor, no Republican of sufficient independence and pluck having come to light to inform his brother Senators that the country sends them here to perform public service and not to wrangle and haggle over petty patronage. Schurz, who comes back after a week's business in St. Louis, is astonished and shocked at this state of things and Garfield's administration is in a fair way to be discredited and ridiculous. No one doubts that Blaine is the responsible party and egged on this fight with Conkling. I hope it will end in driving Blaine out of the Cabinet. If Chandler and Robertson are not confirmed it can hardly fail to; he might take the English mission as a sop.

We took Charley to the Senate on Wednesday; Bayard and Sherman and Burnside spoke. The latter is a dear old soul, but he got into such a muddle and contradicted himself till the galleries roared with laughter. Bayard is not an orator, is not quick and has a disagreeable nasal twang, and Sherman swallows his sentences, perhaps fearing no one else will. Mahone looks like a weasel, is very small, proud of his feet, one or both of which lie on his desk.

Yesterday we went to the Bernhardt matinée to see her in *Camille*; were not impressed and had no reason to reconsider our Paris convictions that to us at least "she says nothing," to borrow one of her own idioms. She is startlingly like Emily Beale, though without her snap and "slope" characteristics.

Hepaticas have come,—Henry brought me a bunch from the woods last week,—but you must wait till the dogwood is fully out. Ellen Parkman[1] is at Mrs. Wadsworth's. I've asked her to top off her visit here, but her hostess is to be alone this week and can't give her up. Love to the families in Cambridge. Affectionately yours

MARIAN ADAMS

1607 H STREET, WASHINGTON,
Sunday, April 17th, 1881.

DEAR PATER: Our lagging spring is not far enough on for your visit yet; magnolias in the park in front of us a month behindhand and dogwood only faint swelling buds; anemones, bloodroot, and mayflowers in plenty and a blush of red maple flowers over the hills.

We've beat you on weather this week. Sunday a heavenly warm day, long ride in the country; Miss Bayard and Randolph Robinson of New York to dine. Monday a three hours' ride in Virginia; a new road over which I'll drive you soon comes out at the Virginia end of the Chain Bridge. Tuesday a rainy morning but warm; sunny P.M., tried my new cart. Daisy liked it, so did we, though it jiggles a good deal at first. Wednesday rain; since then good weather. We have seen by our daily map that you had snow and northeast gales. A storm centre reaches you seven hours after us unless it goes to sea. Today is like summer. I'm much interested in planting out my garden here. It's a patch about seventy-five by fifty feet and, the centre being grass with a red maple in the middle, I'm having border filled with early spring and late autumn plants—lilies of valley, daffodils, roses which in ordinary winters will bloom until Christmas, and lots of new chrysanthemums. I've engaged Bancroft's gardener to do it for me. It will add so much to our premises. We've got so fond of this old house that we shall never leave it until we are forcibly ejected.

---

[1] Miss Ellen Parkman, daughter of Samuel Parkman; later married William W. Vaughan.

Yesterday we had a very pleasant little dinner of eight; Mr. and Mrs. MacVeagh, Mr. and Mrs. Henry S. Sanford,—just back from Florida en route to their seven children in Brussels,—Miss Bayard, and Senator Allison. It was very lively. Mrs. MacVeagh I'd never seen before, Henry says she looks just like her father, old Simon Cameron. She is tall, spare, superb eyes, quick, good deal of humour, and very straightforward. I like her. He is much disgusted at the state of things but hasn't the pluck to do anything. Miss Bayard and I are to write him a speech which he promises to deliver this week. MacVeagh told a good story which he just got from Judge Harlan[1] of Kentucky and Allison vows he'll begin his speech with it. A week or so ago a man from Kentucky came back from Washington, and when he was asked what was going on in Washington, said, "Nothin'." "Nothin'!" said one of his friends. "Why, there's a nigger in the Senate, Mahone[2] has jined the Republicans, there's four Yankee schoolmasters in the Cabinet, and the country's goin' to hell."

There was some rather amusing discussion of the new 3½% loan which MacVeagh endorses. Allison quoted Fair, the new bonanza Senator from Nevada, as saying to him: "Me and Mackay's[3] got twenty millions in 6's and 5's, I ain't sure just which." Mr. Sanford is full of his Florida orange groves; had one hundred and twenty-five acres in full bloom all at once this winter; is negotiating for the purchase of a million acres; says Sea Island cotton is an exploded industry for our coast—Florida beats the Sea Islands at it but Egypt and the Fiji Islands have undersold them. He is supposed to be campaigning here for a foreign mission, but with little prospect of success. We did a stroke of work in yesterday's dinner. Began by asking Mortons, Thorntons, and R. C. Winthrops,[4]

---

[1] John Marshall Harlan (1833-1911) was appointed an Associate Justice of the United States Supreme Court in 1877, a position which he filled with great ability.

[2] William Mahone (1826-1895), a major general in the Confederate army, served as Senator from Virginia from 1881 to 1887.

[3] John William Mackay (1831-1902), in 1852 went to Virginia City, Nevada, where he formed with James G. Fair, James C. Flood, and William S. O'Brien the firm which in 1873 discovered the Great Bonanza vein, more than 1200 feet deep, in the Comstock lode.

[4] Robert Charles Winthrop (1809-1894).

to all of whom we owed a dinner, and by a blessed stroke of fate none of them could come. L. P. Morton at a small dinner would be too much. We are keeping the Lewenhaupts until you come.

Five o'clock tea is a bore these warm afternoons and I seldom come back in time; did happen to be in on Friday, though, when General Miles came. He gave me an interesting account of his many encounters with Mahone during the war. Tell Ellen I got, after some delay, the Channing Home receipt, as she sent it to 1607 8th Street, which corresponds to Blossom Court in Boston. The Academy meets here this week and we should expect Mr. King for a few days' visit except that he said he should come. Have you read Mrs. Burnett's *Fair Barbarian?*[1] Miss Beale is so cross at supposed portraits of herself in that and *Democracy* that she says she differs from the Biblical gentleman who said: "Oh, that mine enemy would write a book." She hopes hers won't write any more. *Adiós.* Affectionately

M. A.

1607 H STREET, WASHINGTON,
Sunday, April 24th, 1881.

DEAR PATER: From your somewhat ambiguous postal card of Tuesday last I half expect you in a day or two. Will cut this Sunday epistle very short. We are getting greener every hour and if you wait a few days you will find a smiling landscape.

The temptations of riding till sunset have broken up five o'clock tea; it becomes a bore at this season and society is pretty much over. We dined out last night for the first time in two months and though it was nice enough I don't care for it at this season. A dinner of twelve at the new Attorney General's,—Outrey, Sanfords, Mrs. Beale, Parkes,[2] etc.—the host took me in which was quite wrong, and with General Walker on my right I had the best of it.

There is going to be a lively ripping up here by the new Postmaster General of scandals begun under Grant, continued under Hayes, persistently ignored and denied by him. You won't find

---

[1] Frances Eliza Hodgson Burnett (1849-1924).
[2] General John G. Parke, U.S.A., then stationed in Washington as an assistant to the Chief of Engineers; he married in 1865 Ellen Blight, of Philadelphia.

MacVeagh reluctant in exposing corruptions. He enjoys spring cleanings. Public business at a total standstill owing to an utter absence of vertebræ. There are new rumours of a caucus for Tuesday which may break up the machine.

The Academy have had their annual meeting this last week and Mr. King passed two days with us or as much of them as was not taken by Academy meetings. He beams with joy at being out of office. He and Mr. Hay were as eager to get out as most fools to get in; the craving for the meanest kind of official existence is so intense as to form a division of lunacy by itself.

Bostonians swarm here. I tumbled on Mrs. Palfrey[1] yesterday, just arrived for ten days to drive off a bronchial attack. We had an impromptu dinner Wednesday—Schurz, Bayard, Marsh, King, Pumpelly,[2] and General Walker; they stayed till midnight and seemed to enjoy it. But as fires go and the sun blazes like yesterday and today, one's social instincts wane; so don't expect a gay visit. In a few weeks we shall be turning our faces Beverly-ward, and after losing two summers in Europe we expect to enjoy our quiet pine trees. *Adiós*. Affectionately

M. A.

1607 H STREET, WASHINGTON,
Sunday, May 8th, 1881.

DEAR PATER: You are "resting and screaming" among your granddaughters today and we peacefully reading and writing and reading under the bluest of skies and greenest of trees. Of course nothing has happened since you left. Our daily three to four hours in the saddle of afternoons, Friday morning's good rain making the roads quite perfect. Yesterday tried to find our old Bladensburg road but missed it and so have added a new road to our list.

---

[1] Mrs. Francis Palfrey (Louisa Bartlett).
[2] Raphael Pumpelly (1837-1923) from 1879 to 1881 was with the U. S. Geological Survey, in charge of the census of mineral industries exclusive of precious metals and mineral oils; from July 1881 to 1883, he was employed by H. Villard on the Northern Transcontinental Survey.

Met Mr. Bayard[1] yesterday; he thinks now the deadlock is broken that the Senate may get away in two to three weeks. General Armstrong dropped in for an hour's chat after breakfast yesterday; is full of interest in his experiment of educating young Indians; has now three hundred negroes and a hundred Indians at his school; finds the latter much the brighter of the two, and stimulating to the darkies. We have had no great heat since you and Ned left, but today rather suggests a warm week ahead. Our signal map gives us daily about fifteen degrees of heat more than Boston. You will hardly get apple trees well out before 18th, except in very sheltered places. Hope to get a note from you Tuesday telling me all the family are flourishing. Ask Betsy to look out for a good cook, laundress, and waitress for me; the latter must be nice-looking. Should like Protestants if any turn up. *Adiós.* Affectionately

M. A.

1607 H STREET, WASHINGTON,
Sunday, May 15th, 1881.

DEAR PATER: Our proud spirits are so broken by the heat of the last week that you needn't look for a gay bulletin. How we long for the bare branches of Beverly today! Spring is a fraud here. One jump from cold and ice to 97° is too much and we are so afraid of a continued repetition of the day and night furnace that we think of pulling up stakes at the end of this week—perhaps Saturday, taking two days or three for New York, and then Beverly as soon as new majesties can be found.

Boojum is in misery; we thought he was dying this morning but he has rallied somewhat. A huge woodtick buried in his ear which we can't get out is one source of his misery but just discovered. We are trying injecting sweet oil into it, which two years ago dislodged one. Have seen almost no one lately. Last Sunday Mr. Walker dined with us quietly, MacVeagh dropped in in the evening. He had a big fight on his hands; if only Garfield has the pluck and decency to support him he may yet provide the late

---

[1] Thomas Francis Bayard (1828-1898), Senator from Delaware from 1869 to 1885, when he resigned to enter President Cleveland's Cabinet as Secretary of State, 1885 to 1889; was Ambassador to Great Britain from 1893 to 1897.

Senator Dorsey[1] with board and lodging at the public expense. The scathing attack on Garfield in Tuesday's *New York Herald* made a great stir here; no one doubts that Conkling inspired it. All denials of his are useless and it is conceded by everyone that— facts or lies—he has overshot the mark this time.

Thursday we made some moonlight calls, sat with the Bayards for an hour on their piazza with fans and Apollinaris; they leave on Wednesday of this week. Yesterday we had a cooling breeze all day and a teaspoonful of rain at sunset. Mr. Nordhoff came in for a chat in the evening—political of course. The rest of the time it's read, read, read, till I loathe the very sight of a book, and yet how nicely sold we shall be if our impatience to get away is rewarded by a cold wet June at Beverly Farms. The weather prophets can't help our doubting minds; 83° today only—in our coolest room! Sich is life. *Adiós.* Affectionately

M. A.

1607 H STREET, WASHINGTON,
Sunday, May 22d, 1881.

DEAR PATER: I think I wrote you that we meant to leave for New York yesterday, but finding that if we sent the horses to Norfolk on Friday they must wait till Tuesday boat from there to Boston, we decided to ship them tomorrow P.M. from here to meet the Norfolk boat. The bill of lading we shall send you. Will you be kind e- nough to tell someone to meet them and take them to Beacon Club stables? The boat is due in Boston on Thursday; box with saddles and harness will be with them, which can be taken by express wagon to the stable, and from there we can either send it as it is to Beverly Farms or use it if we find it best to drive or ride down. *You* must do nothing about this. If William has the time to super- intend it we will settle with him to his benefit.

Have had a cool pleasant week since a thunder shower a week ago tonight. Some long and charming rides four hours each the last two days—yesterday by bridge at Arsenal to Maryland side

---

[1] Stephen W. Dorsey (1842-1916), formerly Senator form Arkansas, was secre- tary of the Republican National Committee which managed President Garfield's campaign; he was involved in the Post Office fraud.

and home by Bladensburg. Air laden with flowering locust trees. Hope for one more ride this P.M.

Conkling's somersault took us all by surprise.[1] It is thought that he really wants an excuse for getting out of public life and making money at his profession. Is said to owe L. P. Morton thirty thousand dollars, and as the Sprague suit comes off in a week or so, unless he lets the charges go by default, that fight will cost him a good deal. It's good riddance, and now if we can get Blaine relegated to private life or a foreign mission we may clear up things a bit. Blaine does not carry much weight in the Cabinet and may resent it by and by. Mr. and Mrs. MacVeagh were here Friday evening and he had much to say that interested us.

We have had enough rain this past week to refresh us without wearying us, and wood fires at evenings off and on. Our plan is to go by Limited to New York on Tuesday, two days in New York, and to Boston Friday in time to dine with you. Hope to move to Beverly Farms by Wednesday, June 1st. Boojum accepts your kind offer with pleasure, is quite well again—a case of Mother Hubbard's dog, tick and all. My roses are budding finely and it's sad to part from them. *Adiós.* Affectionately

M. A.

[1] Senator Conkling's attack on President Garfield was followed by a further attack in the letter of resignation which he and Senator Platt sent to Governor Cornell, which was transmitted to the Legislature at Albany on May 16. On the same day their resignations were announced by the Vice President in the United States Senate and were "followed by a hum of astonishment."

CHAPTER II

WASHINGTON

OCTOBER 1881-JUNE 1882

BREVOORT HOUSE. 2 P.M.,
Sunday, October 23rd (1881).

DEAR PATER: We've got so far in safety. Had a charming lunch with the Searses. Adie came up from Hanover to meet me "by particular request" and was as nice as possible in a pretty russet gown. Then I got three quarters of an hour of the Higginson rehearsal[1] for twenty-five cents and it was *fine*; mind you go in now and then. Got to Quincy at dusk. Very smart dinner in Charles's[2] baronial hall which would not be out of place at Chatsworth. Having turned a deaf ear to a sick headache all day, when bedtime came I paid the bill nature sent in with many a groan too; then travelled nine hours on a piece of toast. I prefer a Morocco mule to travel on, after trying both. Found a lovely Japanese farewell in silver and enamel from Ned waiting for me, and as always happens when we get here the play began at once and the curtain rang up promptly. Tumbled plump on the very most lurid of all our pyrotechnic friends,— or acquaintances rather,—Mrs. E., a lady with a most plethoric past, a precocious present and a future which would baffle and bankrupt any clairvoyant. She tried Cheyenne as a residence; it knows her no more and more than enough; tried Denver, and Denver rebelled; they think after all *Washington* is what they want now. I expect her in every minute for a talk, as she said last night she would come. There are all sorts of rumours about her; one that she owes her existence to Lola Montez,[3] whom she much "features." *Quien*

---

[1] The Boston Symphony Orchestra, organized by Henry Lee Higginson, began its first season in the fall of 1881, and the initial concert was given Saturday, October 22; the regular concerts on Saturday evenings were preceded by public rehearsals on Friday afternoons.

[2] Charles Francis Adams, Jr.

[3] Lola Montez, stage name of Marie Dolores Eliza Rosanna Gilbert (1818-1861), dancer and adventuress. She had two matrimonial adventures; a divorce ended

sabe! Her husband is good and sweet, and stands by her—defies his family's anathema—and as he is an old friend of Henry's we must accept his view—externally.

Mrs. and Miss Clymer came as we did en route for Washington—cordial and staid as ever. Clarence King has been with us all the morning; he and Henry have gone off to lunch with John Hay at the Union League Club. Tuesday and Wednesday we are to carouse with them alternately, and see a famous danseuse and *Patience*. A bunch of roses which Mr. King sent to meet me has never come, having fallen a prey to some æsthetic housemaid; here they come with a Celtic explanation evidently lame from its birth; they must have figured at a ball in the Bowery last night, they are so wan and drooping.

I put myself at your feet. *Adiós*

M. A.

See how much more moral I am than that contrary young man who said he would and then didn't write to his Pa!

1607 H Street, Washington,
Sunday, October 30th, 1881.

Dear Pater: I hope you got my last Sunday's letter which I sent to Beverly Farms. We had a pleasant four days in New York. Went to see Miss Palmer Sunday P.M. and found she had come home from Europe the day before and seen in London some old friends of ours, bringing latest news, also a tulip-coloured silk neckerchief as a present, and some gloves as a commission, twenty-four inches long—I must wear sleeve garters to keep them up! Tiffany has diamond-set leg garters!

Sunday evening at home, with Clarence King to amuse us. Monday, he went to Philadelphia on business. We moused all day and went to Madison Square Theater to see *The Professor*—very absurd and amusing. Tuesday, John Hay and his wife, King, Henry, and I dined at Delmonico's—guests of Mr. King—and went to see *Olivette* afterwards, *opéra bouffe* with some delightful dancing. Delmonico's was very gay. Mr. Jim Keene was giving a

---

the first in 1842 and her second husband was drowned in 1853; between times she became notorious as the mistress of King Ludwig I of Bavaria, 1847-1848.

dinner to celebrate his last victory—Foxhall, the Newmarket stakes—cabled that morning.[1] He came over to see us, and his brother Harry, who took us to the Derby. He's been ill and missed all his races. He's a pleasant well-bred man; if he turns up in Boston do look after him.

Wednesday, lunched with Effie Lowell, then we all five dined again at Delmonico's and went to see *Patience*. What will Ned say if we confess that it bored us a good deal? The real thing in London was convulsing, but no American *actrices* would consent to make such guys of themselves as the women we know. Shade of Lady Catherine Gaskell in her poppy gown and poke bonnet! If she could conceive such lovely crêpe gowns we wouldn't murmur. Thursday, we left early, but not too early for Miss Palmer to bring me all the way from 32d Street a big bunch of red roses, and she and Mr. King amused us while we fed. The former has had a most vivid experience of aristocracy this summer. A youth who was making her young brother a visit in Étretat fell ill of a fever, and his mother, Lady Susan Milbank,—sister of the Duke of Leeds,—came with a son and made and quartered on them as guests for some weeks.[2] She found much fault with the French cooking, which "we are not used to," she explained, "it's so very messy, you know." When she took an egg she sweetly remarked, "An egg is always safer when one is in France." And my friend said her patience gave out suddenly and she answered, "Yes, I suppose even *French* hens don't lay messy eggs." But she said her impatience was not understood or resented. She can't forgive Henry James for his *Daisy Miller*,[3] and, when I said he was on his way home, maliciously asked if he was coming for "*raw* material."

Coming on in the train met ex-Senator Kernan[4] of New York and General Walker, had a good deal of chat with both; the latter goes soon to settle in Boston.[5] Mr. Lowndes came in that same

[1] The *Nation*, October 27, 1881: "Mr. J. R. Keene's colt Foxhall scored his seventh victory on the English turf on Tuesday by winning the Cambridgeshire Stakes—thirty-two horses started."
[2] Lady Susan Georgiana Godolphin Osborne, wife of Henry John Milbank.
[3] *Daisy Miller* was published in 1878.
[4] Francis Kernan's term as Senator from New York expired March 3, 1881.
[5] General Francis A. Walker resigned as Superintendent of the Census to take charge of the Institute of Technology at Boston.

P.M. to welcome us, inquired tenderly for you, says he is afraid he bores people by prating too much of the delights of Beverly. He and General Walker are coming to dine today. John, the waiter, has gone home ill so we must get Wormley to lend us a man. Found the house in perfect order, fires burning, dogs in ecstasy, roses in bloom in garden, maples red and yellow in front and behind. Margery gave us a very nice dinner and, in short, all our plans were carried out. Brent met the horses at Norfolk Monday night; they both have coughs but it's epidemic here and we hope will break up soon. Took a drive Friday with Prince; country looking its best, weather very warm and muggy—in the seventies—and summer showers all day yesterday and today. Have got a bad cold—so has Henry—caught in draughty theatre Wednesday night. Madison Square is the only perfectly ventilated one in the world, they say; every lady's programme had a fresh rosebud fastened to it with a bit of ribbon!

Yesterday P.M. Mrs. Senator Don Cameron and Miss Beale rapped on Henry's window with their umbrellas and of course got in; as Miss Beale explained, "It's better than ringing because you can't say engaged." They were very jolly and begged for some good tea as they'd been to a house where the tea was too bad and the sugar impossible. Miss Beale's description of Mr. Edward Austin's way of greeting her in his own house was irresistible. Mrs. Wadsworth, to cover the retreat, offered her strawberries and cream; but she said, "No, keep them in the refrigerator where they *may* be warm."

Boojum sits on the window ledge and gets greetings from all his old friends as they go to church. The Nick Andersons came to tea yesterday full of the new house which Richardson[1] is planning for them here. *Adiós.* Affectionately

M. A.

---

[1] Henry Hobson Richardson (1838-1886) was born in Louisiana, and graduated at Harvard College in 1859. He then studied architecture in Paris, remaining there until the close of the Civil War, when, returning to this country, he began the practice of his profession in New York. In 1867 he married Miss Julia Gorham Hayden of Boston and in 1878 moved to that city. In Washington he designed houses for Nicholas Anderson, John Hay, and Henry Adams; the last two were completed in 1885. At college, he and Henry Adams were contemporaries and Adams states in the *Education* that he made there no acquaintance that he

1607 H STREET, WASHINGTON,
Sunday noon, November 6, 1881.

DEAR PATER: I hope you are basking today on Ellen's piazza in this heavenly sunshine. After a week of gray skies we revel in it. The hills round about are ablaze with red and yellow and purple, the horses have got over their coughs and leave me to sniffle in solitude.

"All quiet on the Potomac." Senate gone; President in New York; carrion crows hovering in expectant patience. Some wise men say there is brewing the biggest kind of a row in the Republican Party; the Stalwarts think they're going to bag Arthur whole; the Independents fear it. MacVeagh has gone[1] and the press here is tearing him to shreds. I fancy he is justified. If Arthur really wants to convict Star-route thieves he has only to appoint a fit man. Don Cameron is waging a boss-machine war in Pennsylvania and MacVeagh, his brother-in-law, is fighting hard against him. There is much talk of Beale in the Navy and Timothy Howe[2] in the Interior. We ought to see soon. Miss Beale and Mrs. Don Cameron come to tea every day and are great fun; the latter is very pretty, not more than twenty-four, is staying with the fair Emily while she gets her big new house in order; they are deep in politics and "Stalwart" to the finger tips.

---

valued in after life so much as Richardson, although the college relation had little to do with the later friendship. Adams also says that when he was at the American Legation at London in the '60s, "as often as he could, Adams ran over to Paris, for sunshine, and there always sought out Richardson in his attic in the Rue du Bac, or wherever he lived, and they went off to dine at the Palais Royal, and talked of whatever interested the students of the Beaux Arts."

[1] The *Nation*, November 3, 1881: "On Thursday the President nominated Judge Charles J. Folger of New York to be Secretary of the Treasury and Mr. James to succeed himself as Postmaster-General.

"Great pressure has been brought to bear upon Mr. MacVeagh by the President and his friends to persuade him to remain in the Cabinet until the completion of the Star-route prosecutions. Mr. MacVeagh has, however, absolutely refused. He says that the prosecution is in the hands of lawyers of eminent ability, and that his supervision will be entirely unnecessary to secure its successful termination."

[2] Timothy Otis Howe (1816-1883), a United States Senator from Wisconsin, 1861-1879.

Thursday, it rained cats and dogs and I asked them to stay and dine, and they accepted promptly on condition that I would send over for their chicken, etc.; which I did. Then Miss Beale's faithful Sambo flew over to say that the cook was drunk, but if she could cook the chicken he thought it would be nice, and she rallied enough to send spinach done in cream and a nice apple pudding, so we had *two* nice dinners!

Countess Lewenhaupt is sweet and cosy as ever; we owe them a dinner which we'll pay as soon as I can get a new range in. My man-servant is very ill, I fear he is not going to get well; he is valuable to us and we shall miss him—have borrowed David from Wormley's, who is good but under-witted. Mr. Lowndes and Mrs. Craig Wadsworth are to dine with us today. The latter is house-hunting, having decided that there are more cakes and ale here than in Europe, which she tried for many years. She has remains of much beauty, a charming voice, dresses well, is quite pleasant. It will be a happy hunting-ground for dashing widows this winter—the President a widower, also Vice President, and the new British Minister[1] who came yesterday. Miss Beale says Arthur is the *cup* and those who are to run, of every age and weight. Mrs. Cameron, on being annoyed at some feminine stab from Mrs. Blaine, tenderly asked her a few days ago, "What are your plans, Mrs. Blaine? Shall you pass the winter in Augusta?" Aristarchi Bey and Count Lewenhaupt say Blaine has lately been offered and refused the English Mission. He is a crafty old bird and will now pose as Garfield's immediate successor. No one knows that better than Arthur. With MacVeagh and Walker and Mr. Nordhoff gone, we have not one single Independent left to speak to; Stalwarts, and Democrats, such as Mr. Bayard and Mr. Hewitt, will make up our list.

Get Nanny Wharton to go with you to see Genevieve Ward[2] in *Forget-me-not*. She is playing it in Boston; we saw her in London and thought it thrilling. Best love to Nanny. If you wish the latest Delmonico touch with ducks, have hominy fried in small pieces—about two inches square, less than half an inch thick—not too

---

[1] Sir Lionel Sackville-West (1827-1908).

[2] Lucia Genoveva Teresa Ward, Countess Guerbel (1833-1922), actress and singer.

crisp, but light and dry, in a *wire* fry-basket so that they can drain—you must be "ultimate"—and be sure to stuff your turkey with chestnuts (the common little ones will do) mashed like potato.

I've got a sweet new bonnet, all covered with steel beads and wide red strings; Polly would find it "very stylish." Tell her and Ellen, Jr., that I didn't get the dress they advised, but a prettier one, and will send them a bit to see if they approve—blue, Russian gray, trimmed with ruby velvet, sash and pocket, very smart. By the way, I want you to do something for me the next time you go to Worcester. Dear old Tom Kinnicutt is there, broken down and paralysed, in bed; all his profession gone, and money too, I am told. I'm going to write to him. I know a visit from you will cheer him up. The Salisburys[1] are very kind to him; they can tell you where to find him. Do go, and write me how he is. How is your cold? Ned wrote me you had one. Love to Betsy and Aunt Eunice. *Adiós*. Affectionately

M. A.

1607 H STREET, WASHINGTON,
Sunday A.M., November 13, 1881.

DEAR PATER: Still another brilliant summer's day—over 60° in the shade, garden gay with yellow and red chrysanthemums and would be with roses but that the gardener has gone in too much for early spring ones. We pass by Uncle Sam's grave[2] in our ride very often, and see that a great bunch of white roses is blooming over it.

No news here. The papers are denouncing MacVeagh as "coward, liar and rascal." The volume of howls shows that the Star-route thieves and their gang were hit hard and may yet see the interior decorations of the penitentiary. A story is travelling through the papers of a late Cabinet meeting in which Arthur and MacVeagh had a stormy scene. It is somebody's lie, for we know as a fact that MacVeagh and the new President parted in a most friendly manner, Arthur promising to send in the name of his successor the following day, which he apparently did not do. I wrote

---

[1] Stephen Salisbury (1798-1884) founded the Worcester Museum. Stephen Salisbury, Jr. (1835-1905).

[2] Her uncle, Samuel Hooper, died February 14, 1875, at Washington, and was buried there.

to Mrs. MacVeagh yesterday and hope to get a line from her before long. Last night dined with Captain and Mrs. Story[1]—dinner for the Andersons of Cincinnati—small and pleasant. Story tells me his family came from Marblehead, his grandfather being Judge Story's[2] brother; he came from a branch which settled in Wisconsin. His wife is very young and pretty, a Miss Sherman.

I heard last night of some old lace for sale here sent by a decayed Southern lady; I shall go to see it tomorrow. I think it is a *duty* Ellen and I owe to our many nieces to lay in a goodly store. Would that mine had! I send the enclosed song for Loulie to learn for me. Tell her my memory has gone or is full of holes—Lord Houghton said the lines had never been traced, were probably some old epitaph—the last two, that is. See if Bartlett has them in his latest edition; they're not in the earlier. Also for Ned, this instructive and warning tale, which may be of use to him. Horses all well again; Possum has dyspepsia and I am treating him and Mr. Herbert Wadsworth with lacto-pepsine—puppy adores it.   So Henry Cabot Lodge is thrown out. I'm sorry for him, but wonder that he should want to go into politics. *Adiós.* Affectionately

M. A.

Later—8.30 P.M. *edition.* As a special correspondent I think it only fair to give you an "Extra!" Before I sealed this the bell rang and in walked the MacVeaghs as cheery and jolly as you can imagine. They came on last night in the President's private car, and he and Blaine, Folger,[3] and G. C. Bliss[4] coming from New York, picking Mr. and Mrs. MacVeagh up in Philadelphia. They stayed to lunch and we had a long intimate talk; they couldn't dine but are

---

[1] John P. Story, then a First Lieutenant in the 4th Artillery and on duty at the Signal Office of the War Department. His friends gave him the brevet rank of "Captain."

[2] Justice Joseph Story of the United States Supreme Court (1779-1845).

[3] Charles James Folger (1818-1884).

[4] George Bliss, Jr. (1830-1897), held a dominant position in the councils of the Republican Party; from 1872 to 1877, he was United States Attorney for the Southern District of New York and successfully prosecuted the "Custom House frauds." In 1882, he was retained as special prosecutor to assist the Attorney-General in the Star-route cases.

coming at nine o'clock for tea and more talk. It is, as we hoped, all a *lie*, an infamous lie, about the Cabinet scene given by one Ramsdell to the *Evening Star* here, he vouching for the truth of it—it came to him from *Blaine*. That man is committing suicide day by day and is evidently desperate.

MacVeagh to his surprise found in the car a little lobby thief named Painter, whom he warned Arthur against, much to the latter's surprise, and when later in the day Colonel Bliss, Arthur's chosen friend, called the man a thief, poor Arthur said wearily, "This is the damnedest world." Arthur declares that the country generally believes him to be "a kind of Bowery boy who wears his trousers inside his boots and his hat on one side." The MacVeaghs say he has been most kind and cordial to them and their relations are extremely pleasant. The reason he did not send in Timothy Howe's name as he promised was that he found him to be a kinsman by marriage of Brady, the chief Star-route conspirator. They say Folger is very nice. Blaine has *not* been offered the English Mission; as Mrs. MacVeagh tartly observed, "He would take *anything*." I said I was writing you a letter and how much might I quote? They said, "Quote anything you like." In fact, it's much better that Blaine's lies should be belied.

Had a long enchanting ride in Virginia from two-thirty till five; heaven has no such weather as today. Herbert Wadsworth dined here; has just left to go by special night train to Atlanta with General Sherman and party. Save this letter. It may be *olim* interesting to me when I'm old and wizened. My facts are facts, too, which all the special correspondents' are not. *Me pongo a los pies de v. que beso.*

M. A.

We are so glad the Gurneys[1] have settled on the Commons; it will be charming to have a foothold there.

---

[1] The Gurneys purchased fifty acres of the Commons, a wild tract of land at Beverly Farms near what is now Pride's Crossing; they employed Mr. Richardson to design them a house which was completed some four years later.

1607 H Street, Washington,
Sunday, November 20th, 1881.

Dear Pater: It is with heavy heart that I take up my pen today, for my dear, sweet stylographic is out of order and must be sent to New York to a pen-doctor. This is the eighth day of gorgeous weather. Yesterday, above 70°, so that one was glad to creep along the shady side of the street. Rides have been lovely. General Parke has sent us a small army map made during the war, with military lanes and crosscuts and forts. We had eighteen miles on Wednesday, doing the four miles from Riggs's farm to Soldiers' Home in twenty minutes, which is not bad for riding. Daisy has got a bad trick of pulling. General Beale, who is most learned in horses, advises me to have her teeth examined—probably filed— says as they grow older that is a common reason for pulling—and then to use a *leather* bit only. That may be Kitty's[1] trouble. He says horses suffer very greatly with their teeth. I think we could have saved Waggle with strychnine pills, which the head army surgeon used for the dog of a friend here which was suddenly paralysed. She says the dog had three pills a day and it was funny to see his own surprise as first he stuck out one paw and then another. He lived eight years after getting well.

Nothing up here, politically or socially. It is certain that Frelinghuysen[2] succeeds Blaine. He amounts to little or nothing, but his daughters socially will add much to our small clique; the mama keeps in the background and Lucy, who is our friend, will do the honours. It seems to be still uncertain if Mr. Beale gets into War or Navy; the appointment, we are told, would be far from pleasing in California, from which he chiefly hails. Guiteau[3] is

---

[1] Kitty was Dr. Hooper's favorite trotting mare and Daisy Mrs. Adams's saddle horse.

[2] Frederick Theodore Frelinghuysen (1817-1885), "a man of conservative turn of mind, a good lawyer, and a politician of experience," had served as a Senator from New Jersey from 1866 to 1869, and again from 1871 to 1877. His nomination for Secretary of State was sent to the Senate December 12, 1881, and was confirmed unanimously the same day. Unusually charming were his three daughters, Miss Lucy, Miss "Tillie" (Mrs. Winthrop Gray), and Miss "Sallie" (Mrs. John Davis).

[3] Guiteau's trial began on Monday, November 14, Judge Walter S. Cox, of the Supreme Court of the District of Columbia, presiding; Messrs. Scoville and

daily, as you can see, tightening his halter, and I fancy any jury-man who doubts will find it easier to swing too. The beast was shot yesterday. We want to go into court, but it's so jammed and so much sporadic gunpowder lying round that it is reserved for our betters.

Blaine had a big dinner last week for the President and the S——s were there. One of the guests expressed her extreme disgust at that idiot S. wearing an *order* "among all those foreigners." I asked if it was three balls, but she said only a "pawnbroker's pledge," she thought. The alarming rumour that they had come on to take a house is not true. Spare us that element here! Young Blaine—Walker—who is Third Assistant Secretary of State, came to tea a few days ago and is very intelligent and gentlemanly (perhaps Blaine said, "They will reverence my son"). A common friend asked me if he might. I was as civil as I know how, and asked him to come again.

Mr. Evarts too was here—as pompous as ever; said Henry had invited him to bring his bag here next time he came on, and did. I endorsed it with my lips and said "Yes" cordially. He's very witty and a great bore. We are going to have a Thanksgiving dinner as well as you: Mrs. Augustine Heard and a beautiful daughter;[1] the Lewenhaupts; Miss Beale; Counte Lippe; and Kasson of Iowa,[2] if he accepts. Mr. Heard may be here, so I must keep his place open and get another man too. Mrs. Heard is in a stuffy boarding-house, and looks as if life were a demnition grind. They've taken a house here for the winter. Tell Ellen, Mary de Connick, the little sister

---

Robinson represented the assassin of President John A. Garfield. The selection of the jurors was completed on November 16, and the District-Attorney opened the case for the Government on the day following. On Saturday, the 18th, an attempt was made to shoot Guiteau while in the van in which he was being conveyed back from the court to the jail. An earlier attempt on his life was made Sunday afternoon, September 11, when one of his guards shot at him through the window of his cell, the ball grazing the prisoner's head. During the trial Guiteau's conduct was disorderly and unruly; he frequently interrupted the proceedings with abusive remarks; and Judge Cox's patience in the matter was subjected to much newspaper criticism.

[1] Mr. and Mrs. Augustine Heard and their daughter, Miss Amy Heard, who later married Russell Gray of Boston.

[2] John Adam Kasson of Iowa (1822-1910) reëntered Congress after four years in Vienna as American Minister to Austria-Hungary.

was married two weeks ago to a man named Johnson, of Baltimore, without announcing it beforehand, Mrs. Heard says. I thought folks in boarding-houses and stray diplomats might help in a national sacrifice, and Emily Beale is to be all alone; I wish you'd lend me Bil Bigelow, he is just the fellow I want.

Apropos of nothing, I saw in a new greenhouse in Georgetown tother day a plant about three feet high covered with scarlet fruit— size of a mandarin orange. Man said it was an eggplant; seeds had been given him. I said, "Japanese?" He said, *"Quien sabe?"* I showed him my silver Jap match-box, which Yoshida said was an eggplant, and we verified it at once. I'm going to have one for my green Seville jar. Got my first *two* English violets yesterday from the hotbed. Glad your cold is better. Shall write Brooks to come on and convalesce here—he is quite poorly. *Adiós*

M. A.

1607 H STREET, WASHINGTON,
Sunday, November 27, 1881.

DEAR PATER: Another lovely Indian summer day after a cold, windy Thanksgiving. Here I broke off for an hour to take a stroll with Henry and dogs through the President's grounds and down by the river. Like the loveliest September day in Beverly. At two we're going to drive with Daisy, as Prince is nursing a splint. The horse-doctor is enthusiastic over Possum, says he is pure Skye, he has "been in Scotland and knows."

Our Thanksgiving dinner went off gaily; it grew to ten and Herbert Wadsworth came in to dessert and stayed till midnight to tell us about the South and cotton gins. Mr. Heard came with his wife and daughter, Lewenhaupts, Lippe, Miss Beale, and Captain Dewey—all dinnerless folks. Margery gave us a nice dinner. I do not cling to tradition as you do and only gave them one big wild turkey with truffle sauce, the rest of the usual dinner *à la Russe* and a bottle of your Madeira "B," which they appreciated. Emily Beale, in black satin with a big sunflower as her corsage, was as picturesque as Bunthorne's bride. An English female would have made a guy of herself. Here's Madame Outrey in a new Paris walking suit of poke bonnet and pélisse to her feet like a Kate

Greenaway sketch, and it's very nice, but it takes American style to do it.

Kasson[1] wrote me a note of regret worthy of an Iowa politician graduated at Vienna; if he is graceful as a Speaker in the same measure he will win the place he is working for. He had his Iowa colleagues coming to him that day, he said. Mr. Hay, whose labours as editor of the *Tribune* are now ended, had to fly to Cleveland without stopping here, for he wrote me his wife was agitated by a burglar who had robbed her of watch and all her money. He added, "A Cleveland burglar strikes me as a joke. I wonder which church he belongs to." Arthur keeps his own counsel; so do MacVeagh and James, whom the papers owned by Brady and Dorsey here are blackguarding in a way calculated to raise them in the esteem of all decent folks. Mr. Lowndes was here last evening; inquired tenderly for you, the Gurneys and children. My stylo is still in New York and I've nothing to say that would interest you. *Adiós*. Affectionately

M. A.

1607 H STREET, WASHINGTON,
Sunday, December 4th, 1881.

DEAR PATER: I've got a half hour before dinner to send my screed in, or rather write it. Only one friend came to tea and he has gone now. A week of lovely weather, warm and bright; picked a gay bunch of chrysanthemums in my garden this morning of various aesthetic colours. Socially it's quiet as a graveyard. Wednesday Emily Beale and Mrs. Don Cameron came in to dine and were full of talk. Friday we had Eugenia and Edward Frothingham on their way back from Florida, having been turned out of their house on account of young Hammond's desperate illness. She is just the same old sixpence, very amusing, but her teeth need filing, I fancy—Daisy doesn't pull on the bit at all since *hers* were done.

I got a charming present a few days ago from Ohio from John Hay, a bronze bowl stamped on the bottom in Chinese characters

---

[1] "The Speakership of the House of Representatives has been attracting considerable attention in political circles in Washington during the week. Messrs. Hiscock, Keifer and Kasson are the leading candidates for the office at present." (*Nation*, December 1, 1881).

and on the sides Arabic mottoes cut in, made in *Kashgar*, where there was an Arabic settlement. Henry verified the Chinese in a book we have and finds it was made in the dynasty of Ching-tih in 1506. Mr. Hay bought it in New York last summer of Bil Bigelow's great friend, Sichel of Paris, a collector whom we saw there. At the same minute came *Portrait of a Lady*, which the author kindly sent me. It's very nice, and charming things in it, but I'm ageing fast and prefer what Sir Walter called the "big bow-wow style." I shall suggest to Mr. James to name his next novel "Ann Eliza." It's not that he "bites off more than he can chaw," as T. G. Appleton said of Nathan,[1] but he chaws more than he bites off. De Bildt, Swedish secretary, has lent me du Chaillu's new book, *The Midnight Sun*. It's pleasant, dull, cool reading. Have you read it yet?

We are interested in the speaker-fight settled last night—Kasson thrown out, Keifer of Ohio brought in by a combination.[2] He was not friendly to Garfield. Hiscock of New York is too independent and refused to help the senatorial fight of last summer. This is a triumph for Don Cameron and Logan, a boss job. The great Don came to tea a few days since and admired Possum, otherwise I saw nothing to please one. *We*—Henry and I—are more and more convinced of MacVeagh's wisdom both in going out and in holding his tongue, but no one has a good word for him here. By the way, Mrs. Heard was much interested to see Miss Beale on Thanksgiving Day, having heard of her in Newport as the authoress of *Democracy* in collusion with Herbert Wadsworth, whom she accused of it after Miss Beale had gone. He looked very conscious and embarrassed and when we told Emily Beale she only gasped. So her fury of last year may have been a blind. Are you reading Mrs. Burnette's *Through One Administration* in *Scribner's*? We think Miles[3] is in it and Miss Snead is the correspondent of course.

[1] Thomas Gold Appleton (1812-1884) and his youngest brother, Nathan Appleton, both of Boston.

[2] "The contest for the Speakership of the House of Representatives was decided in the Republican caucus on Saturday by the nomination of Mr. Keifer of Ohio on the sixteenth ballot. The largest factor in bringing about this result was the transfer, under Mr. Cameron's orders, of the votes of the Pennsylvania delegation from Mr. Hiscock to Mr. Keifer." (*Nation*, December 8, 1881)

[3] General Nelson A. Miles.

As I never returned her call of four years ago I don't know her personally. I wish you were here to share our dinner today, a piece from a huge haunch of Virginia venison sent me by Mrs. Craig Wadsworth. Folks are very kind and civil here and I must send her a Virginia ham when she moves into her new house. She and Mrs. Heard have taken adjoining ones on Massachusetts Avenue. Have you seen Mr. Kinnicutt yet? Do tell me about him. Love to Auntie and Betsy. *Adiós.* Affectionately

CLOVER

1607 H STREET, WASHINGTON,
Sunday, December 11th, 1881.

DEAR PATER: You must console yourself for the dull letters I send you now in remembering "happy is the man whose annals are dull." There is as yet no society and there are no political excitements. Tuesday Charles Grinnell came to muncheon and again to dinner with Dr. Folsom,[1] and Emily Beale came in after dinner and was quite amusing. Said she was "tired of playing baby-elephant to amuse Bostonians." She says you and Sturgis will both ask her to dine when she is with the Thayers. Do ask Mrs. Bell and a few jolly, gay folks to meet her, but not Mrs. Jack with Mrs. Bell—the latter cannot endure the former; she is eloquent on that subject.

Wednesday morning Dr. Folsom sent in a note to say that, if we would like to go to the Guiteau trial, I could take his seat among the experts, we could go in by the jury door. So we went up about one o'clock. The Court was taking a recess. One of the marshals gave me a good seat by a wide-open window, and Henry sat among the experts. It was intensely interesting. The assassin was in front of me, so I could only get his profile—a large strong nose, a high straight forehead, and a good height from top of ear to top of head. He bullied and badgered everyone; banged his fist on the table; broke off in reading a paper, saying, "Arthur's message has the true ring. I think he'll give us the best administration we ever had." Several nice, intelligent men from Freeport, Illinois, testified, all declaring that no suspicion of insanity had heretofore rested on the family. Said one, "Guiteau's father was the third

---

[1] Dr. Charles F. Folsom was serving on the National Board of Health; he had married a sister of Mrs. Charles Grinnell.

smartest man in the county." And when asked by Corkhill for his definition of a smart man, said, "Well, he *got* all the offices he run for." The witnesses that day smashed the hereditary insanity theory pretty thoroughly.

Mrs. Scoville is a nice, quiet, ladylike-looking woman. Thought she and I were the most respectable-looking women in court. As to the Court being unruly or disorderly, it's all nonsense. How Judge Cox keeps his gravity is a marvel, the beast's sallies are more than unjudicial muscles can stand. Judge Cox is a gentleman and a scholar and the newspaper critics a set of idiots. Every word Guiteau says tightens his noose now. District-Attorney Corkhill is a vile creature in manner; MacVeagh gave us his opinion of him last June and Garfield's last decision the day before he was murdered was to dismiss him. He was one of Hayes's appointments; his first wife's father is Miller of the Supreme Court.[1] Said Guiteau, "Colonel, your record is as bad as mine and as soon as this case is finished you are to go." Only once his acuteness failed him, he expressed his antipathy to the blacks and one of the jury is black as coal. He attempted to explain it away afterwards.

After Court we stood and watched him get into the van, the crowd on the sidewalk jeering and hissing. Then Dr. Folsom said he must go to the jail and examine his eyes once more and asked us to go, so after some hesitation I joined him and Henry. As we entered the jail—a very handsome new building—we came into a large hall. In one corner I noticed a group of four or five men, one sitting in a rocking chair, whose face seemed to me of the Guiteau type, though I had not got a front view in Court. As we entered he got up and came forward very courteously, saying, "How do you do, Doctor?" and shook his hand. Dr. Folsom introduced Henry and me, and supposing it must be the jailer I met his offered hand. I felt rather overwhelmed when it broke upon me who the man was as Dr. Folsom said, "I want to look once more at your eyes." He led the way into the jailer's room and after a short examination sat down to talk.

[1] Samuel Freeman Miller (1916-1890) was appointed to the United States Supreme Court by President Lincoln in 1862.

Said Dr. Folsom, "Well, Grant and Conkling seem to be running things now in the Republican Party."

"I think," said Guiteau, "there is more harmony than there was on the first of July."

Said Henry, "What do you suppose Mr. Blaine thinks about that?"

Guiteau gave him a keen look, remarked drily, "We won't discuss that." Put on his hat, took up his bundle of newspapers, and shambled out of the room without giving us another look.

He's a cunning, shrewd beast, deranged in a sense no doubt, but he miscalculated, believing he could murder Garfield and get off through the gratitude of the "Stalwarts." He told one of the doctors he "thought he should go to Europe when the trial was over." I don't wish to have it repeated that I shook hands with the accursed beast, without the context being given. Someone would write on that they "were sorry to hear that I had asked Guiteau to tea."

Richardson came on Friday to the Andersons'; came in that same evening late for a chat. Yesterday A.M. we studied the new house plans, which are quite charming, and he dined quietly with us, the Andersons having a dinner engagement. We tried to get Senator Bayard and Mr. Randolph Tucker and Mr. McLane,[1] but they were all away or engaged. He was most entertaining and full of talk; if Mr. Anderson can cut the plan to suit his limit it will be the house of Washington. Ultimate to a degree! Love to Auntie and the Cambridge family. Yours affectionately

M. A.

1607 H STREET, WASHINGTON,
Sunday A.M., December 18th, 1881.

DEAR PATER: No winter yet, but one beautiful autumn day after another; such weather for saddle was never seen and we scour the country on Prince and Daisy. Sunday the dogs claim so we take them to drive.

---

[1] Robert Milligan McLane (1814-1898), following two terms in the House of Representatives, became Governor of Maryland, March 4, 1883, and twelve years later United States Minister to France, where he died.

We are much interested in the new make-up of the Cabinet as it develops day by day.[1] Arthur is astonishing all lovers of clean, strong government by the good quality of the new timber he is putting in. Frelinghuysen is not a big gun in any way but a gentleman and a lawyer of training and intelligence, and not a blunderbuss of the Blaine caliber, who has done more bad work in his brief term of office than even his enemies feared. Bancroft Davis[2] gladly leaves the Court of Claims to serve as Assistant Secretary of State, which no persuasions could induce him to take under Blaine, though they raised the salary to tempt him. He is not suave or attractive, but his wife is, and will keep a charming house now that two years of deep mourning for her mother are over. Hitt of Illinois goes out with rejoicing; he gave a small farewell dinner on Thursday—to which Henry went—to meet Eugene Schuyler,[3]

---

[1] After Garfield's death on September 19, his successor showed no haste in reorganizing the Cabinet, and except in the case of the Treasury, where Charles J. Folger succeeded William Windom on October 27, President Arthur awaited the reassembling of Congress in December before announcing other changes. Freling-huysen succeeded Blaine as Secretary of State, December 12; Brewster was appointed to the Department of Justice, December 15, and five days later, Howe to the Post Office Department; no change was made in the Navy and Interior Departments until April, when William E. Chandler and Henry M. Teller were appointed; Robert T. Lincoln retained the War Department through both administrations.

[2] The *Nation*, December 22, 1881: "The appointment of Mr. Bancroft Davis as First Assistant Secretary of State is undoubtedly the best that could have been made. There is probably no man in this country more conversant with the business machinery of our diplomatic and consular service in all its branches, as well as with the history and traditions of our foreign intercourse. He possesses at the same time great working capacity and knows how to give his work a useful direction. In all these respects he is just the kind of a man a Secretary of State should have at his elbow to furnish him with information, and to guard him from those mistakes, which inexperienced zeal is apt to fall into. The only complaint that was ever made of Mr. Davis when he held the same place under Mr. Fish, was that he lacked that smooth pleasantness and unruffled affability which makes a man in such position a favorite with the diplomatic corps as well as his subordinates. But his other qualities are so valuable that they far outweigh this little defect of temper or manner, if defect it be."

[3] Eugene Schuyler (1840-1890) entered the consular service in 1866, and thereafter, until his death, was almost continuously employed as consul, consul-general, secretary of legation, or minister-resident at various stations in Russia,

Consul at Bucharest, and his brother, an officer now stationed in Kansas. He, by the way, told Henry a curious thing. He says they now get trout and sea bass in the upper part of the North Platte River, two thousand miles or so from the Gulf of Mexico. A few years ago the Fish Commission sent a quantity of fish eggs for breeding to California; the train went through a bridge, and the eggs were drowned! So these engineers "builded worse and better than they knew."

Last and not least is Friday's nomination of Benjamin H. Brewster,[1] of Philadelphia, to succeed MacVeagh. He is a widely known and respected lawyer; was chosen by MacVeagh last spring as associate counsel in the Star-route prosecutions, and it seems as complete a recognition and vindication of MacVeagh to the yelping public as he could wish. Some good influence has been at work lately which does not appear. The jump from Timothy Howe to Brewster is too wide to be a natural one. Arthur is on the "road to Damascus," and if he doesn't put the scales, which seem to be falling from his eyes, into Boutwell's[2] hands, Judge Gray[3] may get a seat on the Supreme Court bench after all. Folks are waiting with bated breath to see. Poor Garfield paved his way to the grave with good intentions, and fell so body and soul under Blaine's influence that he lost his moral scent. Today's *Capitol*—a ribald, amusing, blackguard paper—begins to attack Arthur, especially for putting an Eastern man into the Treasury.

Turkey, the Balkans, and Egypt. He married, in 18787, Gertrude Wallace, daughter of Charles and Henrietta (Low) King.

[1] Benjamin Harris Brewster (1816-1888) had been Attorney-General of Pennsylvania in 1867, but otherwise had not held public office before; his nomination was confirmed December 19, 1881.

[2] George Sewell Boutwell (1818-1905) had been Governor of Massachusetts in 1851-1852, a member of Congress from 1863 to 1869, when he was appointed Secretary of the Treasury by President Grant. This position he resigned in March 1873 on being elected to the United States Senate, where he served until March 3, 1877. In 1880 he was appointed counsel for the United States before the French and American Claims Commission.

[3] Horace Gray (1828-1902) graduated at Harvard College in 1845; was an Associate Justice of the Massachusetts Supreme Judicial Court from 1864 to 1873, and Chief Justice of the same from 1873 to 1881, when President Arthur appointed him one of the Associate Justices of the Supreme Court of the United States on December 19, 1881.

Today, Mr. Hitt and Perry Belmont, M.C., were to have dined with us, but Mr. Hitt has just given out. Perry is very solemn, so we must drum up a frivolous fourth. Thursday, we are to have a small dinner for the Andersons—the Bancroft Davises, Aristarchi Bey, Miss Bayard, and a ninth and tenth if any very festive turn up. The Yoshidas give a farewell party on Tuesday—he is recalled to be Finance Minister in Japan. As we hate crowds, I don't think we shall add to his of Tuesday. Madame Lewenhaupt took me yesterday to call on the new Italian Ministress, Baroness Fava,[1] and on Madame Barca,[2] new Spanish; the former lively and amusing; the latter stout, jolly, and common—I would swear the twin sister of our landlady at the Fonda de la Paz in Madrid. They are newspaper people in Spain; that class now get the diplomatic appointments, so the dips here say. They offered us tea and marmalade, which Madame Lewenhaupt ate with a knife, for want of a duller weapon, with naïve Scandinavian simplicity.

Mr. Dwight,[3] Librarian of the State Department, sent me a French book a few days ago which he picked up in Geneva last summer; it is charming, do get it and lend it to Adie and to Mrs. Bell, *Le Crime de Sylvestre Bonnard*, by Anatole France, 1881. There is a French Betsy in it who hides her master's cravats and rules him with a rod of iron with unfailing devotion. I didn't think anything French could be so sweet and charming. Mr. Adee[4] has sent in a new Spanish novel—*Marniella*, by Galdos. It begins well; Ellen may like it, as she is on the lookout for Spanish. My letter is getting garrulous. Goodbye, yours affectionately

M. A.

---

[1] Baron Saverio Fava, Italian Minister at Washington from October 28, 1881, to June 14, 1893.

[2] Francisco Barca del Corral, Spanish Minister at Washington, April 30, 1881, to July 1883.

[3] Theodore Frelinghuysen Dwight (1846-1917).

[4] Alvey Augustus Adee (1842-1924) was Chief of the Diplomatic Bureau in the State Department. He had previously served in Spain as Secretary of Legation, and at times as Chargé d'Affaires, from 1869 to 1877; then, on his return to Washington, Mr. Evarts appointed him Chief of the Diplomatic Bureau, and subsequently, in 1882, he was made Third Assistant Secretary of State, and in 1886 Second Assistant Secretary of State, which position he held until his death.

P.S. I find this page empty on reading it over. Keep me a little posted in deaths, I only hear by chance from the Heards, etc., of Powell Mason's loss[1] and Tom Curtis and John Cushing. Remember that I am so "far from the door" that I can't hear the knocks, and in June I do not dare to ask any old friend for husband or wife or child. The *Herald* doesn't record any but O'Hara and Flanagan deaths. When you have your next Club notify me, and I'll send you a glass jar of terrapin *à la crème*.

1607 H STREET,
Christmas, Sunday, 1881.

DEAR PATER: You will have got my thanks for your delightful "potential"—as the Jameses say—Christmas present. I think of writing to my friend Phillips in London and asking him if he has anything more *ultimate* than the Tudor rose in enamel—I yearned for it in 1879 but took water colours instead. Henry thinks we will have something ahead of that. The gold Tudor rose Mrs. Jack Gardner will show you; the white and red enamel one was copied from an enchanting portrait by Holbein exhibited in loan exhibition in 1879 in Piccadilly. Bil Bigelow has sent me a charming shiny green card-case ornamented with wrought iron which matches my street costume exactly; Mrs. Chardon Brooks a box of pretty things last night; Ned some wonderful leather; Mrs. Campbell brandy peaches of her own making; and little Ellen a handkerchief bag. So we feel almost young again.

I wrote you Friday that our Thursday dinner went off nicely. Friday, Miss Dulaney to breakfast, then Boojum and I to her lodgings, where she played and sang to us. E. to dinner; he is to bring his wife here—has taken a house close by in 16th Street; she is the lady who was too much for Cheyenne and Denver. Washington harbours lions and lambs. She has sold hers, by the way, as it went back on her suddenly and tore her face; that made her very angry and she sold it. She said it was satisfactory to get back the original purchase money and cover the surgeon's bill too!

The weather is better than ever—no winter yet, had a gorgeous ride yesterday. Daisy is becoming a gymnast; first she flings *me* up, then her *heels*, then flies to the side. I have given her fair

---

[1] Powell Mason's son was drowned October 22, 1881.

warning now that she will get no carrots if she breaks my neck, and it seemed to impress her. No news here, the politicians lie low till January 5th and Arthur has gone away. Do get the last *Puck*. Blaine is delightful—"I go but I return!" I hope New England will cut his throat in convention in 1884 as it did in 1876. Henry resumed work at the State Department the day Blaine went out; the new régime is a great relief to us. The Guiteau trial drags on wearily, but for all that the newspaper fire keeps up. Mr. Godkin has made very foolish remarks about the presiding Judge—Cox. If he would trouble to come on and see for himself he might modify his criticisms; he would carry far more weight if he made fewer snap judgments! Poor Boutwell has been hanging round here for some time past; he didn't want anything except what he couldn't get. I hope Judge Gray will be suave and good-tempered here; people expect a great deal from him.

You think I have a "taste for horrors" because I want to know the barest statistics of death and marriage. It is only to save time, otherwise in June I must visit Somerville and ask to see the patients' book, and then explore Mt. Auburn for new-laid graves. I don't dare to ask for a friend or foe's wife or husband when I go back. I *could* take the Daily, but will resort to no such desperate measure if I can accomplish my object by fair measures.

Whom do you think we are to feed today? "Say not, oh! fountain, I will not drink of *thy* waters." I said it at noon yesterday; at twelve-fifteen I dipped in my cup. William Everett!![1] He came yesterday to stay here with his niece Mrs. Hopkins,[2] and she came in so blue and full of small worries that I offered to ameliorate her Sunday dinner; so she and her husband and Piggy are coming. They may say in derision "rolling stones gather no moss"; if not

---

[1] William Everett (1839-1910), a brilliant but irritable scholar, too much absorbed to pay attention to mere matters of personal tidiness, familiarly known as "Piggy," was the son of Edward Everett and Charlotte Gray Brooks, a sister of Henry Adams's mother; he was graduated at Harvard College in 1859, from Trinity College, Cambridge, in 1863, and from the Harvard Law School in 1865. He was licensed to preach in 1872; however, he turned to teaching and from 1873 to 1877 he was an assistant professor of Latin at Harvard; from 1878 to 1893 he was Headmaster of Adams Academy, retiring to serve a term in Congress, 1983-1895.

[2] Mrs. Archibald Hopkins (Charlotte Everett Wise).

moss, every stick and pebble and foreign substance comes to them. You are "eclectic," we truly "all-o-pathic," which means all-suffering; "home-o-pathic," those who suffer from family dinners at home—I don't dig Greek roots for nothing! *Adiós*.

M. A.

1607 H STREET, WASHINGTON,
Sunday, January 1st, 1882.

DEAR PATER: A happy New Year to you and Dandie and let us hope a sunnier one than ours today; it looks snowy in the sky, and is raw and disagreeable. Mr. Lowndes has just sent me in a box of sweet roses; he came in after ten last night to chat the old year out over our fire.

The week has been a quiet one. Sunday, as I wrote you, we had Mr. Everett and the Hopkinses. I subpœned Miss Randolph, who was passing a few days with Mr. Corcoran, and the restraint subdued the pedagogue to decorous and civilised behavior—he talked well and quite amused us. Tuesday, a birthday party, in honour of Mr. Corcoran's eighty-third year, at the Louise Home,[1] his almshouse for some forty decayed gentlewomen. It was from eight to ten and really very pleasant; the Solid South of course, but others beside; a handsome supper in the large central hall, which was dressed with evergreen. Mrs. Rives[2] looked very charming. They have taken a house here not far from us, and though I never exchanged a word with her in my life—only pasteboard certificates many years ago—when I called on her last week, it seemed like the meeting of Charley Ross and his mother. The Bostonian off his or her native granite is a new being; her extreme deafness is a great barrier.

Wednesday, someone to dine——? Thursday, Professor Marsh of Yale, full of interesting new talk. Friday, some folks to dine, to adjourn to the Vokeses—Mrs. Don Cameron and Aristarchi Bey, both ill, gave out just at the last, so I got Miss Heard

---

[1] Mr. Corcoran founded and endowed the Louise Home in memory of his wife, Louise Amory Morris, daughter of Commodore Charles Morris.
[2] Mrs. William Cabell Rives (Grace Sears, of Boston); her granddaughter, Amélie Rives (Princess Troubetzkoy), became well known as a novelist.

and Laughlin,[1] and Mr. de Bildt and Miss Beale were on hand. Tell the Gurneys I give in to "Fun in a Fog"; nearly had hysterics. General Sherman sat in front mopping his tear-stained face. "The Bell in the Kitchen" bored me so that I thought the Vokeses were not for me. Victoria is so like Katy Bayard! Sherman, on the strength of it, took her behind the scenes and introduced them to each other, and they've exchanged calls. Miss Bayard asks tenderly for you, says you are a "most congenial spirit."

Yesterday Miss Howard[2] came for a week's visit; I hope it will interest her, as it is her first. I went to meet her at four, but finding the train to be one hour late, I came back here. West,[3] the new Minister, and his daughter, who has just come over, came in while I was waiting, and I thought her charming; she is the daughter of a Spanish ballet dancer, now dead, has been educated at a convent in France, is quite pretty, rather elegant, and speaks with a most charming foreign accent. It's a curious position for a girl of eighteen to be put at the head of a big establishment like the British Legation. She is delighted with her first week here. As I can't endure English misses, it's a great relief to have this pretty girl after Lady Thornton with her neuralgia and sharp tongue. Tomorrow, we are to dine with them at the Bancroft Davises'—I shall heave Miss Howard in someone's care. Mr. Kasson asked us for Friday

---

[1] James Lawrence Laughlin (1850-1933).

[2] Miss Catharine L. Howard (1833-1897), daughter of Charles Howard and Elizabeth Buckminster Dwight, was a teacher at Mrs. Agassiz's school in Cambridge, where Marian Adams met her and formed a strong attachment to her. When Miss Howard's health broke down in 1869, Marian arranged to have her spend a year in Europe.

[3] Sir Lionel Sackville Sackville-West (1827-1908), the fifth son of the fifth Earl of Delawarr, entered the diplomatic service in 1847; was British Minister at Buenos Aires 1872-1878, at Madrid 1878-1881, at Washington 1881-1888. He succeeded his brother as the second Baron Sackville.

"In the early days of his career, while secretary to the British Legation in Madrid, Lionel Sackville-West fell in love with a Spanish dancer, Josephine de Ortega. As she was already the wife of her dancing master, marriage was impossible, but he lived faithfully and devotedly with her from the middle fifties until her death in 1871. They had a number of children, their eldest being Victoria, who has just died (January 30, 1936). As they grew up the daughters stayed with their father in Madrid and Washington and in 1890 Victoria was married to her cousin, who eventually succeeded her uncle and father-in-law as third baron." (*New York Times*, January 31, 1936)

last, but we couldn't go. Tonight, Mr. Nordhoff and Marsh are to dine here, and Miss Howard is anxious to see both of them, knowing them well by hearsay.

We have it on good authority that the pressure on Arthur to appoint Boutwell to the Supreme Bench was very great. Boutwell swore he would have "that or nothing." As he is a warm personal friend of Arthur's it is very creditable to him that he resisted it. It is still a matter of speculation whether Mr. Beale is made Secretary of the Navy; the appointment of Sargent[1] of California would be very bad. I had a long horse-talk with General Beale at Mr. Corcoran's party. He is intelligent and would not allow stealing, I fancy; as we've no navy, it is rather a sinecure.

I am grieved to hear from various sources of Mrs. Edward Perkins's fatal illness; it seems that she has known it for a long time. What a cruel blow to Mrs. Wharton, and how little she has to make her life happy. Fate has strange ways of dealing. Poor A. who has and gives no pleasure to anyone and may live to bury all her contemporaries, and others called off from a full feast! The moral is to make all one can out of life and live up to one's fingers' ends. Good-bye. Take good care of yourself. Affectionately

M. A.

Read Charles Grinnell's forthcoming article in *Law Review* on the conduct of the Guiteau trial. I hope the critics will digest it.

1607 H STREET, WASHINGTON,
Sunday, January 8th, 1882.

DEAR PATER: We are in the soft embrace of a dirty January thaw; we got down to 20° above one night. Yesterday a lovely ride through the white country roads, the atmosphere like essence of opal, brooks still running.

We've had a quiet week for Miss Howard. As she seems to have enjoyed it, that's all I care for. Sunday, Mr. Nordhoff and Professor Marsh dined here and were most agreeable. Monday, we

[1] Aaron Augustus Sargent (1827-1887) at different times represented the State of California in the House of Representatives and in the Senate; President Arthur appointed him United States Minister to Germany, where he served from 1882 to 1884.

dined at the Bancroft Davises', providing Miss Howard with a friend at home. The dinner was for Minister West and his young convent-fledged daughter—a sweet little Kitty McLane from Baltimore, a plain-faced Miss King whose pleasant father, John A. King, tells me he met Ellen and Whitman on the Nile, Kasson of Iowa, and a Mr. Gherardi Davis. The dinner was lively; Henry and I both fell in love with Miss McLane, he going to the length of waltzing with her while Miss West played for them. We have had various people to tea and dinner every day. Thursday, Henry James put in an appearance; that young emigrant has much to learn here. He is surprised to find that he can go to the Capitol and listen to debates without taking out a license, as in London. He may in time get into the "swim" here, but I doubt it. I think the real, live, vulgar, quick-paced world in America will fret him and that he prefers a quiet corner with a pen where he can create men and women who say neat things and have refined tastes and are not nasal or eccentric. "Let every man be fully persuaded in his own mind," we say.

Mr. Nicholson[1] came on Friday with a note from Gurney; he's a handsome, manly, intelligent fellow. He dined with us that evening and came to tea yesterday, where he found the "team"—the Miss Bayards, Miss Beale, Jinny Davenport, Henry James, et al. Tonight, I've promised to take him and Mr. James to the Larnies' at nine-thirty, Miss Howard going home on the 10 P.M. train. Judge Gray and Miss Dulaney just tumbled in—the latter is to dine with us, Henry says. The combat thickens; I've set up a kitchen-maid and Margery Lite to cook. Tell Ned I've put your thousand-dollar cheque into bank to pay bills, so shall not want any for six weeks or more; shall wait till I really want some monkeys. Love to folks. Ask Nanny Wharton to give her Aunt Mary[2] my very dear love and sympathy. *Adiós*. Affectionately

M. A.

---

[1] Joseph Shield Nicholson (1850-1927), professor of political economy at Edinburgh University from 1880 to 1925.

[2] Mrs. Edward Perkins (Mary Spring), whose fatal illness was referred to in an earlier letter.

1607 H STREET, WASHINGTON,
Sunday P.M., January 15th, 1882.

DEAR PATER: This being a dull gray P.M., I've let Henry go off for
a ride alone and have been reveling in Hans Andersen and *Dr.
Breen's Practice*, Howells's last. It's charming. I shall send it off
to England as I do all his stories now, those hungry Islanders long
so for a new flavour. Two letters this week from both Mr. and
Mrs. Woolner, he begging us to accept as "an expression of gratitude" for our "kindness" a small picture—which is on its bounding
way—found in an old shop in Highgate, *suggesting* Bonington.[1]
He cleaned it himself and to his great joy found Bonington's
monogram under the dirt and varnish. That makes our fourth; and
in Europe Bonington is "heads even" with Turner in reputation.
We shall at this rate leave fine pickings for our heirs. Mrs. Bancroft said the other day, "My dear, I dislike auctions very much,
but I mean to go to yours after you die." I've no doubt she will,
and George too will chip in.

The lesson for the week is as follows: Sunday, Judge Gray and
Mr. Lowndes came to dine; the former has not gained in charm of
manner in the years since we last met. The MacVeaghs came in
and passed the evening and were most amusing and gay.
MacVeagh and Horace Gray fell on each others' neck—the former,
luckily, was the top one; the appointment of the latter had been
MacVeagh's one request of Arthur—to their joint credit, be it
known. I asked Mrs. MacVeagh where they were staying. To
which she answered with grim Cameronian humour, "With my
brother Don; we hear so much of you from them that we thought if
you associate with them we can." I hear that old Simon[2] adores his

[1] Richard Parkes Bonington (1801-1828) painted coast and street scenes.
[2] Simon Cameron (1799-1889), the father of Mrs. MacVeagh and of Senator
"Don" Cameron, accumulated a substantial fortune in railway and banking en-
terprises. He first served in the United States Senate from 1845 to 1849, having
been elected to fill an unexpired term. He was again elected to the Senate in
1856, as a Republican. Lincoln appointed him Secretary of War in 1861, and in
January 1862 United States Minister to Russia, where he remained for a year. In
1866 he returned to the Senate and served there until his resignation in 1877,
when his son succeeded him as a Senator from Pennsylvania. From 1854 on, he
ruled the Republican Party in Pennsylvania; a politician of the old school, he
was by no means enthusiastic about the reform element in the party.

fearless, bright-witted daughter; she's a reform chip of the old block. Henry James pleased MacVeagh by telling him that Matthew Arnold thought him the pleasantest American he ever met. Monday, the MacVeaghs came to breakfast at twelve and left at two for Philadelphia.

George W. Bliss, who is following up Dorsey and Brady relentlessly, is now coming in for daily vitriol from our morning paper owned by Brady. Friday it wound up with this sweet question: "Shall this carbuncle be allowed to fester longer on the body politic?" "That is *wealthy*," as Aristarchi says, when he thinks a thing a good hit. Two weeks ago Bliss was a jewel of a lawyer—a carbuncle in its real sense.

Tuesday, a very pleasant dinner at the Lewenhaupts' for the Wests. The host took me in; a Russian—Willamov[1]—on my right. He fled when the Bartholomeis[2] came, and has been traveling in Cochin China and Ceylon until his chief's peculiarities should force his recall—which has now come, and he and his irregular consort and sinister offspring have fled, leaving only debts to mark their steps. Thursday, we had a small dinner here and, thanks to Miss Dulaney and her delicious singing, it went off nicely. Miss Beale's father went home and told her it was "the nicest dinner he ever went to and the *only* one he had ever enjoyed." And Miss Bayard quite roused up the quiet, sad-eyed British plenipotentiary. I gave the ingenuous little daughter a thimble and needle and silk—as if she were Polly or Lou—and she embroidered a small flower while Miss Dulaney sang French songs to her; she is a funny little church mouse in contrast with the sharp-clawed grimalkin who preceded her.

Friday, a dinner of twelve at Mr. de Bildt's (First Secretary from Sweden and Norway). He took me in, and a shy young Briton on my right, Lord George Montagu,[3] whom Mrs. Mason was so very kind to last winter for Posey's sake. We got on to the subject of titles, and the funny confusions as to his. When he said,

---

[1] Grégoire de Willamov, Secretary of the Russian Legation, and from time to time Chargé d'Affaires *ad interim*.

[2] Michel Bartholomei, the Russian Minister at Washington from November 15, 1880, to January 18, 1882, was succeeded by Charles de Struve, April 11, 1882.

[3] George Francis Montagu (1855-1882), Third Secretary of the British Legation, died two months later, March 12.

with a hesitating furtive voice, "I think they are all very absurd"; I said, "I quite agree with you." Then, emboldened by my sympathy perhaps, he said, "You can't fancy anything so dreadful as the family burial vaults at Kimbolton." Kimbolton Castle is the family Asylum, he being half-brother to the Duke of Manchester. I longed to tell him of Constance Ysnaga's[1] outburst of real feeling to Elsie Barlow, when she told her of her engagement to Mandeville, the Duke's eldest son. "Oh, Elsie! How soon *do* you suppose the Duke of Manchester will die?"

"Don't touch the reins, your honour, they're as rotten as pears." To fortify which quotation I enclose this cutting about our late friend, the Marquess of Huntly,[2] whom we met at Glen Tanner in August 1880, when we lunched with the pa-in-law, Cunliffe Brooks.[3] He had made his comely daughter a wedding present of this same noble marquess, for whom he had paid two hundred thousand pounds sterling down. I shall never forget how, as we drove away that lovely summer evening, the Huntly Victoria with its pretty horses stood at the door, while the daughter and son-in-law stood waiting for a cheque. Because, as Sir John Clark told us

[1] George Victor Drogo Montagu, Viscount Mandeville (1853-1892), married, May 22, 1876, Consuelo, daughter of Don Antonio Ysnaga del Valle.

[2] "A SCOTTISH MARQUESS.—The Marquess of Huntly, Premier Marquess of Scotland, Earl and Baron of more places than can be specified, late a lord-in-waiting to the Queen, was yesterday charged before the Lord Mayor of London with obtaining money on false pretences from Mr. Benjamin Nicholson, a bill broker. The plaintiff had, a fortnight ago, shown that he had made vain efforts to find the Marquess; that he had applied at his town house, club and country house; that he had traced him to Constantinople, Cyprus and St. Petersburg, and still the Lord Mayor showed an extreme unwillingness to grant a warrant. Part of the money had been recovered by civil process, and there was no reason why the criminal machinery should be used to obtain the rest. Lord Huntly had lost money on the turf and elsewhere; he had fallen into the hands of money lenders, and, though these transactions between noblemen and usurers sometimes end in pugilistic encounters and sometimes county courts, they rarely take the form of extradition warrants. The Marquess is the chief of one of the oldest families in the United Kingdom; he descends in direct line from the famous Huntlys of Scottish story; but the plaintiff must think the security particularly bad or he would not risk a scandal which would be pretty sure to hurt one side as much as the other."

[3] Charles Gordon, Marquess and Earl of Huntly (b. 1847), married on July 14, 1869, Amy, daughter of William Cunliffe Brooks, Esq.

on the way home, the sheriffs were camping in Aboyne Castle, which waved its proud old flag at us as we drove by. The young fellow was handsome and had nice manners, but, as Dr. Holmes said once, it had "taken a thousand years to get them up; we can do it in five."

Mrs. Woolner writes, "I wish you would come back to England. Perhaps we shall want you to assist in establishing a republic here in place of these German humbugs, who feed like drones in our hive. I can hardly think of any sight more delightful that would be the family portmanteaus and plate-chests and cradles labeled 'Guelph' 'Passenger to Anywhere.'" She's getting uneasy, it seems. *Adiós.* Affectionately

M. A.

1607 H STREET, WASHINGTON,
January 17th, 1882.

DEAR PATER: You poor old thing! We are very, very sorry for you. Shall I take the train on to see you? I will at two hours' notice if it would amuse you or give you any pleasure. Boojum and Possum will take good care of Henry, and I can go in twenty hours. Betsy is, as you say, a ghastly failure in illness, her ghoul-like whispers make my flesh creep as I remember them. I think Mrs. Watson's cheery face and voice should "reduce you to a simmer," as T. G. Appleton said of Jean Ingelow's mother, when the London footman said, "She can't see you, Sir, her mother is suffering with a boil."

This is something good to eat—very: a dozen picked oysters, the liquor stewed with a little curry powder, and a rim of dry boiled rice round the edge of the dish. I sent some to Mrs. Beale last week, and her daughter said she ate every bit and it was the only food she had fancied for weeks. Try this too, it's my London cook's best "go-to-meetin'" soup: wash, clean, and boil half peck of spinach and, when well drained, rub through a sieve and place the pulp in a stew-pan—be sure all the water is squeezed out and not a bit of stem in it—it takes *one* hour to boil well and a little soda in it to keep a bright green colour; then add three pints of veal stock to your spinach and let it boil until it is reduced to one quart, a little salt and pepper to season, and serve with crisp toasted crumbs. Richardson said, when he dined here, it was the best soup he ever ate, and it is as pretty as it is good. Get Ellen to stand over the cook.

Lillie Winsor[1] came to tea Saturday and again Sunday. She makes a handsome matron. You can refer to her for a character if you find yours called in question. She told us the one bright spot in the sad Boston winter has been R. H. White's accusing Mrs. C. of shoplifting, and that the pleasure was deepened by the stolen lace being found in her pocket! "There is a time to mourn and a time to rejoice." Never will we lose our faith in human boy-nature so as to harbour the vile suggestion of some craven aristocrats that the cash-boy stole the lace and put it where it would do the most good. That granitic female drove Mr. R. out of Boston by spreading blackmailing charges about him, now let her reap as she has sown and share the harvest with her lovely sister. There has been a tender, happy glow on Henry's face ever since he heard this "tale of doom."

Mr. Hewitt, Henry James, and Miss Dulaney dined here on Sunday. Mr. Hewitt full of interesting talk; he told us a new story of William R. Travers—the last. Don't repeat it to Ellen—'cos she and Miss Ashburner think me blasphemous. Mrs. Travers, on Christmas Day, told her husband that she felt their home life was not all it should be; and suggested that it be made sweeter and holier. So she hung up in their parlour an illuminated text, "God Bless Our Home"; and Travers melted, and said he felt regenerated. The next day, on going into her dining room, Mrs. Travers reeled as she saw, in low-toned colours, another text, "God Damn our Cook." As Bret Harte says, in his fable of the "She Elephant," what is home without a mother?

Last night we went to drink Russian punch at Mr. Williamov's rooms; no one but Senator Bayard and his two daughters, and Mr. and Mrs. Bradley—she, Don Cameron's elder daughter, married to a son of Judge Bradley, whom Judge Hoar sat on the bench, saying to him, "Mind, now, you vote to reverse Chase's Legal Tender decision"; and it was reversed. Miss Bayard was very pretty and charming in white, sitting, as we went in, on a low wide divan covered with Eastern stuffs, playing on her banjo; she and Mabel sing-

[1] Mrs. Henry C. Winsor (Lillie C. Jackson).

ing love songs about "Susan Jane." It was as good as the Vokeses; and Bayard, stern as Ramses, amusing himself with Jap photographs. Then the punch was brewed thusly: from a stout wire on the mantel-shelf was hung a lump of sugar as big as Boojum's head; under it into a large porcelain stew-pan our Kalmuck host put slices of banana and pineapple, then champagne, and then brandy, setting fire to the latter. Miss Bayard left her banjo and stirred it with a silver spoon three feet long, from time to time pouring some over the sugar, which then dripped into the pot— Fortuny would have made a charming picture of it; then we drank it and it was like nectar. We had cakes and fruit, and Jap curios to look at and Ceylon cat's-eyes, and at eleven we broke up. Our host was very gracious and courteous and it amused us like a bit of travel.

This unseemly screed is in place of a call. My love to Adie, tell her my letters are written to her as well as you, only she must skip the cuss words. Love and sympathy from Henry, who says, "Tell him to come on here and get rid of his troubles." *Adiós.* Affectionately

M. A.

The newspapers haven't got scent of Henry James yet; he is sheltered under an alias—the Postmaster General, late acting!

1607 H STREET
January 18th.

DEAR PATER: How are you today? Are my yarns too much for you? I'd rather you had the reading of them than I, peace to their ashes.

Yesterday Nogueiras,[1] Portuguese Minister, and his wife came in before tea-time; *he* is very nice, she colossally dull but a Vicomtesse, to keep the balance socially. I asked *him* about the Comtesse d'Edla, wife of ex-King of Portugal.[2] He says it's *not* a morganatic marriage but a square out-and-out first class "A No. 1" marriage.

---

[1] Visconde das Nogueiras, the Portuguese Minister at Washington, 1878-1888.
[2] Ferdinand II (1816-1885), titular King of Portugal, was the son of the Duke of Saxe-Coburg-Gotha, and married in 1836 Maria II of Portugal; on her death in 1853 he was regent for two years for his son, Pedro V.

His eyes glowed as he described her magnificence and surround-ings. I began the story, how when I first knew her in Boston her father was a poor German tailor and the stepmother a laundress, and how my *"bon pasteur"* (E. W. Peabody) taught them and helped them. *"Mon pasteur"* sounded so sweetly that I lugged it in as often as possible, it replaced recalcitrant subjunctives and made me feel like a *brebis*. Nogueiras was so thrilled and excited that he nearly fell out of his chair. Suddenly in flew Emily Beale to ask "candidly" was I willing to have her bring Nelly Grant Sartoris[1] to tea? She took it amiably and flew off, but did not reappear. Nelly has taken to frescoing her face till, as Henry James says (he knew her in England), she looks like a ceiling of Michael Angelo.

I have asked Henry James *not* to bring his friend Oscar Wilde[2] when he comes; I must keep out thieves and noodles or else take down my sign and go West. I have just written a note of regret "couched in elegant language" to Lord George Montagu, who in the name of the "Bachelors" was bidden to invite me to receive the guests at their next ball on Friday! A merciful Providence has in-terposed a dinner engagement at the Bayards'. I addressed my note, "Lord George etc.," but within I wrote, "My dear Mr. Monta-gue"—*vide* letter of January 15th. How should you have felt to take up next Sunday's *Herald* and to have seen in the Washington letter:—

"The Bachelors' German on Friday was a brilliant social event. All of our best people were there. The guests were received by Mrs. Henry Adams of Boston, married to the scion of a once-honoured race. Mrs. Adams has a most queenly presence, an aqui-line nose rendered less prominent by full cheeks and wealth of

---

[1] Mrs. Sartoris, a daughter of General Grant.

[2] Oscar Fingall O'Flahertie Wills Wilde (1856-1900), son of Sir Wiliam Wilde, a distinguished Irish surgeon, went to Magdalen College, Oxford, where in 1878 he won the Newdigate Prize and took a first-class in classical Moderations and in Literæ Humaniores. At Oxford he adopted what to undergraduates appeared the effeminate pose of casting scorn on manly sports, wearing his hair long, de-corating his rooms with peacock's feathers, lilies, sunflowers, blue china, and other *objets d'art*, which he declared it his desire to 'live up to,' affecting a lackadaisical manner, and professing intense emotions on the subject of 'art for art's sake'—then a new-fangled doctrine which J. M. Whistler was bringing into prominence. Wilde made himself the apostle of this new cult. Its affectations were burlesqued in Gilbert and Sullivan's travesty *Patience* (1881).

chin. She was magnificently attired in ruby velvet, the gift, as she proudly told us, of her father, one of Boston's eminent oculists. Jewels flashed from her raven tresses and she had a winning Beacon-Street welcome for all. By her side stood her husband, a man of superb physical proportions, two well-set eyes surmounted by a brow of great height and lustre; he ably supported his lady by his genial bonhommie—hereditary it may be, but none the less his own."

"Some are born to greatness, and others have it thrust upon them"; only fools thrust it *from* them!

Tonight, we go to a banquet at Mrs. Bancroft's. I have a feeling in my bones she will send me in with Blaine or Robeson; I shall leave my purse and amethyst smelling bottle at home as a precautionary measure. Henry James passed Sunday evening at Robeson's, and dines tomorrow with Blaine.[1] "And a certain man came down to? from? Jerusalem and fell among thieves . . . and they sprang up and choked him." Boojum and Possum send you much love. The latter is misunderstood here by the gamins; they cry out as we pass, "Look at that little *hog!*" Good-bye. Affectionately

CLOVER

1607 H STREET, WASHINGTON,
Sunday, January 22, 1882.

DEAR PATER: You will say, as you see this fat envelope, in the words of Mrs. Callender, "There comes that tiresome Eddie Hooper again." But be long-suffering; and what ears so ready as a parent's to the weekly cry of its young?

---

[1] "As usual Mr. James G. Blaine excelled everybody else in the entertainment which he gave this week. It was not the magnificence of his hospitality this time, but the small and noted company that gathered round his board which made the dinner party Thursday evening the most interesting social event of the week. Among the guests were the President of the United States, the British Minister, the Governor of California, Generals Sherman and Hancock, Senator Hale, Murat Halstead, Andrew Carnegie, Hon. S. B. Elkins, the editor of Robert Ingersoll's organ, the *North American Review*, Mr. Allen Thorndyke Rice, and that eminent novelist and anglicised American, Henry James, Jr., besides several ladies."

If I am not mistaken, I wrote you last on Wednesday, the 18th, just before going to a feast at Mrs. Bancroft's. As I wished to make a pleasing figure before the new Cabinet and the President, I dressed myself in my old-gold brocade—Mr. Worth's happiest *bon mot*; pinned against my beating heart a large snow-white camellia in its green leaves—which I walked far in a pouring rain to buy at a smart florist's; over all I laid a new evening cloak—made by Pingat and quite "utter"; then we hied through a driving storm to the scene of impending revelry. We were first on the battlefield. And just as I was displacing Pingat to reveal Worth, a middle-aged and extremely florid lady entered the dressing-room, enveloped in what is known to the trade as "a rubber gossamer" and a black bonnet upon whose sides clustered bunches of black grapes—not Hamburg, but black glass. I wondered which new "Cabinet lady" it might be. In the entry stood her hemisphere, a manifest judge— suggestive of Pufendorf in the flesh. He was simply and inexpensively attired in a rusty brown beard of unusual length. Only Senator and Mrs. Edmunds had arrived. When the rosy-cheeked lady entered, Mrs. Bancroft led her to me and presented *me* to her, as "Mrs. Adams, Mrs. Gurney's sister." I said very sweetly, with the innocence of childhood on my lips, "And to whom are you introducing me, Mrs. Bancroft?" "Oh! Mrs. Freeman," she said, as if the name were of barren importance to me. My heart thumped wildly against my twenty-cent camellia as she said, in accents of astonishment, "*You*, Mrs. Gurney's sister! Really?" Then I saw that Ellen had withheld from her friend an inventory of the gifts of Providence. In short, I was to her only a very well-dressed impostor.

At dinner, the great historian of the Norman Conquest[1] was on my right; Henry, *one* removed from my left. Ye Gods, what a feast

---

[1] Edward Augustus Freeman (1823-1892), from 1854 on, Regius Professor of Modern History at Oxford, author of a *History of the Norman Conquest* in 15 volumes (1867-1876); in it he stressed the idea "of the permanence of the Anglo-Saxon elements in spite of the Conquest, and their continued importance as the basis of constitutional development." Henry Adams, writing to Gaskell, January 29, 1882, refers to this same dinner, "The other day we went out to dine, and to my horror I came face to face with your ursine and ursa-maximine countryman, Edward A. Freeman. I say 'to my horror' because I had reviewed very sharply two of his books when I edited the *North American* and he knew it. He

it was! No stylographic could narrate it. Let us draw a veil over nine-tenths of it. When Freeman informed us that the Falls of Slap Dash—or some such name—were better worth our seeing than Niagara "for the reason that many several streams like your States end in one great *fall*," we let the vile insinuation pass, and Edmunds, with his best senatorial courtesy, said very gently and with no passion in his tones, "Where is this fall, Mrs. Freeman?" "On the *H*adriatic," she said, as most Englishwomen would. There was a deathly stillness, unbroken save for the winter rain beating drearily against the windowpanes. On we went. The canvasbacks entered. *Three* of them—fresh and fair, done to a turn; and weltering in their gore. Says Mrs. Bancroft, with a growing hauteur of manner as of a turning worm, "Do you appreciate our canvasbacks, Mr. Freeman?" "I cannot eat raw meat," he said angrily, while a convulsive shudder shook his frame. Then the *picador*, which is latent in me when nature is outraged, rose in me, and I said to him, all unconscious of his theories and the scheme of all his writing, "I wonder that you do not like rare meat. Your *ancestors*, the Picts and Scots, ate their meat raw, and tore it with their fingers." At which he roared out, "O-o-o-o! *Whur* did yer git that?" Unheeding, careless of consequences, I said, "Well, your Anglo-Saxon ancestors, if you prefer." He thereupon pawed the air and frothed at the mouth.

The funniest remains to be told, but it must be done viva-voce. It was a dialogue between him and George Bancroft when the latter was tired and sleepy and at the end of his forces, as the Gauls say. Never having read one line of Freeman, I did not know until the next day the exquisite point of my historical allusions. As I casually repeated them Henry became purple in the face and rolled off his chair, and he, the husband of my bosom, who is wont to yawn affectionately at my yarns, he at intervals of two hours says, "Tell me again what you said to Freeman about the Picts and Scots

---

made himself as offensive as usual at dinner. At the end he attacked me, as I knew he would, and told me he had replied to my charges, as I would see in the Preface to the first volume of the third edition of the *Norman Conquest*. I felt not the slightest curiosity to see the reply, and should not know what to think of it, but if you wish to see the *disjecta membra* of your friend scattered among the other bones in this 'Zummerzetshire' bear cave, you can some day glance at the Preface in question and shed a tear over my untimely fate." (*Letters*, p. 334)

and Anglo-Saxons." I send this to you for Whitman; to me and to you it is probably without point or flavour. As *we* rose up to go Mrs. Freeman came up to me very kindly and said, "We mean to go *back* to Cambridge before we sail for home to see our friends once more." I smiled like one in a trance and said, "I'm sure they'll be much flattered." That's all; they are at the Arlington, next door, as it were, have been ten days or more, leave tomorrow, and we have neither of us called.

I enclose you some tidbits "culled" from the local press.[1] When you read of the Bachelors' German and shut your eyes, think of me and what might have been. We declined two big dinners last night; we are urged to meet Oscar Wilde tonight at the Lorings'. I tartly remarked "that fools don't amuse me" when a courteous refusal was unheeded. Henry James went to call on him yesterday and says he is a "fatuous cad." Miss Schurz came Thursday and goes next Thursday to Miss Aldis for three weeks, says, "Give my love to your father," adding sotto voce, "I've a great affection for him." Woolner's Bonington came Friday, is charming, all duties and express from London four dollars fifty! I shall write Ellen at Godkins, he expects them tomorrow. They must come on to us. Affectionately

M. A.

Arthur has just given Mr. Lowndes the place of Commissioner of Spanish Claims at a salary of thirty-five hundred dollars!!! Isn't that nice?

---

[1] "THE BACHELOR'S GERMAN. [!!!!]—The popular social organization, the Bachelors' Club, gave a german last evening at Marini's, which was very largely attended by the best element of our society. Everything was done in the best style, and the event was a very enjoyable one. Mrs. General McKeever received the guests and Lieutenant Paine led the german. Mr. Oscar Wilde arrived at eleven o'clock in company with Congressman and Mrs. Robeson, and was introduced to Mrs. McKeever. General introductions followed, and the dancing was suspended for the time and the german was resolved into a reception. He was pleasant and affable, and created a very favorable impression. He remained for some time, and then retired from the hall. About twelve o'clock the dancing was resumed and continued until a late hour." [!!!!!]

1607 H STREET
January 26, 1882.

DEAR PATER: I enclose you a few choice exotics plucked from the parterre of the local press—pressed flowers, so to speak. I want them to "go on the record," as our brevet gallows corps says; when I am old and blind they may amuse me. If I live till Sunday next your letter will be "A. No. 1."

Life is like a prolonged circus here now—I grudge my night's rest. Ask Betsy to look up a red camel's-hair scarf which I wore in childhood's hours and please send by mail or express. Also please copy at once the following on a post-card and mail to me:—

"My dear child: Let me beg of you not to make calls and as few new acquaintances as possible. I know better than you the delicacy of your constitution. Ride on horseback daily but avoid visiting and evening parties. Medicus."

Can you get that all on one card? My next will justify your paternal warning. Shall ask the jury to five o'clock tea. We lost your cold snap—10° above here the worst.

1607 H STREET,
Monday, January 30, 1882.

DEAR PATER: I really was so driven yesterday by people that not one blessed moment could I get even for a note; MacVeagh all the morning and others all the P.M. and evening and today no time either. I've enough to tell you to fill a thousand foolscap pages and will begin tomorrow and issue extras; I am dog-tired tonight. Long ride to Chain bridge and Virginia, quiet dinner, and then a call from Aristarchi Bey—just gone at ten-fifteen—and I can't keep out of bed any longer. This is only to tell you we are alive and well and up to our eyes in papers. This rat hunt by our friend Nordhoff, the special correspondent of the *N. Y. Herald*, is very exciting.[1] Read his despatches in Friday, Saturday, and Sunday

---

[1] The first of several references to a new political attack on Mr. Blaine which had been developing in the columns of the *New York Herald* and of the *Nation* since the death of President Garfield in September. In substance it was alleged that the State Department under Mr. Blaine had pursued a jingo policy in its dealings with Chile and Peru, in the interest of certain claimants to the Peruvian nitrate deposits and Guano beds, which might easily have involved the United

Herald in Athenæum. The scoundrel Blaine is fighting for his life desperately. *Adiós.* Your weary and loving

M. A.

1607 H STREET, WASHINGTON,
Tuesday, January 31st, 1882.

DEAR PATER: Yours of Sunday has just come, it's a relief to hear that dear Mrs. Perkins[1] has ceased to suffer. I've just got a telegram from Mrs. Agassiz[2] in answer to my enquiry last night; she says Mrs. James[3] died Sunday night. Henry James came here at eleven o'clock Sunday night to tell us he had just received an alarming dispatch; he could get no earlier train than yesterday's Limited so he will not reach Cambridge until thirty-six hours. It will be a heavy blow to him, the more so perhaps that he has been away for six years from her and it's the first time death has struck that family. Ellen and Whitman will miss her cheery face and ways. She strongly wished him to live in his own country but I doubt if he can; he confesses to being "terribly homesick for London." He'd better go and lay the ghost, as in the end he must.

Thanks for the notice of Tom Kinnicutt, it is very touching and has the rare merit of being true. After the lying panegyrics on our late chief, it is a comfort to say amen to praise.

We are deeply interested here in politics and hope the rat Blaine[4] is in a corner at last. He is of course lying, and squirming, and bullying, but there is worse to come, and all the press is

---

States in a war. The attack in the press appears to have been largely directed by Nordhoff and Godkin, the proceedings in the House by Belmont and Kasson, and those in the Senate by Bayard and Edmunds.

[1] Mrs. Edward Perkins.

[2] Mrs. J. Louis R. Agassiz (Elizabeth Cary), widow of Professor Jean Louis Rodolphe Agassiz (1807-1873).

[3] Mrs. Henry James (Lucy Walsh), wife of Henry James, the elder (1811-1882).

[4] Mr. Blaine replied to the attacks in an interview published on Monday, the thirtieth, and denied that his instructions to Trescot had been drafted without the knowledge of the President, or that any attempt was made to push the claims of private citizens against Peru, or that he instructed Hurlbut to prosecute the Landreau claim, etc. Godkin joined in the attack on February 2, in a long article entitled "Another Chapter of Mr. Blaine's Diplomacy."

against him but the *Tribune*, whose editor, Whitelaw Reid,[1] is a scheming tramp from Ohio, sold to Blaine body and soul. Hurlbut[2]—brother of W. H., editor of *World*—is in a nasty fix, yet the *World* is turning on Blaine. You will see that the *N. Y. Herald* of January 28 has a savoury letter from one Shipherd[3] to Boutwell—December 10th, 1881—in which he begins, "My dear Governor: There *may* be somewhere a wickeder man than James G. Blaine etc., etc. . . ."; and in the same paper to a reporter, "Mr. Blaine, Sir, is ruined for life. *My* opinion of him? He's the biggest, most infernal liar in Christendom. When the whole thing comes out, he will never lift his head again." It's not sweet or elevating reading, but rather instructive. Bancroft Davis said to me last Friday night, "You will not lack food for interest for a month to come." There are some startling disclosures, we hear, to come, and not in a quarter to break our hearts, either. Nordhoff put a match to the fuse last Thursday, and now that the blast is in full force we remain at a safe distance and watch the splinters fly.

A kind note from Gurney today; he seems to be as eager to see the Blaine-rat trapped and squeezed as we. I am glad indeed that we never broke the man's bread nor so much as pulled his doorbell. Mr. Lowndes and we alone in this society took that stand, and for eight prospective years to cut the Secretary of State was a measure which brought on us much criticism and some ridicule, I fancy, but let me say that we are not now the only three who cry "Stop thief"—not by a long sight. He's down now and so they can safely jump on him. Emily Beale, to do her justice, declares he is not corrupt, that he's no more a swindler than "old man Schurz a revolutionary demagogue," that for her part she "prefers an American swindler to a foreign one," that Blaine is not rich, "Why I've seen the contract of his new house, it's only fifty thousand dol-

---

[1] Whitelaw Reid (1837-1912), principal proprietor and editor-in-chief of the *New York Tribune*; in 1881 he married a daughter of Darius Ogden Mills.

[2] Stephen Augustus Hurlbut (1815-1882), though born in South Carolina, served with distinction in the Union Army; he was United States Minister to Colombia, 1869-1873, in Congress from Illinois 1873-1877, and United States Minister to Peru from 1881 until his death; his brother, W. H. Hurlbut, was the editor of the *New York World.*

[3] Jacob R. Shipherd, the president of the Peruvian Company.

lars!" That fair "hoodlum" can sling epithets when she likes. I think Mr. Bartlett irritated her—she felt he was quizzing her.

To go from the sublime to the ridiculous, "Hosscar" Wilde, as they call him, has been and gone. I escaped his acquaintance, but only by a *tour de force* which nearly frightened my hostess, Mrs. Pendleton, out of the very few senses nature gave her. I'll tell you hereafter; it is a viva-voce tale. Last week on Pennsylvania Avenue I met a tall slender man, *café au lait* in the face, long hair, dressed in stockings and tights, a brown plush tunic, a big yellow sunflower pinned above his heart, a queer cap on his head; turning to look after him,—as you taught me was very vulgar,—I saw a large blue card on his back, "Oscar on a wild toot." When Henry James told him he was very homesick for London, he said, "Really! You care for *places*? The *world* is my home"; and again, "I am going to *Bosston*; there I have a letter to the dearest friend of my dearest friend—Charles Norton from Burne-Jones." Suggest to Ned that the Corporation give him the degree of L.L.D.—long-legged-donkey! Mr. James says he is a fatuous fool, a tenth-rate cad, and we are told that he was carried home drunk in New York after a dinner given him by "wicked Sam Ward"[1] at which a big bowl of punch bore floating lilies!

Mr. Bartlett gave a fine dinner on Friday to the Supreme Court judges and insisted on roping in Henry in spite of entreaties to be let off, but Frank Bartlett[2] mercifully put him next to Justice Miller, whom he found most agreeable. The judge's daughter married District-Attorney Corkhill,—the beast,—whom many of us would like to see flanking Guiteau on the gallows. Poor Garfield had decided to turn him off the very night before he was assassinated.

Simple Mrs. Bigelow Lawrence! I'm curious to see her course as to Blaine; it was thought last spring here that if Blaine were a widower she would not long be a widow. Emily Beale declared at

---

[1] Samuel Ward was a brother of Mrs. Julia Ward Howe and very much a man of the world; preëminent for his knowledge of excellent food and rare wine, he was a master of the art of entertaining; he was known as "wicked Sam" to distinguish him from his much more conventional contemporary, Samuel Gray Ward.

[2] Mr. Adams refers to them in a letter of November 1878 as "Mr. Sidney Bartlett, aged seventy-nine, head of the Boston Bar, rich, eminent, and considered witty. His son, Frank Bartlett, a contemporary of my own."

dinner Sunday that the novel called *Democracy* was "a horrid, nasty, vulgar book, written by a newspaper man not in good society," and added, "Mrs. Robeson is awful mad she's not in it."!! Harriet Loring says, "Clover, your aunt Tappan says you wrote it and that Carrington is Henry Sayles." I said, "Yes, I did, and *you*, Harriet, are the Dare girl. I hope you don't mind." Then she gasps, "Why, no. It's Emily Beale." "No," I answered, "I meant her for *you*." Then I went up the street quietly and she down it *very* softened in manner. Aunt Tappan is *Minerva* in the novel I am writing now—I shall call her Minny for short!

I bought some nice things with your Christmas cheque. A week ago I received an anonymous note in a lady's handwriting saying, "If you will go to 1905 F Street before January 25th you will see an armoire, an ecritoire, and two portraits by Sir Joshua Reynolds which will be sold at reasonable prices." Fearing it might be a clairvoyant trap or Charley Ross scheme, I took Ms. Schurz and Henry as bodyguard. The house was shabby stucco outside; inside, a young African showed us into a long, pleasantly furnished study full of books and etchings and old chairs. At one end was a rosewood wardrobe, handsomely carved, about seven feet high and a little less wide—Henry thought it old Flemish; I did not examine it carefully, thinking I could not find a place for it here, and in Beverly it would be quite out of place; in the opposite corner stood an escritoire about six feet by four, of light wood inlaid with figures and birds, the key lost and it would not open. Black boy knew of no pictures but called a brown maiden, who told him to go to the nursery and bring down "them two little pictures." Whereupon he promptly reappeared bearing two chromos worth five cents apiece, I should think. The whole thing was so ghostly that I did not even ask to whom these things belonged, but Henry saw in a book lying about: "Th. Dwight." So on coming home I wrote to the Librarian of the State Department, whose name that is, and asked if he could give me a clue to the mystery. He came in to tea at five, and told me this: An impoverished lady here, a friend of his, wished to sell them; her father was a Marylander, one Virgil Maxey, sent as Chargé d'Affaires to Belgium in 1832. The armoire was bought then and there—so Henry's guess was correct—price three hundred dollars; five perpendicular barols of flowers, carved, hanging by a ribbon from a ring—beautifully carved; a deep drawer with three carved panels (small); and round balls for feet—about ten-inch diameter. I've bought it, and my bedroom is transformed into a Flemish chamber. Took the escritoire at forty dollars; it's being polished and done up by a German here. The portraits (twenty-four by thirty inches), "Mr. and Mrs. Grover, two of Sir Joshua Reynolds's earlier portraits sent to the owner's great-grandparents, Mr. and Mrs. Sam Galloway, West River, Maryland. That's all we know. They are not *first*-rate; are very dirty, no varnish, and badly cracked. The lady, snub-nosed and pale, in pink satin with blue gauze scarf and pearl ornaments, hair drawn up over a cushion; Mr. Grover, stout and handsome, in powdered wig, gray brocade coat, and white neckerchief. I prefer the woman; Henry, the man, though he wished neither and "hates portraits."

> Jack Sprat dislikes portraits,
> His wife dislikes paysages,
> And so betwixt them both
> The choice is very large.

I mean to sell my Tilton "Venice" if I can, and hang these two between the library windows, side by side; Henry can look the other way. I paid one hundred and fifty dollars for each! I feel as guilty as Blaine ought to. We've a charming new German friend, one Dr. Bessels of Heidelberg; about forty; has been four times to the North Pole; was accused of murdering Hall; is working at the Smithsonian; is an amateur painter. I shall consult him as to washing and varnishing these. Ask Mr. Frank Bartlett about them; he saw them. Will you consult catalogue of Sir Joshua Reynolds's portraits in Anthenæum for Mr. and Mrs. Grover? Do you think I've wasted your cheque? I've still three hundred and seventy dollars left for monkeys. Isn't this a long, tangled, wearisome yarn? How glad I am that fate has denied me garrulous daughters. *Adiós.* Affectionately

M. A.

1607 H Street, Washington,
Sunday, February 5, 1882.

Dear Pater: Thanks for yours of February 3rd in answer to mine of the 1st. Today, I take time by the bang as it were, so as not to get left. I've no news but a few dropped stitches to pick up. Your enclosed newspaper cutting is correct as usual; we *did* dine with the French Minister on Thursday and it was for the Frelinghuysens; the Nogueiras, thank fate, were not there; Count Brunetti[1] has no wife; and we do not tag on to West's heels. I sat between Secretary of State and Mr. John R. King, whom Ellen met on the Nile, and had a charming dinner; not so Henry, who took in Miss Dulaney whom he sees every day and whose voice is better adapted to singing than talking; she's a nice, sweet, good woman, but not too deep for wading; Baroness Fava on his right, a dull Italian lady; Miss Frelinghuysen opposite me and between Count von Beust and Barn Fava, she exhausted all the treasures of Ollendorf on them and half swooned in my arms after dinner. We deplored to each other the vast sums our respective and respected parents had vainly "fooled away" on our education, the dem'd total being useless. "Have you the apricot of my aunt?" "Has the baker the coat of the tailor?" though excellent exercise in themselves, are as useless in the sea of real life as a dory without oars—the sexes of my nouns are as undecided as that of Oscar Wilde or Dr. Mary Walker. Never mind, you meant well and I won't bite off your ear like that rude young man in Æsop who was the terror of my younger days.

The new Secretary of State and I got on swimmingly; we had a good deal of talk about politics. He said, "Blaine may quarrel with me if he likes but I shall not with him." I told him if they went on making such good appointments as Judge Gray and Mr. Lowndes and then smashed Blaine, they would have Massachusetts on their side. MacVeagh vows that Blaine has Bright's disease, and that it has affected his brain; I told Mr. Frelinghuysen that and he seemed rather struck by it. Senator Eugene Hale and his wife were there; he is not to our taste and we avoid him always in so marked a manner that I doubt if he will encourage me much longer; he has taken to a bang, and has very dirty hands physically—morally I

---

[1] Señor Don José Brunetti, First Secretary of the Spanish Legation.

can't say. Miss Beale declares him to be a hedgehog; Mrs. Cameron says he's a brute. He's got 1501 H Street during L. P. Morton's Ministry to France.

Wednesday evening, Mrs. Bancroft's *very* select party. How glad I was that Ellen and Whitman did not come on for it. It was like a wild menagerie. Such yelling I never heard; and it was "culled"!—then give me a mob. We fled at ten-thirty and supped on crackers and milk at home. "Family" and "official position" cover Mrs. Bancroft's guests. As for Mrs. Senator C., you would refuse her as a cook on the ground of her vulgar appearance and the fearful waste of flour on her face; it may have been to counteract the heat, which was suffocating. The President was there and Mrs. Blaine—on his arm, they say; I saw nothing; my sole idea was flight and Miss Beale got away even before we did.

Friday, a dinner of twenty-three at the Secretary of State's; the British Minister took me in. He does not improve on further acquaintance; is *very* dull—no conversation—and it seems to me a nullity. His brother [-in-law] is Earl of Derby, a sort of Jacob's ladder to diplomatic elevation. I pity him too; he is a bachelor and stands so in the British Peerage; had a liaison of twenty years with a Spanish danseuse who had a husband—she has died since we were in Spain, I hear; his daughter, who had been brought up in a convent in Paris, had to be told her history before coming here. He came alone at first, and enquired if she would be received, and was told she would. The Sunday papers opened fire at first but were instantly throttled—probably by Blaine as he holds them all even today, and Mrs. Blaine, so one of her intimate friends told me, was consulted by West, so that she has to stand by him. Luckily for him the girl is sweet and refined in manner and attracts everyone; she will help him rather than hinder him—still, it's a horrid position; there are *three* other children in England. You had better not show this except to the Gurneys; gossip travels fast enough, let Mrs. Rollins Morse take it to Boston.

We've made a most agreeable new acquaintance, one Dr. E. Bessels of Heidelberg, did I tell you?—has been on four North Pole voyages; was accused of murdering Hall;[1] floated *one hun-*

---

[1] Charles Francis Hall (1821-1871) was in command of the North Polar expedition fitted out by the United States in the *Polaris*, and died suddenly on Novem-

dred and ninety-six days on pack ice; is having my two portraits cleaned; is stuffing me an owl; is mending the amber cross of Adie's wedding present to me; brings me Strassburg pâté de fois gras and is full of all human knowledge; is very Hebrew in appearance, with long hair and unkempt garb.

The Cheyenne-Denver lady of whom I wrote you in October has got herself turned out of Wormley's already for misbehaviour; her husband and she came to tea last week—he's an old friend of ours—I've had to tell John never to let her in again even if she came with him. Her first husband, a Connecticut pieman, had to divorce her, and so will poor E. sooner or later. He has taken a pretty new house a few hundred yards from us!!! Every time I see him he asks me if I've been to see his wife and I'm afraid I must tell him that I cannot and that he must not ask any lady to visit her!! To steer one's small cock-boat in these rapids is as difficult in the season as shooting "El Bab" at the First Cataract of the Nile, and there we had a "praying sheik" with a pea-green flag. I cannot legally open a "Home for Sinners" without a license from the District. Two young sprigs of diplomacy here who have dropped me for a year past were concerned in a scandal two months since, which would have sent them to jail but for their "diplomatic privileges," and one has a Boston mother, I grieve to say, and is an only son. I think in America we may dispense with a "trained diplomatic corps" these furringers "train" like the devil.

Dialogue at Mrs. Bancroft's between the blonde widow whom you know and myself.

J. D.—"Mrs. Adams, may I bring a charming man to tea?"

M. A.—"Who is it?"

J. D.—"I'm afraid to tell you for fear you'll say no."

M. A.—"Who is it?"

J. D.—"Captain Lachère, new Secretary of French Legation."

Then I tell her that I prefer to receive no foreigners unless presented by their own Ministers. Met him next day at dinner at the Outreys', but as he was guest at Newport of James Gordon Bennett, I shall wait for more light. Marquis de Chambrun, in answer

---

ber 8, 1871. The vessel was then in winter quarters at Lat. 82° 11'. A few months later, after breaking out of the ice, the *Polaris* was lost, but the whole of her crew was subsequently rescued.

to my inquiry of "why they do not send us better specimens of his countrymen," grinned and said, *"Gambetta les a mangé, Madame!"*

I shall have your terrapin cooked tomorrow or Tuesday, and sent by express Tuesday night in two glass jars—sauce in one, terrapin in the other—packed in *sawdust* as a non-conductor. If the cream sauce is sour let your cook make some fresh by this receipt[1] and be sure to have a dish of potatoes baked in their skins—that is *de riguer*. Henry Johnson says the Bartletts said ours was the best they ever tasted—I sent you Welcker's last time.

Is Mrs. R. C. Winthrop, Jr., alive? her sister telegraphed Friday that she was dying. Whatever is the matter with Boston? It seems to be one big charnel house. *Adiós*. Affectionately

M. A.

Great snow-storm yesterday, bright and warm today, shall get a ride this P.M. we hope.

1607 H Street, Washington,
Sunday, February 12th, 1882.

Dear Pater: Your much garbled note of warning reached me a few days ago; you bid me beware of "partisan" politics. If that means taking pleasure in seeing Blaine shown up, I need the warning, and so do all honest, clean-handed folks who object to seeing their country made ridiculous by corrupt blatherskites, but I will try to keep my Sunday pen free from politics. "Our ways are not your ways nor our thoughts your thoughts." Boston is a more temperate latitude and wit and papers non-conductors of feeling and interest.

---

[1] Receipt enclosed: "Terrapin Sauce. Put in clean saucepan half pint rich cream, half tumbler of sherry or Madeira, a heaping tablespoonful of best butter, half tablespoon of Indian soy, one pinch each of white pepper, salt, allspice, mace, cloves; do not stir it in the saucepan but keep shaking till it simmers up thick; pour over terrapin in a deep *vegetable-dish* and serve."

Monday last, Mr. Lodge[1] came, having invited himself for a week, and seemed happy and occupied. Tuesday, we had General Armstrong,[2] Eugene Schuyler, and Professor Goodwin[3] to dine with some bright talk. Wednesday, Mr. Kasson had a dinner for Mrs. Bob Oliver[4] and her two pretty sisters; we made Mr. Lodge an excuse for declining and stayed quietly at home. Thursday, we had a little dinner here for Mrs. Oliver, having declined a big one at the British Legation and also one at Wormley's given by Mr. Hewett to Mrs. Butler Duncan (sister of late Winthrop Sargent); we had Mrs. Oliver, Miss Lucy Frelinghuysen, Miss Dulaney, Mr. James Wadsworth, M.C., and Lamar, who had, an hour or two before, been knocked down in the street by a horse and stunned. He

---

[1] Henry Cabot Lodge (1850-1924) was graduated at Harvard College in 1871 and at the Harvard Law School in 1875; in his senior year and as a postgraduate student he attended Henry Adams's courses and obtained the degree of Doctor of Philosophy in 1876, meanwhile assisting Adams in editing the *North American Review*. From 1876 to 1879 he taught American history at Harvard and at this time the first of his many literary and historical works began to be published. He served in the Massachusetts House of Representatives in 1880 and 1881, and in 1887 and again in 1887 was elected to Congress; in 1893 he was elected to the United States Senate and served there continuously until his death.

"With Mrs. Lodge and her husband, Senator since 1893, Adams's relations had been those of elder brother or uncle since 1871 when Cabot Lodge had left his examination-papers on Assistant Professor Adams's desk, and crossed the street to Christ Church in Cambridge to get married. With Lodge himself, as scholar, fellow instructor, co-editor of the *North American Review*, and political reformer from 1873 to 1878, he had worked intimately, but with him afterwards as politician he had not much relation; and since Lodge had suffered what Adams thought a misfortune of becoming not only a Senator but a Senator from Massachusetts—a singular social relation which Adams had known only as fatal to friends—a superstitious student, intimate with the laws of historical fatality, would rather have recognized him only as an enemy; but apart from this accident he valued Lodge highly, and in the waste places of average humanity had been greatly dependent on his house. Senators can never be approached with safety, but a Senator who has a very superior wife and several superior children who feel no deference for Senators as such, may be approached at times with relative impunity while they keep him under restraint." (*Education*, p. 353)

[2] Samuel Chapman Armstrong (1839-1893), soldier, philanthropist, and educator, founded in 1868, at Hampton, Virginia, an industrial school for negroes, Hampton Institute, at the head of which he remained until his death.

[3] William Watson Goodwin (1831-1912), from 1860 until 1901, when he retired, was Eliot professor of Greek at Harvard.

[4] Mrs. Robert Oliver was a Miss Rathbone of Albany, N.Y.

sent a note at six-thirty saying he was too much hurt to come; but at seven, he walked in saying "the country had nearly lost one of its more conservative statesmen." There was a reception that same night at the Secretary of State's to which the others went, but I was too lazy, and a big rout at the British Legation which by all, except newspaper folk, is said to have been horrible—they declare it "a most magnificent occasion." We are "blàse," as they call it—an acute accent of criticism or a grave one of disapproval changes any adjective. Friday, Mr. Lowndes invited us to a theatre party, but we begged off. Yesterday, a pleasant tea-party by three young bachelors near by—Richardson, Macomb, and Paine;[1] lots of pretty girls, Posey Mason looking as if the ball and chain were off her ankles; she was gay and gracious—she is paddling her own canoe as a guest of the Pendletons; dined at the Edmundses', sat between Senators Edmunds and Byard, and had a very nice time; was bidden to a feast at Mrs. Bancroft's, to take the Freeman taste out of our mouths, she said, adding that she herself "clung to the memory of that comedy."

I enclose you a snip sent me last week by Aristarchi Bey on Henry James, Jr.; it may amuse the Gurneys if they have not seen it. Last night came a heavenly little brocade silk box—red, blue, and green—with "*mille homages*" from Aristarchi Bey—"*cadeau de mon collègue de Chine*"—he wished to be permitted to offer it to me. It bears on its face its celestial origin and inside a small canister about five inches high, gaily decorated, and what the tea may be the gods in Olympus alone know. So I've written him a sweet note of thanks with appropriate allusions to his fair country-woman Pandora; he is of a very old Greek family. If he comes to-night to vesper service I shall open it. Mrs. Oliver said the other day, "And Sunday I am engaged too," and when I asked where? "Here of course," and Miss Frelinghuysen said she was too. It's a simple form of service but seems to give satisfaction.

Don't imagine I bought the portraits out of charity—far from it, I took a gambler's chance and the old lady has sent me some family papers which back them up strongly. Grove—not Grover—is the name; believed to have been painted in or about 1760; were

---

[1] Clifford Richardson, the chemical expert for the District of Columbia; Lieutenant Montgomery Macomb of the United States Army; Frederick Paine.

hung on the wall at "Tulip Hill"; Mr. and Mrs. Sam Galloway sent their portraits as a return compliment. Mrs. Grove has a "lake"-coloured gown; Redgreave says, "Sir Joshua Reynolds used 'lake' in his earlier portraits but it faded so he gave it up for carmine." He had a hundred and twenty-five sitters at that time. Dr. Bessels has them still. Sir Joshua, when derided for his portraits fading, said, "Yes, I usually come off with flying colours!"

Was the terrapin eatable? *Adiós*, lovingly

M. A.

1607 H STREET,
Monday, February 14, 1882.

Eureka! Eureka! Yesterday came Dr. Bessels to say that, after much inspection and study, he believed my portraits to be genuine Sir Joshuas and never cleaned nor touched before. Miss Markoe—clerk in the State Department, niece of the lady of whom I bought them—said Mr. Groves—not Grover nor Grove—was the London agent of the Galloways, her great-great-grandparents, to whom they consigned tobacco from their plantation in Maryland. Today by chance Henry took up at State Department library *Life and Times of Sir J. Reynolds* by Leslie and Taylor, John Murray, 1865. From Sir Joshua's memoranda, "August 1755 sitters, Lord Bath, Colonel Pearson, *Mr. and Mrs. Groves*, Captain Smelt, Mr. Clerk, Miss Jones"—and Henry coolly remarks—though the man's portrait shrieked Sir Joshua—it's not likely that these have been either autotyped or mezzotinted because they could not have been reached, for they have been for five generations in this family and I am their first purchaser! Shall I have them photographed for you? I'll take them on in June to show you.

Miss Bayard and I visited a charming Hebrew pawnbroker today and went halves on a dressing case full of boxes with silver tops each having French hall-mark of last century, and lovely mirror twelve by fourteen in it,—also a silver cream ladle,—also two Japanese coin-chains (silver coins verified in book here), itzibus of small value but very foxy, and so on. Silver dressing-case pawned by New Orleans lady twenty years ago in the war. Miss Bayard discovered it and took me to her friend's shop. Please send this

note in to Mr. Francis Bartlett, 236 Beacon Street, he was so interested and sympathetic about my Sir Joshuas. Yours affectionately

M. A.

1607 H Street, Washington,
Sunday, February 19, 1882.

DEAR PATER: A high old storm today, luckily rain instead of
snow. We have missed the cold wave which struck you a few
nights since, you were 10° with a high wind and we 27° with very
little wind, dandelions in bloom, buds swelling. We rode to Arlington Friday P.M. and it was lovely with its fifteen thousand quiet
sleepers; no unsightly iron flummery and granite lies there, there's
no lovelier place in the world as I know it than Arlington with a
sunset behind and a view in front. Miss Lee,—Mildred Lee,—who
used to live there, came to tea last week;[1] she's about my age and a
quiet lady-like woman, though Henry complains that her manner
savours too much of those of most "old families." Age is apt to
rust and cool them, I think, which accounts for the failures in England in sundry mildewed specimens exhibited to us who have been
on exhibition so long from father to son that they and their garments strike an American as a trifle shop-worn. What comfort
they must take in the Book of Revelation as they sit in their old
pews in family livings. "Behold I make all things new."

We've had a quiet week though the dancing dervishes of society keep it up night and day; we lie ourselves out of almost all invitations—dinners, lunches, and evening parties. A quiet pleasant
party at General Parke's on Wednesday for Mrs. Frank Peabody,
which I enjoyed, having a seat and pleasant people to amuse me.
Mrs. Craig Wadsworth invited us for that same night and when we
found it was for the Blaines we were glad, as it was too small and
intimate to have made avoidance of them possible. Yesterday we
had a pleasant little dinner here for Miss Hitchcock of New
York—Mr. and Mrs. Randall Gibson[2] of New Orleans, Mr. and

---

[1] Miss Mildred Lee, a daughter of General Robert E. Lee.
[2] Randall Lee Gibson (1832-1892), a Member of Congress. He was graduated at
Yale in 1853; fought with distinction in the Confederate Army, in which he
eventually held the rank of Major-General; elected to the United States Senate in
1883.

Mrs. Randolph Tucker of Virginia, and Dr. Bessels. Mrs. Gibson is the bosom friend of Mr. Richardson's sister, Kitty Labouisse; he was a general under General Taylor in the war, a quiet, gentlemanly, attractive man. The Tuckers are full of fun and very intelligent. They are both members of Congress. Mrs. Gibson talked German mostly with Dr. Bessels and found she had lived for fifteen months in Heidelberg next door to his mother and had many common acquaintances.

Here I was interrupted by a call from Miss Hitchcock, who came to say good-bye as she leaves tomorrow morning. She came like the Greeks "bearing gifts"—a box of Marshal Niels, Jacques, lilies-of-the-valleys, violets and mignonette, so that my vases are filled and my rooms reek with sweet odours. She is a rich New York spinster of forty or thereabouts, lives alone in a pretty house and buys pictures. She was a friend of President Arthur's wife so he gave her and her party a little dinner last week and sends her flowers every day; she has with her two lovely girls from Waterbury, Connecticut, named Kingsbury, whom Sir Joshua ought to paint instead of Mr. and Mrs. Groves. Did you get my note of Wednesday night telling you I've verified them? August, 1755—he was young then, only thirty-two, and just starting in London, too poor even to employ a man to paint in his draperies. Ten years later he had three which Leslie thinks was no gain to his portraits. Mine are "kit-kat" size[1] (see Johnson's Dictionary for curious origin of name); he got at that time twenty-four guineas for a half length; the kit-kat unfortunately did not include hands. Leslie says his pictures from 1753 for ten years are more "safely" painted than the later ones, the note-books with lists of sitters are lost for 1753, 1754, and 1756. How by the skin of their teeth these are verified! Dr. Bessels sent them home yesterday and they are charming; he took off a quantity of dirty brown varnish a hundred and twenty-seven years old! The satin gown is a fresh pink, not purple at all, and the snub-nosed lady has lovely blue eyes. Evidently Mr. Grove was thought to look like his contemporary Edmund Burke and is posing for it, but he looks as if "wittles and

---

[1] "So called from portraits of members of the Kit Cat Club (founded in London about 1700), painted of this size by Sir Godfrey Kneller." (Century Dictionary) The canvas is thirty-six inches long and twenty-eight wide.

drink were the chief of his diet"—portly London tradesman with money, High-churchman and Tory evidently. Among records of many dinners of Sir Joshua Reynolds with his sitters I've come on none so far with the Groves; I fancy they had a smart house in "Wapping," and he seems to have dined west of St. Martin's-in-the-Fields. I've hung them in the library between the windows side by side and Henry even says, "Yes, they are charmingly modelled and very dignified." Thank you so much for so nice a Christmas present.

Get at Williams, *N. Y. Tribune*,—Extra No. 81, ten cents, General Armstrong has sent it to me,—letters from an intelligent correspondent sent on a tour last year through the south, worth reading; I'd send you mine but I'm going to mail it to lady Goldsmid in London. I'm amused by the papers to see that Mrs. Howe[1] and T. W. Higginson[2] have fallen foul of each other in the papers apropos of that vulgar cad Oscar Wilde.[3] That Julia Howe should reform sinners by suppers and flattery is charming on the same principle that her moral brother Sam Ward gave him a feast in New York from which he is said to have been carried home drunk. What a

---

[1] Julia Ward Howe (1819-1910), daughter of Samuel Ward and Julia Rush Cutler Ward; married Dr. Samuel Gridley Howe, a distinguished philanthropist.

[2] Thomas Wentworth Higginson (1823-1911), author and soldier.

[3] The *Nation*, February 23, 1882: "Mrs. Julia Ward Howe has published a letter, with regard to the social treatment of Oscar Wilde, that has attracted a good deal of attention in Massachusetts. Colonel T. W. Higginson, it seems, objects to the entertainment of Mr. Wilde in private houses, and Mrs. Howe, having entertained him herself, feels called upon to make a statement of her reasons. Admitting, she says, that Mr. Wilde is a bad young man, still 'to cut off even an offending member of society from its best influences and most humanizing resources is scarcely Christian in any sense.' Women, she says, are not merely 'the guardians of the public purity,' but they are also 'the proper representatives of tender hope and divine compassion.' Consequently 'if, as alleged, the poison found in the ancient classics is seen to linger too deeply in his veins, I should not prescribe for his case the coarse, jeering, and intemperate scolding so easily administered through the public prints, but a cordial and kindly intercourse with that which is soundest, and purest in our society.' This is a new view of the relation which society ought to adopt toward the æsthete; and that it should exist at all, accounts in a measure for the increasing seriousness of the discussion about him in New England. The suggestion that the author of *Charmides* may be made pure and good by cordial and kindly intercourse with the ladies of Boston, will probably make the young man and his manager weep for joy."

touching cartoon for *Puck*—Oscar presenting Julia with a passion-flower and Julia offering a flower in return. "There's rue for you." I would that I could draw! I would support the family with a daily comic paper.

Miss Beale is in bed with chills and fever; looks like Blake's ghost of a flea; says she made the doctor count her teeth after one bad chill to see how many were gone. Mrs. Don Cameron came home yesterday from a six weeks' illness in New York. I'm going to see the poor little woman now; she's drawn a blank in Don, I fear, for all his money and fine house, and she's not over twenty-three—a mere baby. We want you to try a sea voyage for your "Blaines," the tonic always sets you up. Pass one week in Paris, and I'll write ahead to Worth for some gowns, and you bring them to me. We'll give you some letters to friends in London and you'll have one week of dinners and shopping there, three for both voyages, five in all. Then come on end of April and tell us about it. Go in *Servia* with Cook next trip and take some charming man. Please, please! Clarence King is very ill at Brevoort and had to give up his trip to Mexico, we've just heard; if he can bear the voyage write and ask him to go with you—his little sister is over there and he's never been. He is sewer-poisoned. He'll go anywhere on the spur of the moment. Rain stopped, so must I. Good-bye, *adiós*. Affectionately

M. A.

P.S. This is about L. P. Morton,[1] good if true; will not miss him nor his liveried flunkeys, he's such a snob. What a comfort there is a Paris for hybrid Americans.

---

[1] The *Nation*, February 23, 1882: "More correspondence in relation to Chili and Peru has been sent to Congress; among others letters which passed between Mr. Blaine and Mr. Morton, United States Minister at Paris. From these letters it appears that, in August last, President Grévy had an informal talk with Mr. Morton in regard to the desirability of a mutual understanding between France and the United States in regard to some policy which might be adopted 'to secure an early return of order and stability of affairs in Chili and Peru.' President Grévy also said that 'another attempt at mediation on the part of foreign governments, and especially that of the United States,' might have satisfactory results. Mr. Morton communicated this informal talk to Mr. Blaine, who thereupon wrote a dispatch to Mr. Morton, in which he called President Grévy's proposed mediation 'a concerted effort by France, Great Britain, and the United States,' and

1607 H Street, Washington,
Sunday, February 26, 1882.

My Angel Pa: I am curious to see in your next, if you mean to take my good advice of last Sunday, and try a sea voyage and two weeks in the Old World. In Paris you will find that under republican rule an American, if less amused, is less disgusted, and you can call on Levi P. Morton, Minister dis-credited by the Republic of the United States to the Republic of France. We have, with many others here and in New York, known for some weeks that this scandal was impending. The papers have not *alluded* to it even now; nor the *New York Herald*, because Jim Bennett and L. P. are dining and wining in Paris; but Bayard and Edmunds are ripping it up in the Senate, and Belmont and Kasson in the House. He may be called home to explain to a Congressional committee his low behavior. For Mrs. Morton great sympathy is expressed; she is very ambitious, well-bred, and must go down with her husband. Schurz said, Friday at dinner, "Yes, Morton has a brilliant *future* behind him." Then said Countess Lewenhaupt, "He had better turn round." She's a clever little Swede. In defending Mr. James against the attack of a lady here, who said, "He's a cad," she said, "I like him. He's the nicest Englishman I ever knew."

Lent has set in with its usual gaiety. The principles of agnostics are not respected. On Sunday, a quiet dinner, only Mr. Lowndes. Monday Major and Mrs. Herschel,[1] Mr. Stackpole and Mr. Hewitt; then on to a dance at the British Legation. Henry wouldn't go so I took the Herschels. They brought us a warm letter from Mr. Lowell, who, I find from them, has never seen them; they are quiet, intelligent and well-mannered, socially ineffectual, like the majority of the nation. He has got a room at the Smithsonian for a few weeks and is more interested in heavenly bodies than in earthly ones. They insist on fixing themselves in a cheap hotel in Sixth Street unknown to fame and of course will deduce

---

objected to it. To this M. Grévy replied that he accorded entirely with the position taken by the United States in the matter."

[1] Major Herschel, a son of Sir John Frederick William Herschel, Bart. (1792-1871) and grandson and grandnephew, respectively, of Sir William Herschel (1738-1822) and of Caroline Lucretia Herschel (1750-1848), the sister and assistant of Sir William, all remarkable astronomers.

life in Washington from their experience there. I've remonstrated, but with no effect. They brought letters to their Minister, Mr. West, and I tried to explain to him who they were; from his icy indifference and polar cordiality I fancy he has never heard of Herschel—father or grandfather or aunt. He didn't even shake hands with them! and I've no doubt they thought it good form.

Tuesday, a pleasant party at the Assistant Secretary of State's—Mrs. Davis's house is always pleasant. Our good king Arthur was there, all the pretty girls taken up to him and presented—it was more like royalty than anything I have ever seen—not being a pretty girl I did not compete in the ceremony. Wednesday, Mr. and Mrs. MacVeagh, Mr. and Mrs. Eugene Schuyler, Mr. Schurz and Aristarchi Bay to dine here; Mr. Nordhoff happened in. Kept it up till twelve, very amusing and interesting, not *one* word but of politics from seven to twelve. Thursday, Mr. Agassiz turned up to tea—just from Mexico—weary, ill, and disgusted; made him come to dinner and go first to party at Professor Baird's for the Herschels, and then to the Secretary of State's—the scientific crowd—we found it ghastly, Caroline H. Dall all-pervading in a robe of pure white, tell Ned. She sent me a message weeks ago by Mr. James that it was "my place to call on her but that if I lived in a vortex of gaiety she would waive ceremony and call first on me." I have not gone. I am told that she is to give a lunch to the whole Massachusetts delegation. She lives in æsthetic quarters in Georgetown, I hear; as she is not familiar with my classic features I escaped her notice on Thursday. Friday, dinner at Mrs. Lawrence's,—very jolly,—Lewenhaupts, Aristarchi Bey, Schuylers, Dr. Bessels and Mr. Schurz, who has been our guest since Wednesday; party at Mrs. Wadsworth's afterwards to which we did not go. Yesterday, musical party—very small—at the rooms of Misses Markoe, nieces of the old lady of whom I bought my wardrobe and Sir Joshuas. She is ill in her room and I went to see her for a few minutes as she wanted to tell me her pleasure in their having fallen into appreciate hands; she was very sweet and pathetic. In her parlour is a bust of her by Powers taken in her youth and prosperity; their carved furniture and china-ware is most beautiful. One niece is a fine musician. We thereby escaped a party for Reverend Edward Everett Hale at Henry's cousin's, Lottie Hopkins.

Conkling's nomination is a surprise;[1] Hoar and two or three other Republican Senators will vote against it. Dawes, it is said, will be unwilling to do anything wearing the aspect of courage. The *New York Tribune* of February 25 has a leader beginning, "Guiteau has made a Supreme Judge as well as a President and he is not hung yet." The *Times* is cooler, wiser, and bitterly opposed.

Miss Dulaney goes to Mrs. Robert Cushing this week for one month. Won't you call on her? She is very nice, and I told her you *would. Adiós.* Affectionately

M. A.

1607 H STREET, WASHINGTON,
March 5th, 1882.

DEAR PATER: I'm as sleepy as a cat this Sunday morning and as stupid as an owl, so you'll have a sorry letter. Sunday last had a lovely ride; came home late; tea was like the happy family in a menagerie,—Adam Badeau, Senator and Mrs. Don Cameron, Misses Fish and Beale, Mr. Schurz and Mr. Belmont,—Mrs. Cameron much amused that her husband had himself proposed coming. I spoke warmly of the MacVeaghs; he observed that their politics were "peculiar," and I said, "Yes, I wish yours were peculiar in the same direction." If he doesn't look out a reform wave will sweep over his state and beach him high and dry in Harrisburg.

Sunday, a pleasant dinner,—Carl Schurz, Aristarchi Bey and Mr. Belmont, and Mr. Nordhoff after dinner,—all politics and public affairs. Tuesday, a small dinner for Mrs. Lodge and Mrs. Gardner; took occasion to ask the Favas,—new Italian Minister and his wife, well-bred and intelligent and gay,—knowing the weakness of certain Bostonians for the foreigner. We judged that a Baron, Baroness, and Austrian Count (Lippe Weissenfeld) would please them. They frankly admit that the life of a diplomate is their notion of earthly bliss. A little of that set goes a great way—I mean Beacon-Streeters. Wednesday a feminine tea-party at Dr. Bessels's; among

---

[1] On February 24, 1882, the President sent to the Senate the name of Roscoe Conkling, of New York, to be an Associate Justice of the Supreme Court. The nomination was reported on favorably on February 28, and confirmed on March 2 by a vote of 39 to 12; on March 6 the President received a letter from Mr. Conkling declining the office.

his penates the white pennant of the ill-fated *Polaris*, which, in the allowance of eight pounds of baggage apiece on leaving the ship, he took as a towel and used for months, and its blood-red letters are still fresh.

Warm, sunny days this past week, frogs singing gaily, trees bursting into flower, no ice or snow anywhere, but today a gray sky and impending storm. Blaine won laurels for his oration and even his opponents must admit that it was a very difficult thing very skillfully done. What a pity that so much ability should be unsupported by enough moral sense to make him an honest servant; jobs and shekels have apparently an overmastering fascination for him. There'll be a lively row in Congress soon over the foreign policy. So Conkling can be a Supreme Judge if he wants to! Arthur has lost all the ground he gained.

Let me know, if you can, when Ellen and Whitman will come; we want to keep *both* rooms for them and have no other visitors then, and towards spring guests are more frequent. I hope they will have the energy to do it this time—early April is so pleasant here. Tea, I wrote you, came safely. Am sorry you won't stiffen yourself by an Atlantic voyage. Love to Aunty. *Adiós*, affectionately

M. A.

1607 H STREET, 7th, 1 P.M.

Yours of Sunday received, have written Whitman to come at once with Ellen—do not want Ned with her, she sees quite enough of him at home. We can only make *two* comfortable upstairs and want them to be forced into our interests and not bring their own. You must come later with a stranger,—a New York friend of mine,—not Ned this year; we shall make you come separately, it's much more refreshing all round; Ellen would be miserable without her husband. Tea *tip*-top. Affectionately

M. A.

1607 H STREET, 7th, 1 P.M.

"Mistrusting child," "Suspecting parent." I thought the letter would only bore you and you said, "When I've dined I shall read Mrs. Green's letter" and I thought envelope might never fall in your eyes. Sent you postscript today begging you to send Ellen with her husband. So our map tells us you've snow today! Affectionately

M. A.

1607 H Street, Washington,
Sunday, March 12th, 1882.

Dear Pater: I have no new fact or fancy to give you today for it is Lent. On the surface everything is quiet enough here but slowly and surely the Committee on Foreign Relations in Senate and House are ripping up the brilliant cloth of gold woven by Blaine and his pals since March 4th, 1881. Shipherd is to testify on Wednesday; Blaine is to be called up; Trescot to be sent for probably; L. P. Morton was cabled by Secretary of State last week, and it will furnish lively food for gossip here. There's a hungry, greedy lobby like that of the old Grant days in full force here, but we are told on good authority that members of Congress are getting very shy of jobs and subsidies, and that Eads[1] with his ship-canal scheme and others with Tehuantepec may have to fall back on private capital. Nordhoff is denouncing them day by day in his letter to *New York Herald*, and the Chili-Peru scandals make our legislators hesitate in voting other people's money. Sunday, Mr. Hewitt (Democrat) and A. G. McCook (Republican), both from New York, dined here. McCook is an Ohio man, brigadier-general in army, friend of Garfield; bachelor, forty-seven, intelligent and attractive; as a young man he worked in the mines in California with pick and shovel, side by side with Chinese, and found he could keep even with them. It is doubtful if the bill just passed in the Senate can get through the House—it's so poor and faulty that Edmunds and Sherman had to back out of it.[2] Theoretically and

---

[1] During the first week of March, "Captain Ead's proposition to carry vessels across the Isthmus of Panama on a railroad, as embodied in a bill to incorporate the Inter-Oceanic Ship Railway Company, has been favorably reported to the Senate from the Committee on Commerce. It is stated that opposition to the bill in the Committee was withheld as a compliment to the introducer, with the understanding that Senators who were opposed to it should have an opportunity to manifest their opposition by speech and vote." (*Nation*, March 9, 1882)

[2] The bill prohibiting Chinese immigration for twenty years was passed by the Senate on March 9. The Democrats, with one or two exceptions, voted for the

philosophically it's all wrong, but the Pacific States are solid for it and entitled to a hearing, the Democrats have gone for it largely, and it may turn the next Presidential election in their favour— that's the game.

Dined Wednesday at Randall Gibson's of Louisiana; sat between Mr. Bayard and Eugene Schuyler. A curious dinner: Wade Hampton;[1] Judge Cox; a Kentucky widow with powdered face and hard, loud voice; Carlisle,[2] who is coming to see me, alas! The wife of Senator B., hard-featured, ill-dressed, common-looking woman, like our overworked New England farmer's wife. The tradition of Southern culture, voices, manners, etc., is ill-supported in these post-bellum days; Mr. Lowndes seems "a bright particular star"; Mr. and Mrs. Gibson are better than any I have seen socially, quiet and well-mannered. Eads, the lobbyist, was there—a sharp, keen, common face and manner; what dining and wining can do for his ship-canal will be done. I like to get off our own beat though and meet any man or woman going. Yesterday came Mrs. Tucker, of Virginia, to tea, bringing two bright-eyed, macaw-voiced little daughters; then Miss Beale, bringing a Miss Porter from Louisiana, a nice bright woman whom I've often heard of; and Perry Belmont, with the latest news from his Foreign Affairs Committee. Aristarchi Bey comes often in the evening and tells us of more politics in Europe than a dozen newspapers.

Of private news nothing new. The Outreys are recalled. He is sixty and they want his place for Roustan, who got into a scandal in Tunis, so they quietly extinguish poor Outrey, and he can educate the three babes and stroll on the Boulevards. It's a great blow to them and they will be a loss here. Roustan is a widower or

---

bill, and the Republicans, with the exception of the Senators from the Pacific Coast and Senator Cameron of Wisconsin, against it.

[1] Wade Hampton (1818-1902), though not in sympathy with the prevailing State rights' views in South Carolina, espoused the Southern cause in 1861, and served brilliantly as a cavalry officer, rising to the rank of lieutenant-general; after the war his attitude was conciliatory, and from 1876 to 1879 he was governor of South Carolina; he served in the United States Senate from 1879 to 1891.

[2] John Griffin Carlisle (1835-1910) served in Congress from Kentucky from 1876 to 1890; was Speaker of the House of Representatives from 1883 to 1889; in 1890 he went to the Senate, and was Secretary of the Treasury in President Cleveland's second administration.

bachelor or both or nothing—a Frenchman can be single or double so easily. In my heart of hearts how I sympathise with grandfather Sturgis's prejudices, and yours too. To Mrs. Gardner and Mrs. Lodge a diplomatic existence is the sum of earthly bliss! "We might marry. Polly's had an offer." Frelinghuysen has offered Henry the Mission to Costa Rica; Logan[1] has just been transferred to Peru. Think of us in Guatemala City! I wish we wanted it, it would be so new and fresh; it includes Guatemala, Honduras, Nicaragua, and Salvador. I told Mr. Frelinghuysen it was an unwise appointment, that Henry would be in a railroad or job of some kind before he knew it.

They had a pleasant reception Thursday evening, one always meets worth-while people and it's not crowded. Friday, Miss Lucy Frelinghuysen and I went to Vorhees's[2] room in Capitol to see the plan for the new library building by one Smithmeyer of this city— a meaningless, tasteless, pepper-potted plan like a great railway hotel. We surveyed it in silence and shall do our best to scotch it. Voorhees—alias, the tall Sycamore of the Wabash—is an inflated, bombastic, ignorant man too uneducated to build a pig-pen. This scheme *must* be blocked. It is stated on good authority that Smithmeyer is to marry Voorhees's daughter—"there's millions in it." Show this part to Ned, please. *Adiós.* Affectionately

M. A.

1607 H STREET, WASHINGTON,
March 20th, 1882.

DEAR PATER: I could not get a clear half hour yesterday in which to write to you so I'll send off a scrap this A.M. to say that we still live.

A week of raw, cold, dull weather behind us though yesterday we got a warm blue-sky ride of two hours in the back country. A raft of people to tea—S. L. M. Barlows, Eugene Schuylers, Hewitt, Belmont, Judge Gray, Mrs. Don Cameron, Austin Wadsworth,

---

[1] Cornelius A. Logan.
[2] Daniel Wolsey Voorhees (1827-1897), a Senator from Indiana; he was chairman of the joint select committee on additional accommodations for the Library of Congress.

Mrs. Craig Wadsworth,[1] etc. At ten minutes to seven I had to suggest to some lingering guests that as we had some people coming in to dine I needed ten minutes to dress in. I fear we shall be driven to dining at eight as in London, people so often hang on till seven; if Margery is not loath we should much prefer it. We dined on Saturday at the Andersons' to meet Mr. Richardson. The other two guests were two Cincinnati men, Mrs. Burnett the novelist, and a Miss Stevens, a smart lively person. Last night we had the Randall Gibsons and T. F. Bayard to meet Richardson and they were all full of talk, especially Mr. Bayard, whose growing deafness throws him out at a large dinner. If Mr. Frelinghuysen had the tenth part of Bayard's sense of humour and decency Morton would have been sent home long since. There seems to be a certain moral malaria here in official life which few escape. Bayard not only calls a spade a spade but dirt dirt. That L. P. Morton should have proposed to risk a war on the chance of stuffing the pockets of his gabardine with guano, is revolting.

Have the Herschels taken letters to the Gurneys? I don't think they will find him very effectual socially; he is not popular here, few Britons are. Miss Herschel is a good, plain, sensible woman. Miss Dulaney writes me she was much disappointed at losing a call from you and hopes you will go again. Love to the Cambridge colony. Yours affectionately

M. A.

1607 H Street, Washington,
Sunday, March 26th, 1882.

Dear Pater: I can only send you the record of a quiet week; if we were "stalwarts," devout worshippers at the Grant throne, this might reek with orgies and incense. On Sunday, as I wrote you perhaps, we had a quiet dinner for H. H. Richardson. On Tuesday, Sturgis Bigelow turned up; he seems to find endless solace and amusement in Miss Beale's company, and has had some parties and a daily chance dinner guest to prevent our dining with a "dummy." I fancy the amount of politics he hears between five

---

[1] Evelyn Willing Peters (1845-1885), a daughter of Mr. and Mrs. Francis Peters of Philadelphia, married, in 1869, Craig Wharton Wadsworth, of Genesco, N. Y.

and eleven daily bores him a good deal, but that is the inevitable fate for those who come to this latitude. Thursday, we kept Dr. Bessels from tea to dinner and he and Sturgis fraternised on science—molecules, bacilli et al. The S. L. M. Barlows left yesterday. Mr. Barlow tells me that Mr. Morton's famous Regnault, the "Automedon," which has just been sold for five thousand dollars and over in New York, was cut by Morton about one foot from each end in order to fit it to an alcove or space in his Newport dining room! that it was put together again before the sale. Ned will enjoy that.

Richardson was much pleased with the Sir Joshuas and has inspired the Andersons with wrath at their blindness in rejecting them as rubbish, though offered to them at the same time they were offered to me. I'm going to sell my Tilton; Mr. Barlow thinks I could sell it for eight hundred dollars in New York and is going to speak to Schaus; I gave two hundred and fifty, years ago, and am tired of it, though as a Tilton it is a good one. Mr. King bought Gérôme's "Red Flamingoes" at the Morton sale, a picture he has long fancied. Sturgis was to leave today but has changed his mind; the two Adams boys come for a week on April 8th and after the 15th Brooks Adams, whom we postpone till then. He is much out of sorts and spirits; I must get a young woman to leaven the family dough when he's here—a stranger. A late spring, one yellow shrub in flower in the garden, but cold and dusty. *Adiós.* Affectionately

M. A.

1607 H STREET, WASHINGTON,
Sunday, April 2d, 1882.

DEAR PATER: I trust you are all basking in summer heat today on Ellen's piazza and the babies rolling in the grass. Wild flowers are out in the woods here and birds and frogs singing popular airs all day long. Would that the sap which makes the trees and bushes so lively in the springtime ran as gaily in human legs and arms.

Our great law-makers having trampled on Chinese and Mormons are wrangling genially over tariff charges.[1] Mr. Hewitt has, as you will have seen, made an important speech in favor of modifying taxes, and as he is one of the largest iron and steel makers in the country his opinions and suggestions have weight. He is to dine with us today, also Miss Bayard, Dr. Bessels, and a Mr. Griswold of Bangor, one of Henry's old scholars now in a niche in Library of Congress. We seldom dine alone; often we keep Aristarchi Bey from tea to dinner, or Mr. Belmont or Dr. Bessels— stray bachelors like to dine in human habitations, I find. I think the sawdust came out of W. S. Bigelow's California doll towards the end of his stay, and was not sorry. Game that flies into the bag, without a shot being fired is less exciting than coyer birds on higher branches. *"Faîtes vous rare et on vous aimera."*

Mr. Lowell seems to be a target for the papers, perhaps he has let the social half of his duties outweigh the public, for John Bull must be kept up to the mark and forced to try suspects.[2] The British Government only lately complained of one of their subjects not having been brought to immediate trial in Michigan, and the State Department sent, within twenty-four hours, telegrams to London that the case was on trial by request. A man needs all his wits

[1] The Edmunds Anti-Polygamy Bill passed the House of Representatives on March 14. The Anti-Chinese Immigration Bill passed the House of Representatives March 23, but was vetoed by the President on April 4. The Tariff Commission Bill passed the Senate March 28, and the debate upon it in the House began the same day and continued intermittently until May 6, when the bill was finally passed without amendment. Mr. Hewitt advocated a repeal of the duties on raw materials and the implements of manufacturing industry with a corresponding reduction of the duties on the manufactured articles; he opposed the creation of the proposed Tariff Commission as unnecessary and likely to delay such necessary legislation.

[2] The *Nation*, March 9, 1882: "Mr. Lowell has got into a 'dungeon' trouble with an American Fenian named MacSweeny, who returned to his native country to engage in political agitation, and was arrested under the Coercion Act, and was, when he brought his case to Mr. Lowell's notice, confined in what he called 'Victoria's dungeon,' at Dundalk. Whenever an American Fenian is arrested by the British Government he is, curiously enough, always put into a 'dungeon,' the ordinary jail being apparently reserved for British subjects; and when he begins to call for deliverance at the hands of this Government, by the invasion of England, or the bombardment of London, as may be deemed most expedient, it is from a dungeon that his cries always issue."

about him who takes a situation in a big country. Dined on Tuesday at the Bancroft Davises' to meet Mr. and Mrs. Hamilton Fish; he took me in and was very chatty and agreeable—chiefly politics. The "Grant crowd" has eaten and drunk its fill and gone its way—to us a great relief.

My mind is as dry as a biscuit today, lay the blame on the Lenten season and the heat. *Adiós.* Affectionately

M. A.

1607 H STREET, WASHINGTON,
April 9th, 1882.

DEAR PATER: I'm glad to hear from Miss Dulaney that you are well and gay. Which of us does she flatter most in saying that "it's ridiculous that any man and woman should be so like one another" as you and I are? I wish I were sure of being so congenial to my fellow critters as you are when I've turned seventy.

I find, Sunday last, Miss Bayard, Mr. Hewitt, Dr. Bessels and a youth named Griswold dined here—Mr. Hewitt full of his late speech. Tuesday, Henry went to a man's dinner given by Dr. Bessels to Captain Hooper, who went in search of the *Jeanette* last summer—Schwatka,[1] famous for his sledge journeys in the frozen North, Weckerlin, the new Dutch Minister,[2] etc. Aristarchi Bey came in and talked over the fire till ten-thirty with me; he has been in correspondence with Mr. Norton lately in regard to the Archaelogical Society who wish certain digging privileges from the Sublime Porte. He tells me his father once owned a large estate by the Sea of Marmore, just over the site of old Perinthus, and he and his brother dug up many treasures—I think he said it had never been explored. Wednesday, the John Hays turned up from Cleveland; he will be here on and off for a month, has had diphtheria and is rather run down; we see them daily. Thursday, our nephews came; George is a broad-shouldered boy of nineteen, very Crown-

---

[1] Frederick Schwatka (1849-1892) was graduated at West Point in 1871 and resigned from the Army in 1884; he commanded an arctic expedition in search of traces of Franklin, 1878-1880.

[2] Guillaume Ferdinand Henri von Weckerlin was the Minister-resident of the Netherlands at Washington from 1882 to 1889.

inshield, jolly and ready to be amused; Charley quiet and non-committal.[1]

We are much interested in your politics in Boston. Boutwell seems to be at the bottom of the change of Collectorship;[2] it's a brutal slap in the face of all decent men in the party and Mr. Arthur may live to find his mistake. His highfalutin phrases as to civil service reform were mere buncombe; he is a ward politician, neither more nor less, and the daily widening breach in the Republican Party may give the Democrats a clean walk-over in 1885. We know none of the Cabinet except the Frelinghuysens and have no desire to seek the acquaintance; chance may bring us together but we shall wait for that. Mrs. Bancroft, who is an old courtier, fancies qualities of intellect and manner in the President which his high seat has brought to light. Things are getting mixed here and we look on with indifferent curiosity. The twistings and turnings of many machine politicians won't kill this big country.

Brooks has just turned up from Fortress Monroe via Baltimore; we tried to postpone him till the middle of the month but he couldn't stand "Hygeia" any longer; so I've laid in an extra bed, got a new man to fill the place of one who was suddenly taken ill, and so on we go. If I can keep the commissariat up we shall have no trouble. A dull, warm day this, peach trees and pears in full bloom and dogwood swelling fast. *Adiós.* Affectionately

CLOVER

1607 H STREET, WASHINGTON,
Sunday, April 16, 1882.

DEAR PATER: No news, no warm weather, no excitement of any kind. I cannot see that the trees have grown any greener for the past two weeks—it's a slow, late spring.

---

[1] George Caspar Adams and Charles Francis Adams, 3rd, the sons of Henry Adams's brother, John Quincy Adams.

[2] The *Nation*, April 13, 1882: "The President sent a large batch of nominations to the Senate on Thursday (April 6th), among which were those of Senator Henry M. Teller, of Colorado, to be Secretary of the Interior, William E. Chandler, of New Hampshire, to be Secretary of the Navy, William H. Hunt, the Secretary of the Navy, to be Minister to Russia, and Roland Worthington, to be Collector of Customs at Boston. The last nomination has been received with a general feeling of disapproval throughout the country."

The two nephews went home Wednesday and professed to have enjoyed their week's outing very much. Brooks Adams is still with us and I fancy means to stay through the month; he eats and sleeps like a viking and is gaining daily—if he had quiet nerves and peace in his soul he would gain faster. Tomorrow the "Academy" meets in Washington and Mr. Agassiz comes to us for a few days; probably after him at the end of the week Miss Palmer of New York. We want to ask Mr. Hay, who comes back tomorrow alone, for a stay of two or three weeks, but we've no room—unhappily. It's no sinecure to run a house here, but as we are too old to be ornamental we may as well be useful.

Had a long talk with Mr. Nordhoff at the Frelinghuysens' on Thursday evening; he belongs to the crowd who expect little good of this administration—we shall be lucky if we escape the corruption of Grantism. MacVeagh has broken his long silence at last in his speech at the public dinner in Philadelphia last week. Evidently Mr. Lowell is to be crowded out.[1] That he made a mistake even his friends can't deny; socially he is a success, but that's not enough. There is more or less talk about Bancroft Davis as his successor—but it may be mere talk—he has far more experience than most men in this country but his manners are not good and the British hate him for his work at Geneva. I think Mrs. Davis is too good for the situation, it's a mean existence for any man or woman—exile in livery at best.

I'm glad you've bullied Aunt Eunice into black silk stockings and I quite agree with you that one should dress better as age steals on. Mrs. Bigelow Lawrence and I have agreed that one can do nothing except to keep many interests and keep very clean, and certainly when an old age is serene like Madam Cabot's it's as

---

[1] The *Nation*, April 13, 1882: "The President sent to the Senate on Wednesday (April 5th) a report of the Secretary of State relating to the three American citizens imprisoned in Ireland, from which it appears that all but three of the prisoners have been set at liberty in response to the request of Mr. Lowell. Mr. Frelinghuysen further states that the negotiations have been carried on for some time 'in a spirit of entire friendship.' The London *Times* says the Government holds all persons resident in Ireland liable to British law, and to be treated as British subjects, and that the naturalized subjects of the United States who have been released, were released for reasons entirely unconnected with their citizenship."

pleasant as an Indian summer day. The monograph you ask for, Henry has, and will keep for you or send—it's rather heavy for the mail. Much love to Adie. Ask her if she'll have me at Hanover in June for two days. *Adiós*, affectionately

CLOVER

1607 H STREET, WASHINGTON,
Sunday, April 23rd, 1882.

DEAR PATER: The dogwood trees are white at last—with snow and not flowers! We are today the victims of a miserable practical joke—a good, hard, driving snowstorm all this morning, now at two P.M. turned into rain and slush under foot *à la rigueur*, etc.

We've had a busy week. Alex Agassiz came on Monday. Tuesday we had an impromptu feast for him—Admiral Rogers, O. C. Marsh, Mr. John Hay, and Senator Fair of Nevada, whom Mr. Agassiz wanted to see. The Corporation of Harvard College are robber barons bold and always seeking whom they may devour. Fair and Mackay were grocers together in Virginia City not so very long ago and Mrs. Mackay is remembered by Mr. King as a pretty barmaid rinsing glasses. Fair is neither spicy in his talk nor gingerly in his methods, as one might expect. He reported to Miss Bayard that he had "dined with Charles Francis Adams"; that your humble correspondent was a "splendid woman"; that among the guests was "Mr. Hay, who made the corrupt contract for the East River bridge"; that he "seemed a pleasant fellow" but that he was "surprised they should ask such a man" (he is in jail for forging), etc. etc.!

Wednesday, Bessels and Hay. Thursday, Major Powell and Hay; the former is Mr. King's successor as head of the geological bureau and a very intelligent man—lost his right arm at Shiloh. Wednesday evening, a reception for the Academy given at Wormley's by Professor William B. Rogers—a scientific crowd, always very dreary for social purposes, to my thinking. Friday, we bid good-bye to Mr. Agassiz and offered his room to Mr. Hay, but he is too ill to come and is languishing in a stuffy hole at Wormley's. Brooks is still here waiting for weather to venture north in. Bostonians swarming and New Yorkers; I fear they expect civilities which we are too tired to wrestle with. I must do something for the

Schuylers, but their thirst for light is so exhausting that I try and frame excuses. Miss Frelinghuysen invited us all to go with her to the White House on Tuesday to the official reception, but our dinner stood in the way. Henry hasn't left a card yet, which is not over-civil to a new opposite neighbour who likes social attention. No news, as you see. *Adiós*, affectionately

M. A.

1607 H Street, Washington,
Sunday, April 30th, 1882.

Dear Pater: Thanks for yours of the 27th though you don't tell me what ails Adie. Is she seriously ill? As to the note from Mr. Lowndes, Henry advises me to withhold it until I hear from you again—Mr. Lowndes has no connection with any French claims, nor with any Spanish of the period of which you speak. Those old claims still lie before Congress as they have for many years, and will, it is thought here, until we are all in our graves. The two commissions here now working concern modern claims. I hope the Hichborns will not build Spanish Castles off their claims and be sadly disappointed at the hopelessness of any prospect of getting them.

Senator Fair made a "visit of digestion" a few nights since and amused us much by his naïve and frank account of the way politics are carried on in Nevada. He and a few of his friends—some ten in all—arrange the tickets and issue their orders all over the State and their "ticket is always voted." "Why," said he, "I've seventy-five miles of private wires in my office alone." In answer to the question why Senator Jones might not checkmate him, he smiled sweetly and said, "I've more wires than Jones." I suggested that was monarchical rather than democratic; to which he rejoined, "I don't care what you call things so's you get the results you want." A small tea at Mrs. Bancroft Davis's Tuesday night; talked with various Ministers—Swedish, Turkish, Belgian, Dutch, and Austrian, the two latter new arrivals. New Russian Minister came in to tea a few days ago, has been in Japan for several years; his wife has made a collection there of teapots—*nine hundred and seventy-three* so far—and has sent them to St. Petersburg, I'm sorry to hear. She and I have exchanged calls but not met. She is well-born and a lady, it is said, and will, it is hoped, atone for the short-comings of her predecessors.

Thursday we had Mr. Schuyler and Louisa to dinner, Miss Ellen Mason, Miss Frelinghuysen, and Mr. Lowndes—which with us made up eight. It was purely a duty dinner and I thought deadly dull except for Miss Frelinghuysen, who came up to the scratch like a heroine. Whatever vivacity Mr. Schuyler once had has yielded to time and the loss of two helpmeets. His daughter is estimable, more than most, but for social purposes I prefer the vicious and frivolous. Miss Mason is a sealed book to me. Friday Richardson turned up at tea time, gay and full of life; he is to dine here today with Mr. Bancroft, Professor Marsh, and Hudson—*Herald* correspondent—a motley crew! I've been in my room and bed for three days with a heavy cold which caught me ten days ago; in spite of persistent and vigorous defiance on my part it got the upper hand Friday night, so Henry sent for Lincoln and he for aconite and quinine and mustard plasters. I'm so bored with coddling for two days that I shall try to go down to dinner—my own company is not amusing. Boojum never leaves me and was unwilling to eat yesterday, owing to my staying in bed, except what I gave him. Possum has no sentiment in his nature and would cheerfully eat me if mixed with potato. Sad it is to lose a visit to Barnum tomorrow evening; De Bildt and Aristarchi Bey proposed to me to chaperon a party. It has grown since Friday, and Kasson came in last night to say that Barnum will reserve seats for it. I shall try and go, and pay for the whistle afterwards if need be.

The Blaine-Belmont affair[1] has interested us much and it's refreshing to have someone to tell that old wretch to his face that he's "a bully and a coward." Belmont came in to tea that same

---

[1] The *Nation*, May 4, 1882: "Mr. Blaine continued his testimony before the House Investigating Committee on Wednesday (April 26th). He stated that in the diary of President Garfield no mention whatever was ever made of Shipherd, the Cochet claim, or the Peruvian Company. He produced the draft of the Trescot instructions, which was shown to President Arthur and amended at the President's suggestion, and denied that he had ever 'interpolated a word, or a line, or a syllable, or an idea.' He also denied that he had assumed to act as President *de facto*, or that he was engaged during the President's illness in 'blocking out a great foreign policy and precipitating it on the country between the lives of two Presidents.'"

P.M. and was warmly greeted by ourselves, the two Miss Bayards and Miss Cameron, the Senator's daughter. The papers, except the *Tribune*, which is now a mere Blaine organ, are all anti-Blaine. Nordhoff pounds away daily in the *Herald*, having at last found Blaine out; a year ago he was impatient with us for declining to visit his house or recognise him socially. Lost a breakfast yesterday at Miss Bayard's; she is always charming and drops in often. Brooks leaves tomorrow for New York to Geneseo; we think him pretty well, on the up-grade steadily. I'm tired now and so are you. *Adiós*, affectionately

M. A.

1607 H STREET, WASHINGTON,
Sunday, May 7th, 1882.

DEAR PATER: We possess our damp souls in patience outwardly while Jupiter Pluvius holds high carnival. For some reason best known to themselves the leaves have all come out—dogwood flowers and apple blossoms—from sheer force of habit as if nature had given a general order to wake them on May 1st. We have had a sniffling, barking household this week and are glad that no guest has shared the infliction.

Sunday we had three or four people to dine with Richardson; he can say truly "I am my own music," for he carries off any dinner more or less gaily. Monday, I had to renounce Jumbo and all his works. Tuesday, Miss Bayard and Oliver Wendell Holmes, Jr., to dine. Had an invitation to reception at White House; as Henry had never even called, it was an unlooked-for civility, he went for a *mauvais quart d'heure* just to bow the knee to Baal and brought away a violent influenza which has laid him low ever since. Thursday we crawled out into the woods late, as it was very warm, and came out after a long scramble through tangles and beds of brooks on the grounds of the new Naval Observatory in Georgetown, a most lovely place. Poor Admiral Rodgers[1] lay dying in the house,—we stopped to get the latest bulletin,—he lingered on until the next sunset. Friday was rainy so we were at home by the fire at

---

[1] Rear-Admiral John Rodgers, U.S.N. (1812-1882), then the superintendent of the Naval Observatory.

tea time; among others came in Perry Belmont. He was so out of spirits that we kept him to dinner and gave him a wooden monkey to jump on a string. He finds politics flat, stale, and unprofitable. The pleasure of calling Blaine "bully and coward" is not an enduring one. He has been deluged with letters of approval and is as well advertised as Lydia Pinkham, but all is vanity to his restless soul.

The District has had a sad loss in Major Twining's[1] sudden death on Friday—caught on Tuesday a chill at the circus and went off in seventy hours with acute pneumonia. He was so sympathetic and courteous when I went to his office to state Boojum's grievance three years ago that I've loved him ever since. Everyone respected and trusted him; he was only forty-five and full of wise plans of improving the city. It will be very hard to fill his place. Among other plans was one lately submitted to Congress for draining and filling the flats south of us; as he was a trained engineer his suggestions carried weight.

This morning comes the sad news of Frederick Cavendish's murder,[2] which will have endless consequences to Ireland and the English Liberals. It seems to come home to one when you know personally the victim. I remember his taking me down to dinner at W. E. Forster's in London and Henry took in his pretty, kindly wife. I remember the dinner very well; Cavendish was gayer in his manner than most Englishmen and full of talk. He and I concocted a scheme by which he was to send a quantity of hansom cabs to this country and we to import English cabmen to drive them and so help the surplus population to earn a living. His death will be a great shock to many of our good friends over there and especially to the Forsters. For two years we have expected to hear of Forster's assassination and now his escape seems all the more marvelous. It seems now as if the extreme radicals—such as

---

[1] W. J. Twining, Major of Engineers, United States Army, was one of the Commissioners for the District of Columbia.

[2] Lord Frederick Charles Cavendish (1836-1882), the second son of the seventh Duke of Devonshire, had married, June 7, 1864, Lucy Caroline, the second daughter of the fourth Lord Littleton. He was murdered in Phœnix Park, Dublin, a few hours after his being sworn a Privy Councillor, on his appointment as Chief Secretary to the Lord Lieutenant of Ireland, May 6, 1882.

Chamberlain,[1] Dilke, John Bright[2]—must take the helm and hand over Ireland to Parnell[3] and his friends, and the often-repeated prophecy of the Prince of Wales bids fair to come true—that he would never come to his throne, that England would be a republic before his turn came. France and the United States are ghosts at noonday to the English aristocracy.

I read last evening a book of Spanish travels by an Italian, De Amicis—have you seen it? It bored me a good deal, except the Granada chapter. He gives one page in that to a description of a cinque-cento house on the Dairo at the foot of the Alhambra with its motto over the doorway—"Esperando la del Cielo." He hadn't been to tea there several times as we have, and knows no charming Don Leopoldo; confesses that he knew no one in Granada; and has a low opinion of the people. If we get out of health, or money, or both, we'll go to Spain and write a charming book of travels or die in the attempt. Don Leopoldo offered me any quantity of old Arabic legends if I would stay there a few months and use them.

Clarence King sailed for England yesterday; wrote for two letters; has never crossed the big pond before; comes back in July or August. We shall miss him sadly as we go through New York in June. Is T. going to mind that idiot doctor? Malaria at Beverly Farms is a wise invention. Some of your colleagues are asses, methinks. We shan't hurry to go there, it's dull and cold in June. We prefer it here till roasted out. *Adiós*

M. A.

---

[1] Joseph Chamberlain (1836-1914) and Sir Charles Wentworth Dilke (1843-1911), representing the Radicals, entered Mr. Gladstone's ministry after the general election of 1880, the former as President of the Board of Trade and the latter as under-Secretary for Foreign Affairs. Mr. Chamberlain was opposed to coercion and negotiated an arrangement with Mr. Parnell resulting in the latter's release from jail on May 2, 1882, on his agreement to advise the cessation of outrages and the payment of rent, and in return the coercive administration was to be relaxed. As this did not meet with the approval of Mr. W. E. Forster, the Irish Secretary, he resigned, and his successor, Lord Frederick Cavendish, was immediately murdered on taking office.

[2] John Bright (1811-1889).

[3] Charles Steward Parnell (1846-1891).

DEAR PATER: Yours of Sunday just come. After days of damp and cloudy skies we've got a summer sun which will soon throw out our colds. Had three hours in the saddle yesterday; are to give the Outreys a little dinner on Friday; as Outrey lost a very dear brother two months ago, a small dinner suits them best. I doubt if we get up steam for any more, it is getting too late for dinners. Affectionately

M. A.

1607 H STREET, WASHINGTON,
Sunday, May 14, 1882.

DEAR PATER: Every fool becomes a philosopher after ten days of cold rain, so I spare you the inside view of my heart. Tuesday, we got up to 86° with the bluest of skies and drove out to Silver Spring, in spite of the heat, to make a call; it's a lovely farm at the head of Rock Creek Valley. Since then the poor beasties have mildewed in their stable. We have been very glad to have no visitors to pine and peak at the rain, they would have been sadly on our minds.

I'm glad to hear that the Cambridge colony is so flourishing and babies all jolly. Tell Ned two of the four frocks are done and the other two will be in a few days. I hope they will prove decent, though they are Spartan in simplicity but the latest dodge, so he can ask no more. I will keep them till we go north or send them, as he prefers, but in this cold wet spring they may as well scrub out their winter things.

Had a little dinner Friday for the Outreys—Mrs. Lawrence, Miss Dulaney, Aristarchi Bey, and Mr. Hewitt; Mr. Bayard was engaged. It went off very well for that kind of dinner, which is not inspiring—to us at least. Miss Dulaney sang for us charmingly in the evening. I gave Mr. Lowndes your note, after all, as he wished to "have the pleasure of writing to Dr. Hooper." Nothing up politically; Congress muddling away its time and our money in empty wrangling. The Chili-Peru matter drags on; the general public cares little and knows less. Jim Blaine is a shining light or a pretentious blatherskite, according to the point of view you choose to

take. So is Jesse James,[1] for that matter. If he had not fallen a victim to the vengeance of a reform clique, he might have represented
Missouri in the Senate and filled society columns with his charms.
Apropos of Jesse, I had a farewell letter from Henry James, Jr.,
written Tuesday at midnight on the eve of sailing. He wished, he
said, his last farewell to be said to me as I seemed to him "the in-
carnation of my native land"—a most equivocal compliment coming from him. Am I then vulgar, dreary, and impossible to live
with? That's the only obvious interpretation, however self-love
might look for a gentler one. Poor America! she must drag on
somehow without the sympathy and love of her denationalised
children. I fancy she'll weather it!

As to America, there is a curious picture at Barlow's on the
Avenue sent for sale from Mississippi (don't count the *s*'s if you
love me), signed by Audubon;[2] an oil painting about twenty inches
or more, of dead birds, some in an overturned basket, some on the
ground, a spray of purple convolvulus on the left background,—
painted in oils with great delicacy and accuracy rather as one
would paint who was more used to the handling of water colours;
three hundred dollars is the price asked. Neither of us cares for
"still life" in any shape—on canvas or off—but the Art Museum
might do very well to buy what is on internal evidence a good and
unusual specimen of Audubon. It was left as a legacy to the ser-
geant of the Senate by a Mississippi relative, so Barlow says. The
signature may be forged of course, but if any artist in America
could paint birds as well as that, except Audubon, he ought to be
spotable and a bird savant could easily identify the birds. There is
also a very striking and powerful oil painting from one of the de-
scendants of Robert Gilmore, who had a famous collection many
years ago in Baltimore. This purports to be a Salvator Rosa. It is
weird enough to suit Vedder, reminds me strongly of Allston's
Elijah in character, is about five feet long by two or more high—a
storm-bent tree in left foreground, a high bank on the right, a bril-

---

[1] Jesse Woodson James (1847-1882), a notorious American outlaw, the leader of
a band of bank and train robbers, as the result of a reward for his capture, dead
or alive, was shot and killed by two members of his own band, in his home,
April 3, 1882.
[2] John James Audubon (1785-1851).

liant blue sky with one great hot white cloud cumulus rolling over it, a flock of far-off birds and a group of figures in robes watching them. It tempts me very much. I hate Salvator's molasses pictures as a rule; we both went to scoff and remained, if not to pray, at least to respect and like. If you or Ned telegraph an offer of two hundred dollars for the Audubon I dare say the coon might come down, but I will take no responsibility. Were I a dealer I should grab both. Salvator is five hundred dollars; S. L. Barlow, who has not seen it, has telegraphed an offer which is rejected as too low. *Adiós*, affectionately yours

M. A.

1607 H STREET, WASHINGTON,
Sunday, May 21, 1882.

DEAR PATER: Thanks both for your letter and postcard. Your patience has been even more sorely tried in the matter of weather than ours. Your fierce east winds come to us, but so tempered that they hardly chill. Yesterday we got up to 78° and today is as warm with a gentle shower now and then to lay the dust for our ride this P.M. My first tea-rose opened today in the garden and now I hope a good crop will come along. Last June was so wet and cold and solitary at Beverly that we are not anxious to repeat it and shall hang on here until fairly roasted out. We get the wild country every P.M. and have society for rainy days; and the effort of pulling up stakes and getting a new household together is not tempting. Please ask William to be on the lookout for a nice man for us, not a surly, lazy American such as we had last year. If ours here were white we should send him on with the horses, but I fear trouble with Irish if we try to mix races.

Richardson is expected here tomorrow, but he is so uncertain that one never counts on him. Monday a small toot at our neighbours', the Bancroft Davises; I prattled mostly with diplomates who have not yet mastered the Anglo-Saxon idiotisms—more exhausting to me than hoeing potatoes. Friday another toot there for Mr. and Mrs. Nicholas Fish—he has got the Brussels mission—Miss Dulaney sang from time to time and it was informal and pleasant. Yesterday afternoon a kettledrum at General Sherman's—not exhilarating; escaped with the Outreys after a very short time. Henry did buy some Madeira after all; Outrey had sent it to John Cadwallader, who is considered the best taster in New York and, following the lead of Aristarchi Bey and Count Lewenhaupt, Henry got two and a half dozen averaging from two-seventy-five to four dollars. He says they are not, to his mind, nearly as good as your "Tartar." There were few bidders and little competition. Brewster has sold my village cart at last; sent me a cheque for one hundred and seven dollars, which, as they have dropped to one hundred dollars and he had to deduct for repairs and freight from here, was better than I had hoped. I shall leave my phaeton here; the cost and wear and tear of sending it on and back twice a year are more than it's worth, so shall try and find a light one in New York or else one like this at Kimball's again; it is very satisfactory. The victoria I left in Beverly Farms. Why don't you replace your beach-wagon this summer? It seemed hardly safe last year; a victoria would be charming for your pair and so easy to get in and out of.

Tomorrow we are going to have a small dinner of eight, the last effort in that line; Mr. and Mrs. Charlton (he has come back to the British Legation from London), Captain and Mrs. Story, Mrs. Craig Wadsworth, and Baron Schaeffer,[1] the new Austrian Minister, who has brought a letter to Henry—has been for some years Consul-General in Cairo, is a bachelor and speaks English.

We don't believe anything is coming out of the Shipherd investigation, so-called. The Committee—except Belmont—are in terror of any disclosures apparently and don't understand the drift of such testimony as they have got. We hear on very good authority that Morton-Bliss's five percent contract is sharply criticised among business men in New York. Randall used the cipher of the firm in cabling from Paris and the answers went to Morton, who very wisely denies all knowledge or part in the affair. No news from any quarter. Love to the Cambridge colony. *Adiós*, affectionately

M. A.

---

[1] Baron Ignaz von Schaeffer was the Austria-Hungarian Minister at Washington from 1882 to 1885.

1607 H STREET, WASHINGTON,
Sunday, May 28th, 1882.

DEAR PATER: This is a later date than my Sunday's letters have
borne before, but we should be foolish to leave this pleasant place
in such perfect weather. I wish I could send you a bunch of red
and tea roses which came from my garden today; they would delight your eyes and nose. The apple blossoms here dropped off
weeks ago and dogwood and azalea are nearly gone. We hope to
get the laurel, though, which is very fine here and which I have
never seen; the woods will soon be white with it. We ride or drive
daily, sometimes not getting home for dinner until eight. One
great advantage in coloured cooks and waiters is that they never
look black at any unpunctuality—a few shades browner one does
not notice.

Our final dinner went off pleasantly last Monday; as it was
cool and dull the effort was not great on either side. We are rein-
forced as to dinners by soft-shell crabs. Can't you get them at this
season? Shall I send you some alive? Tuesday Mrs. Lawrence and
Miss Chapman went home to Doylestown, and Mrs. Craig
Wadsworth and I drove down to say good-bye in the early morning
and then loaded up in the market with flowers and early vegeta-
bles. It's a pretty sight on market day. Yesterday we joined a
party to Mt. Vernon got up by Miss Frelinghuysen. The day was
perfect though rather too warm; the grounds looked charmingly,
and we had a long table under the elms; the men half American,
half diplomates. It takes more youth than I have to really enjoy a
picnic. I sat under a green tree and prattled gravely with a Mr.
Trenholm of Charleston, a friend and contemporary of Mr.
Lowndes and not unlike him in good breeding and intelligence.
Mr. and Mrs. Nick Fish were of the party; he is quiet and gentlemanly and his wife seemed to talk German and French glibly to the
foreigners. It is a very suitable appointment,—Brussels,—I fancy.

The newspapers keep on raging at Mr. Lowell, as you see. The
New York Herald declares that "Conkling would be an ideal appointment"; the Western politicians clamour for a Western man;
Williams, of Foreign Affairs Committee, says the "woods are full
of 'em"—i.e., men better fitted than Lowell for the place. One
would think that he would find the U.S. livery irksome and long to

be "lord of himself" again. I should strongly advise any man or woman who pines for office in or out of this country to move here and see the cloud to the silver lining. The great Holmeman, whose philosophy you reject, is justified here.

We have been basking in 84 degrees today with a mild shower now and then to cool the trees. Boojum is suffering with rheumatism and yells wildly every now and then and is terribly depressed. He had a sharp chill in the morning, so that I made him take a quinine pill at lunch, and he revived so that he danced off and killed a rat in the harness room. I shall give him quinine again at bed time, he is so sensitive to malaria. I saw in a New York paper today that Dr. John Brown[1] is dead, so that his pen will give us no more dog sketches. His life was so full of suffering and clouded with attacks of insanity that one cannot be sorry it is over. I used to hear of him in Scotland from friends of his.

As to the Hichborn claims of which you wrote, they probably belong to the same batch as those Mr. William Gray has been pressing here this winter. The Peter C. Brooks estate has heavy claims against the government; the bill is now before Congress, but they are so behindhand with their work that it's not likely anything will be done. Take good care of yourself; be as gay as you can. I shall get a few quiet days with you at 114 before long, I hope; Henry must look after his Quincy people—his mother needs him now. *Adiós*, affectionately

M. A.

1607 H Street, Washington,
Sunday, June 4th, 1882.

Dear Pater: Today belies the weather map of yesterday by which we should be in the lap of a big storm. It seems to me to be heading straight for Boston. It is cool and fresh and at four we go off for three hours in the saddle. Aristarchi Bey has just gone, having dropped in for a chat and stayed to lunch and talked American and European politics for two hours or more; showed me too how to burn a charming little perfume lamp which he sent me last

---

[1] John Brown (1810-1882), a Scottish physician, the author of *Rab and His Friends*, died on May 11.

week—I find it's Swedish and not Turkish, as I supposed. Henry had a chat with Mr. Trescot early this morning on the doorsteps. He will not, I fancy, quarrel with the State Department, which is the source of all his bread and butter, of which he has learned to know the value. Does not seem to think the South American countries desirable to live in. Wednesday, Lowndes dined quietly here; asked if you had received a note from him and I could not say if you had or not. Friday, the Moscow professor turned up with his note from Whitman and dined with us that same evening—only Mr. Hewitt to meet him. We found him most agreeable and intelligent. Mr. Hewitt asked us all three to dine with him yesterday. I gave out, as my Sinbad cold got a grip on me, but Henry went. Sunset Cox[1] and Manning[2] of Mississippi were all who could be got together. He left (Russian) for the South today frightened by our tales of the great heat in store for him. Yesterday Sandy Bliss had a picnic to Great Falls by canal-boat; we made herculean excuses and got off. To be at Georgetown at 8 A.M. and bake all day on the deck of a canal-boat may appeal to some brave spirits; we are of softer mould.

People are beginning to move now. Aristarchi goes tomorrow to Saratoga, etc., etc. In answer to my question of what he does there, he replies, "Madam, I go to 'ops and see the learned pig and the fat woman." The Lewenhaupts go to Pittsfield this week for the summer. But the political wretches must stay on for weeks—heat or no heat.

Our present plan is to leave here on the 15th, pass Friday in New York and go to Boston Saturday. Henry will have to go to Quincy and I shall be glad to settle on you for a few days. The dogs will be expressed to Boston and Henry can take Possum to Quincy if you will suffer Boojum over Sunday until I can take him out to join Possum at Quincy. The horses leave on Friday, 16th, for Norfolk and will be due by Monday or Tuesday following. Can they be boarded as of old at the Club stable? We shall send our groom to Norfolk with them to transfer them from one boat to another and would take him for the summer except that there

---

[1] Samuel Sullivan Cox (1824-1889), a member of Congress from New York City, 1875-1885.
[2] Van H. Manning (1839-1892).

would probably be a conflict with Irish servants. Shall be very glad if William has a good man for me; I hope he's nice-looking, too. Have written to Mrs. Chase and to an office, and in no case will allow a flood of applicants at your front door as last year. It is a great nuisance to change every year but in part, at least, inevitable.

I had hoped to hear from you that Mrs. Bell was coming to Beverly Farms, but I fear there's no such neighbour in store for us. Ned writes me that the Tweed-Evarts ménage is going, they will not add to us nor we to them, but at that distance nothing will be expected beyond one call. Shall I look for a surrey at Brewster's and report to you as to colour, lining, price etc.? I will with pleasure if you say so. As John Hay is ill in Cleveland, and King is in England, there is nothing to tempt us to linger in New York beyond one day. My roses are so lovely here that I can send them off daily for presents—I wish you were near by. I am glad you are going to have a yellow porch and house; the brighter the better. Good-bye, yours affectionately

M. A.

1607 H Street, Washington,
Sunday, June 11, 1882.

Dear Pater: Thanks for your last two postals. We have begun to break up and start on Thursday—dogs and horses waiting over till Monday, that the former may not be a bore to others, or not be on the road over Sunday. Our past week has been very comfortable. Tuesday, raw and cold even in the saddle, so had a gay fire to cheer our evening. Wednesday evening, to Miss Dulaney's rooms with three or four others for music and tea. Tomorrow, the same party at the Bancroft Davises', our next neighbours. Strolled up to the Bayards' last night; the young women go this week to Delaware to their great regret. Yesterday we ran up to 86° until a sudden wind dropped the mercury to 73° and our sunset drive was cool as one could wish, with a lively shower to come home in.

Congress drags on accomplishing little; if they manage to pass the needful appropriations bills we shall be glad. MacVeagh was here on Friday at noon and breakfasted with us; he was summoned to testify in the Star-route cases but dismissed under some pretext.

It is thought by people who know the wires that Dorsey and Brady are not anxious—their friends are well placed and to err is human.

Don't trouble yourself to meet me Saturday. I will drive at once to you only asking time for a bath before dinner—Henry goes that evening to Quincy. *Adiós* and *au revoir*, yours affectionately

M. A.

1607 H STREET, WASHINGTON,
June 13, TUESDAY.

DEAR PATER: We've decided to let our groom, whom we like very much, go on with horses and dogs by Norfolk steamer and keep him this summer if it works well. In engaging new kitchen ladies I can prepare their minds for a coloured brother as messmate.

Yours of Sunday came today. We have such perfect weather that it seems folly to leave it—cool and fresh and cloudless. Why shouldn't you and I invite ourselves to dine with Ellen on Sunday and so drive home in the gloaming instead of going back for dinner to town, which would seem so like winter? We have not got into early dinners here this season but linger late till our hour is British rather than American. It's a quarter to nine and we just finished and are bidden to carouse at Arabia Felix's.[1] We must go as we've not been very responsive to his hospitality. *Adiós*, affectionately

M. A.

---

[1] A nickname for Alexander—"Sandy"—Bliss; "Arabia is sandy and Felix is bliss."

CHAPTER III

WASHINGTON

OCTOBER 1882-MAY 1883

1607 H Street, Washington,
Sunday, October 29, 1882.

Dear Pater: Here we are again shaking into our old haunts, horses and dogs none the worse for a rough four days at sea; as for us, the few days in New York were full and pleasant. On Sunday we lunched with the Schurzes and dined with Mr. Godkin, a very bright and amusing dinner of eight. Mrs. Baldy Smith[1] we thought charming. Monday morning bought a pretty new victoria—a trifle higher and stouter than the Beverly one—and ordered a new gown which, if not a failure, ought to be tiptop. Took the three P.M. train to Philadelphia. Mr. MacVeagh waiting for us, got to Bryn Mawr for late dinner. They've a dairy farm of two hundred acres and send a hundred thousand quarts of milk to the city every year. The house is a roomy one of gray stone just rebuilt after being burned a year ago. Tuesday was a fine day and we drove about the country both morning and afternoon, the rest of the time sat over the fire and talked politics mainly.

Got here Wednesday P.M., found everything in order, fires and a nice dinner. Engaged two new women servants and have had to fill the man's place as he is ill. Am having a nerve killed with arsenic and so the past three days have been chequered, but after four months of nightly toothache all summer anything is a relief which ends it.

Mr. Lowndes was here Thursday evening and gave us a full account of his trip to the Yellowstone, begged me to say to you that he had seen nothing so charming as the drive from Beverly Farms to Gloucester. Miss Beale has been in to tea twice at twilight, en-

---

[1] Mrs. William Farrar Smith (Sarah Ward Lyon), daughter of Samuel Edward Lyon and Katherine Cooper Ward; wife of General William Farrar Smith, a graduate of West Point.

155

quires anxiously for "Billy." The city is very quiet, the country roads very lovely. I'm forbidden to ride today by dentist so must take the doggies to walk. Take care of yourself. Ever affectionately

M. A.

1607 H STREET, WASHINGTON,
Sunday, November 5, 1882.

DEAR PATER: I was glad to get your note on Thursday and find that you had only forgotten to write on Sunday and were not ill as I half feared. You must enjoy your Cambridge drives if you have such lovely weather as we have for the past week. Wednesday at 80° it was rather oppressive, but in the saddle towards sunset very pleasant. Riding and nerve killing have divided my time—and it is still dying.

Thursday evening Richardson and the Andersons passed here, the former gay as always. Friday we dined there quietly with only Mr. Frederick L. Olmsted[1] and Richardson. The Anderson house is a subject of much discussion and very opposite opinions are held about it; it is emphatically a gentleman's house and the lines are very fine; it is very stern and severe as a whole, but H. H. Richardson is satisfied and says windows and grading will give it all it now lacks.

Blaine and Robeson[2] have put up huge piles of brick. The Democrats in New Jersey are trying to defeat Robeson's reëlection by issuing photographs of his new house as an answer to his plea of having left the Navy Bureau a poor man. We hear no politics

---

[1] Frederick Law Olmsted (1822-1903), the landscape architect. During the Civil War he was secretary of the United States Sanitary Commission; as a landscape architect he first attracted public notice by his success in superintending the execution for the plan for Central Park, New York City, which he and Vaux had designed; thereafter he was engaged in most of the important works of a similar nature in America.

[2] The *Nation*, November 9, 1882: "The defeat of Mr. Robeson in New Jersey shows that he was wrong when he said that not only was he what he had been, but that what he was he was going to remain. What he was—a member of Congress—he ought never to have been, and is not going to remain. He will now go back to the position which he ought never to have left—that of an industrious country lawyer."

here as yet, the mangers are all away "fixing" things. Our German friend Dr. Bessels came in last evening; has been here all summer writing science; now finds excellent shooting—pheasants, wild turkeys, etc.—in Virginia in the early mornings, is going to bring to tea this P.M. an engineer, attaché of the German Legation, Langer, who he says is charming. There is to be a new German Minister in January—Eisendecker,[1] very nice we hear. Tonight Mr. Olmsted and Judge Gray are to dine here. Mr. and Mrs. Bancroft seem younger and better than last year—he still rides daily; popped in yesterday P.M. with a New York paper containing two columns of praise of Henry's *Randolph*.[2] The Virginians are very angry with it—not that they defend Randolph, but the picture of his surroundings is not pleasing, though true. The Canadians liked Francis Parkman till he criticised Canada, then they foamed and swore. Love to the folks, affectionately

MARIAN ADAMS

1607 H STREET, WASHINGTON,
Sunday, 10 A.M., November 12, 1882.

DEAR PATER: How has the tidal wave of Tuesday last[3] left you all? I shall go to Commencement next summer to see Charles Eliot

---

[1] Captain von Eisendecker was the German Minister at Washington from February 14, 1883, to June 11, 1884.

[2] "My John Randolph is just coming into the world. Do you know, a book to me always seems a part of myself, a kind of intellectual brat or segment, and I never bring one into the world without a sense of shame. They are naked, helpless and beggarly, yet the poor wretches must live forever and curse their father for their silent tomb. This particular brat is the first I ever detested. He is the only one I never wish to see again; but I know he will live to dance, in obituaries, over my cold grave. Don't read him, should you chance to meet him. Kick him gently, and let him go." (H. A. to J. H., October 4, 1882. *Letters*, p. 341)

[3] The *Nation*, November 9, 1882: "The elections on Tuesday resulted in a 'Democratic deluge.' As we go to press it is impossible to give the result in all the States, but the Democrats have undoubtedly carried New York, Pennsylvania, Massachusetts, Connecticut, Delaware, Arkansas, and Texas. Both parties claim the victory in Colorado and California, but the Legislature of the latter State is probably Republican.

"Gen. B. F. Butler has been elected Governor of Massachusetts by a majority of about 10,000. His Council and the Legislature are Republican."

kootoo to Ben Butler.[1]   Ask Ned if he remembers the proverb, "Say not, I will never drink of thy water, oh! fountain." Ben Butler, Leopold Morse, and Theodore Lyman![2] what a curious combination as the result of an earthquake. It's going to be tough work for the Administration to get through two and a half years more with no party to back them and a contemptible Cabinet. Of the Attorney-General one hears much scandal. The story which was disbelieved in September about his being very drunk at Chamberlain's restaurant and expressing his maudlin sympathy to a gang of the Star-route thieves is true. He is given to drinking sprees *à la* Grant. He has been turning out old officials from his department lately and made things so hot that it will not surprise some people if the President has to get rid of him.

The town is filling up by degrees. I had quite a frisky tea-drinking yesterday at five o'clock. People who come for one winter seem to end by buying or building; Mrs. William C. Rives has bought a house and the John Fields are talking of buying. Mr. Field has made two long calls on Friday and Saturday and at that friendly rate we shall get intimate. He reports James Russell Lowell as very happy, immensely popular with the Britons, dressed to perfection by Poole; Mrs. Lowell quite recovered from an attack which came on last May, absorbed in painting, for which she has developed a wonderful talent and to which she gives four hours a day. She has defied death and disease like a demi-goddess. I see that your good friend Mr. Sargent has gone. But the saddest death of all is Elsie Barlow—Mrs. Olin—last week, leaving a baby a week old and another not much more than a year. The blow will nearly kill her father and mother as they idolised her and she was their only daughter. You remember how handsome and gay she was and how superbly she sang. I must stop now as I am off to the dentist; nerve not dead yet. It's a slow process—can give no atten-

---

[1] Benjamin Franklin Butler (1818-1893), "an able but erratic administrator and soldier, and a brilliant lawyer. Many charges of corruption were made against him, apparently well substantiated." The custom of giving an honorary degree to the Governor of Massachusetts at Commencement was not followed in the case of Governor Butler in 1883.
[2] Leopold Morse, a successful retail merchant of Boston, was elected to Congress; so too was Theodore Lyman, an intimate friend of the Adamses.

tion to my ear till tooth is done, so they both say; meantime it roars like Boston. But I'm used to it. *Adiós*, affectionately

M. A.

1607 H STREET, WASHINGTON,
November 19, 1882.

DEAR PATER: My mind is as bare of news today as the trees over the way are of leaves. We hear no politics talked as yet; with those now in office it is not a pleasant subject. I see the papers are trying to start an Edmunds boom for 1884, which may force a good candidate from the Democrats as Edmunds would carry a strong independent vote and all the anti-Blaine men, Blaine being in Edmunds's estimation a leader among thieves. Wormley is overwhelmed with letters for rooms, could fill a whole block of houses if he had them. The "Blonde Widow" says the hotel is transformed—an indefatigable white housekeeper who keeps her underlings scrubbing all day and it is neat as wax.

The Commissioners are consulting as to letting out the "Flat" dredging and in a few years all the land from the White House to the river's edge will be a beautiful park. Even now you'd see great changes. Rents are going up and we were very lucky to get this nice old trap for twenty-four hundred dollars a year for six years; they'd not do it now. Brent has fitted up a room over the laundry with his own furniture and looks as smart as Cuffy—three windows with fresh lace curtains, a couch, stove, pictures, etc.—it saves him rent and is better for us. The indoor man and kitchen maid go home every night so I've only three women in the main house.

Miss Beale is almost a daily visitor; tells me she's had a letter from "Billy"—as she elegantly calls him—from China, is coming home next spring. Some superb old tapestry from Spain is offered for sale here by the butler of the British Minister who brought it from Madrid—I wrote Richardson about it; since then have seen another piece of it even better than the first. It's absolutely cheap being what it is. Tell Ned the Art Museum ought to get one of the nine pieces—measuring about eleven feet six inches by ten or eleven feet; one thousand dollars. In London it would be bought at once, here no one sees it and few care for it.

Have heard from Miss Martin, who was with the Barlows; Mrs. Olin was beyond all danger, as they believed, when suddenly was struck with paralysis—speechless for five days, though conscious until almost the end. The doctors did not give up hope till the last day. Has Betsy come back? When she does I want my brown Chinese silk. *Adiós*

M. A.

1607 H STREET, WASHINGTON,
Sunday, November 26, 1882.

DEAR PATER: It's a dull cold day and at this hour—one P.M.—a few flakes of snow are trying to fall, as yet in a most amateur fashion it must be said, but enough to prevent our giving the dogs their Sunday drive.

"All quiet along the Potomac" except that the President has exploded a local bombshell by turning out some four or five improper officials,[1] one of the gang a personal friend of Garfield. I fancy the Attorney-General is frightened by the growing feeling against him, and indeed the Administration must unload fast if it doesn't want to sink out of sight.

Hudson, the editor of the *Capitol*, is to dine with us today, and Miss Beale, who wishes to be favourably noticed in future. Friday, we went to a pleasant dinner at the Lewenhaupts';[2] several new

---

[1] The *Nation*, November 30, 1882: "On Saturday afternoon much excitement was caused in Washington by the announcement that the President, after consultation with the Cabinet, had ordered the removal from office of C. E. Henry, Marshal of the District of Columbia; D. B. Angier, and M. M. Parker, Postmaster and Assistant-Postmaster, respectively, of the District of Columbia; M. D. Helm, foreman in the Government Printing Office, and in charge of the *Congressional Record*; and ex-Senator Spencer, Government Director of the Union Pacific Railroad, for obstructing in various ways the course of justice in the Star-route trials."

[2] There is a description of this dinner in a letter of Adams to Hay of November 26th: "We have been here a month and have seen no one. I have no gossip to tell you, for I am not now intimate with the powerful. In your ancient throne sits Johnny Davis, but I see him not, nor yet his wife. Miss Lucy is *my* friend, for she reads my books—my poor black-eyed Susan, J. Randolph—and she reads your books too, for the night before last when we were all dining at the Lewenhaupts'—The Sackville-Wests; Roustan; Dalla Valle the Eyetalian Charged; Willamov and his new sister Mme. Catalano, whose Italian dragoon-husband ran

people, Madame de Catalano, a young Russian—sister of Willamov, the Russian chargé here—she married an Italian cavalry
officer about four years ago, who has run away with another
woman and left her with three babies and no money, so her brother
has kindly set up a small home here for them and himself—she's
rather pretty and gay; Miss West and her father; Miss Lucy
Frelinghuysen; Miss Beale; the new French Minister, Roustan,
who was the author of the grand row in Tunis—he is about fifty,
not ill-looking, good manners and quiet, not monkeyish in appearance; Willamov; de Bildt; and a strange French youth, a lieutenant
of dragoons, son of the Duc de Fitz-James, a lineal descendant of
James II (Fee-jarm he is called);[1] has been sent away from Paris by
his pa. In Newport he was looked askance at, I hear, but as he's a
kinsman of the Countess Lewenhaupt, and the King of Sweden especially recommended him, they had to dine him. They had the
tact not to introduce him to us, and Miss Beale in answer to de
Bildt said sweetly, "Yes, by-and-by, not just yet, please." He's   a

---

away and left her with three children and *cent livres de rente* for poor Willamov
to take care of, which he is doing; De Bildt and a sous-lieutenant de hussars
named Feejam, which is some relation to Boojum, being legitimist French for
the Comte de FitzJames, as I am told, and much addicted to games of chance;
and besides these great people, Miss Beale, Miss Lucy Frelinghuysen and ourselves—amid this gay scene, I say, Miss Lucy remarked in a sweetly meditative
manner that she wondered you had not been credited with that much discussed
story *Democracy*, and I hastened to assure her that the newspapers had done you
honor, nor had you, I believe, thought it necessary, any more than my wife, to
deny it. As, at the same moment, my wife, unheard of me, was denying it at the
other end of the room under the Argus eyes of Lewenhaupt and West, I hope we
did all we could to maintain your reputation. By the bye, we are told that the
work is being translated into French. For the love of fun, send me a copy. It
must be droller than a Palais Royal vaudeville on the English. You seem to
think I am going to make myself ridiculous by denying its authorship, but, oh,
my poet of the people, I have printed volume after volume which no one would
read, and now if the public choose to advertise me by reading as mine Shake-
speare, Milton, Junius, Don Quixote and the *Arabian Nights*, shall I say them
nay? Not so, by Hercules!   I will let them give me Little Breeches, Castilian
Days and the Report of the 40th parallel rather than lose a single possible adver-
tisement for *Anglo-Saxon Law* and *New England Federalism*." (*Letters*, p. 342-
3)
[1] Jacques Gustave Sidoine de Fitz-James (1852-1919) was the son of Edouard
Antoine Sidonie duc de Fitz-James and Marguerite Augusta Marie, daughter of
Count Loewenhielm, the Swedish Ambassador in Paris.

handsome youth and perhaps you'll yet see him in Mrs. Jack's train.

Then Wednesday Perry Belmont turned up in search of winter quarters; he dined here twice—as he sat till a few minutes of seven of course he must dine as well as take tea. He gave us the latest New York gossip and seems to have been so encouraged by his political success as to be able to take a human interest in other people. He had given Mrs. Langtry a supper, had driven her and dined with her at Hurlburt's with Mr. Evarts and old Sam Ward! But, alas, Mrs. Paran Stevens won't call on her and Mrs. Langtry says Mrs. Stevens is only a cook, and Lady Mandeville—late Irenne McGillicuddy[1] and one of the swiftest of all the swift American women in the Marlborough House set—won't call on her either, and that settles her fate in New York socially, and really she's a bad lot and it's a wise decision. Mr. West was somewhat chaffed at Friday's dinner as to the attention the Legation will show her when she comes here and he took it seriously and con-fessed that he was in a difficult position, as she has brought him letters from a "near relation"—that must mean his sister-in-law, Mrs. Cornwallis West,[2] who is very pretty and very rapid. She went to stay at the Legation in Madrid just before we were in Spain and they told us he had to send her home. Among other enormities she frisked off to Toledo in a green gown and tried to flirt with the Archbishop, who probably was enchanted, but the Spanish ladies were not. If Lord Dufferin[3] were here he could snap his fingers and do as he chose, but this man is not very firm in his saddle and his poor little daughter can take no initiative. She passed a week last summer at the Glades with Fanny Sturgis and seems to have found my nephew George and blind-man's "duff," as she calls it, more amusing than any experience she has ever had. Little Polly is

---

[1] *Tender Recollections of Irene Macgillicudy*, a novel by Laurence Oliphant, published anonymously in New York in 1878. It is about a New York society girl in London society.

[2] Major William Cornwallis Cornwallis-West (1835-1917), a second cousin of Sir Lionel Sackville-West, married, October 3, 1872, Mary, eldest daughter of the Reverend Frederick FitzPatrick.

[3] Sir Frederick Temple Hamilton Temple Blackwood, Marquis of Dufferin and Ava (1826-1902), then the British Ambassador at Constantinople.

far more suited than she to be at the head of a big legation in this maelstrom.

By the way, the only letter in Harry James's "Point of View" in the last *Century* that can hit me is that of Hon. Marcellus Cockrell. Some of the remarks—as that about "Hares and Rabbits Bill and Deceased Wife's Sister"—I plead guilty to, but that it should be spotted as "one of mine" I can't imagine. The whole article seems to me, with one or two exceptions, a dilution of his "Bundle of Letters" of 1879. The suggestion that "an aristocracy is bad manners organised" is very good. To my surprise Count Lewenhaupt had picked that out to chuckle over; said he, "I told it to de Bildt and he could not understand it." Perhaps Fee-Jarm wouldn't either, as he's a vicomte. The new dinner dress you have given me is very fine, I couldn't have done better at Worth's. Did Betsy show you the patterns I sent her? Nerve dead, tooth finished; shall begin tinkering Eustachian tube this week. This drivel will weary and disgust you—never mind. Yours affectionately

M. A.

1607 H STREET, WASHINGTON,
Sunday, December 3rd, 1882.

DEAR PATER: It's a cold, windy, brilliant day following a week of cold raw weather—except yesterday, which was Indian summer. As to public news, there is none. As our lawmakers meet tomorrow I suppose they'll start some news soon. Tuesday went across the street in a snow-squall to a mild musical party at Mrs. Beale's; as not more than one person in ten will listen on those occasions I think they are always a failure, like Sidney Smith's brandy and water. Wednesday Count Lippe stayed so late at tea that I had to ask him to stay and dine to help us eat some quails he had sent me as the result of three days' shooting in Virginia. He sat late over the fire and gave a most entertaining and interesting description of the small German principality of which his cousin is the reigning prince, with a little army and a little court and a little miniature parliament—Lippe-Detmold, where Varus lost his legions. This man lives in Austria and comes as diplomate from there, he is not an *esprit fort*, but well-mannered and full of small talk.

Yesterday for my sins I had to go to a feminine lunch, a style of killing time which I detest, but as Miss Frelinghuysen made it a personal favour I had to accept gracefully. She said, "Come, if it's only to show that you don't despise us after the elections." There was the usual mild gabble, but I was amused when a lady on my left rehearsed to me the charms of a California woman with a big fortune and cream-coloured ponies who is cutting a dash here, and who, she said, had her head perhaps a little turned in London by the devotion of the Duke of Abercorn[1] and Mr. Gladstone.[2] I turned to Miss Frelinghuysen and said, "Do you know this charming Mrs. So & So?"   "Oh, yes," frankly rejoined our Miss Frelinghuysen, "I know every crank in Washington!" Upon which my left-hand neighbour became pensive. I see by today's *Tribune* that Sir Coutts and Lady Lindsay of Balcarres have separated. It will be a great blow to one set in London, as their Sunday teas were very entertaining. Lady Lindsay is very plain, very dowdy, and has no manners—was of a rich Jew family, a friend of Henry James; neither she nor her husband is young—he is near sixty and I fancy not at all fast. No reasons have yet been given by Smalley, who mysteriously hinted at it in last Sunday's letter.

The S.'s are here and being lunched and dined vigorously. I am sorry to find them both very antipathetic—to me, that is—there is a jaunty *ci-devant* young-man-of-fashion air about him which riles my sweet temper. She is a silly, stout bore. They rave about Aunt Tappan and the "depth and freshness of her mind." As I've not seen her for seven years and a half, my impressions are dim; she must be more amiable and patient than I remember her, to have housed and fed Mr. and Mrs. S. for two mortal weeks. This coming week we are in for two dinner parties given to them, on Wednesday Mrs. Bancroft, on Saturday the George B. Lorings! Will Aunt Eunice ever speak to me again if you tell her we are to dine with Dr. Loring? Neither Henry nor I ever spoke to him, but I called on his new wife last week; she's quite pleasing and we met so often that it has grown to be awkward not to call.

Dr. Bessels tells me both the Smithsonian and Major Powell are going to publish extracts from the twenty pages of Grandfather

---

[1] James Hamilton, Duke of Abercorn (1811-1885).
[2] William Ewart Gladstone (1809-1898).

Sturgis's journal you sent me—part relating to the vocabulary and part to the value of fur trade. He has returned the original to me. When you want a mild but readable book try George Sand's *Histoire de Ma Vie*—lots of volumes but very quick reading. *Adiós*

M. A.

I'm glad you like Henry's *Randolph*; the *Burr*[1] is much better; he'll publish that next spring on his own hook. Dr. Loring is tinkering me, drum of ear sagged in, blows it out, a horrid process. I expect to be very deaf by AND by.

1607 H STREET, WASHINGTON,
Sunday, December 10, 1882.

DEAR PATER: The past week has been a very dissipated one for such tame cats as we are. Monday a dinner at British Legation, small one of ten—Lewenhaupts, Emerys, Miss Frelinghuysen, Charlton and Saurin,[2] British secretaries, Heredia, a new Spanish secretary.[3] Mr. West too me in; his conversation is as brilliant as Asa Larcom's and somewhat similar. After dinner, representatives of all the nations of the earth filed in—Ministers from France, Austria, Belgium, etc., little secretaries with handles and spouts to their names. These guileless youths whose family trees were green in the carboniferous period remind me of T. G. Appleton's cook when he showed her his three-thousand-year-old pottery. "Lor, sir! What improvements we have made since that day." Not that their manners have suffered, for I think as a rule they are better, but their brains are attenuated to a startling degree. Said one foreigner to us the other day, "Count Lippe is a howling idiot. It took me six months to find out what an idiot he is." We, on the contrary, find the accused more intelligent than the accuser.

---

[1] There are several references to the "Aaron Burr"—which was never printed. The manuscript was probably destroyed. In the published letters of Henry Adams, October 8, 1882, writing to Hay, he said: "Houghton declines to print Aaron Burr because Aaron wasn't a 'statesman.' Not bad for a damned bookseller! He should live a while at Washington and know our *real* statesmen. I am glad to get out of Houghton's hands, for I want to try Harper or Appleton."
[2] Dudley E. Saurin, Secretary of the British Legation.
[3] Don Emilio Heredia y Livermore, Second Secretary of the Spanish Legation.

Tuesday Mr. Hewitt and Saurin, the new British Secretary, dined here and we shied a musical party at the Beales'. Wednesday a Belshazzar of twenty-two at the Bancrofts'; Senator Pendleton took me in, Secretary of State on my left; it was very long, very warm. I was so faint for the last three courses I could hardly sit it out. I prefer the dinner of yarbs "where love and wit are" to stalled filet and terrapin. Thursday we invited to dine a Mr. Forbes-Robertson who brought a letter of introduction from London. He wrote to regret that he was previously engaged and we were amused to find later in the evening at a little party at the Frelinghuysens' that he is an actor in Modjeska's company and so of course was engaged. The party was given—tell Ellen—to the brother and daughters of the Ardtonish and Edinburgh Sellars, who came here for two days. Friday a dinner of ten at Mrs. John Davis's—the latter Assistant Secretary of State. Yesterday a dinner of fourteen at G. B. Loring's; sat between a mild and dull New Yorker named Jay and the Secretary of State. At last in desperation I spoke across the table to General Sherman and he became very lively over his "march to the sea" and repeated it with knives and forks on the tablecloth. Finally he swept the rebel army off the table with a pudding knife, much to the amusement of his audience.

I've just cut from a New York paper the sad account of a suit being tried in the Supreme Court of that State, brought against one Cynthia Shillaber for swindling in a sale of mining stocks. She took twenty-five thousand dollars and refused to give up the stock. Mr. S. ought to defend her. *Adiós*

M. A.

1607 H Street, Washington,
Sunday, December 17th, 1882.

Dear Pater: A postal card would suffice for last week's record but I'm afraid you'd not think it suited to the day. Monday, we shone by our absence at a reception at Senator Pendleton's. Tuesday, we denied ourselves a party at the Beales'. Wednesday, we had a small dinner here: Mr. and Mrs. Larz Anderson and a sister-in-law, Madame de Catalano, Mr. de Williamov, Miss Bayard, Judge Gray, and General Cook—Mr. and Mrs. Jack Gardner, Miss

Howe, and Perry Belmont after dinner. As the Bostonians only came that P.M. and reported for duty at once, I could only ask them to come back after dinner. Mrs. Gardner has been laid up ever since with a swollen face, and so her visit is a sad failure. Miss Howe, whom I never met before, disappoints me much. Her face is handsome, but her intense self-consciousness and hard shrill voice destroy all charm, to my fancy. Thursday, Sandy Bliss had a large party for the Storys; I made Henry take my regrets—hot rooms and crowds always take so much more from one than they give, and I can't cut it down to fifteen minutes, as a man can. Friday, Mr. Lowndes dined quietly with us. He lost his eldest sister a few weeks ago and is not going out at present. Tonight, Mr. Belmont is to bring Herbert of Alabama[1] to dinner—an M.C. Last Sunday he brought Mills of Texas,[2] who was very pleasant, intelligent and amusing.

You will have seen that the French Spoliation Claims got through the Senate Friday without any great struggle. I read the debate in the *Congressional Record*; John Sherman stoutly opposed it, and Bayard as warmly defended it. Of course it may be killed yet in the House or, even if it gets by that, lie over indefinitely in the Court of Claims. Civil Service reform is as fashionable as a "Langtry bang." I fancy Senator Brown of Georgia[3] was only a little more outspoken than his colleagues in saying on Thursday, "It's all a humbug," and maintaining that each party as it came to power must take the spoils."[4]

Long ride Thursday—roads soft and good; yesterday was too cold and windy, though Henry braved it. I'm sorry to see that Dr. Green[5] is beaten; the Democratic tidal wave seems to reflect little credit on Massachusetts brains. You gave me two years ago from a cigarette box a card portrait of Mrs. Cornwallis West, and on Friday I just missed leaving it at British Minister's by mistake for Henry's card, it having by some chance got into an old card-case— his rapid sister-in-law. His red-liveried flunkey would have sold

---

[1] Hilary A. Herbert (1834-1919).
[2] Roger Q. Mills (1832-1911).
[3] Joseph E. Brown (1821-1894).
[4] The Pendleton Civil Service Bill was being debated in the Senate.
[5] Dr. Samuel A. Green, candidate for Mayor of Boston, was defeated.

the joke to a reporter in half an hour. I shudder at my narrow escape! *Adiós*, affectionately

M. A.

1607 H STREET, WASHINGTON,
Sunday, December 24, 1882.

DEAR PATER: I can send you nothing better than many wishes for a pleasant Christmas and a happy New Year. Today is like a charming October one and yesterday even better. We rode for two hours before breakfast over soft roads into which frost has not yet gone and through an atmosphere like liquid sapphire. In the P.M. I had out the beasties again in the victoria you've just given me; it rolls over these superb pavements like a billiard ball on a smooth table. Brent is as smart as "Cuffy." He was deeply depressed at my refusing to let him have shiny nickel buttons on his livery, but rallied slightly at the hope of a large diplomatic cockade on his hat. When that too was denied, he evidently made up his mind that I had no ideas as to style or true self-respect. He has euchred me as far as he dared, though, by sticking a black velvet band round his hat; not for worlds would I sadden him by telling him it's quite out of fashion in Newport or New York.

Charley and George Adams came at dusk yesterday, having written to offer themselves for their vacation. They have outgrown the resources of Quincy and are anxious to see the world. George says, "Ma likes us to come to Washington, she hopes it may *widen* our minds." They've just gone home with Miss Frelinghuysen to call on a friend of Charley's who is staying there; if they chance on Alan Arthur I've no doubt they'll get the run of the White House in a day or two. They are going to the British Legation at one to call on Miss West, with whom they struck up an intimacy at The Glades last summer, and I advised them to accept if they were asked to lunch. Two lively little women are coming in to dine tonight and it will have to do as a Christmas dinner, for as we didn't expect them till Wednesday we let it slide.

Tuesday last we had a pleasant evening at the Beales' over the way. Friday a dinner party at Senator Don Cameron's and reception there in the evening. The house is new and large and handsome—well suited for entertaining. The big oak hall with a blazing wood fire and full of sofas and low chairs looked charmingly. Our host's downfall in Pennsylvania in November[1] has sobered him if not saddened—a "dethroned boss" is an object of pity rather than criticism. Sunday last Perry Belmont brought Herbert of Alabama to dine—a shrewd, uncultivated man of fifty, an ex-rebel colonel. He helped himself with difficulty to the dishes passed and apologized for his disabled arm—his "rebel arm," he called it. Tuesday Mr. Hudson dined here. Wednesday Mr. Hewitt, and so, though we give few real feasts, we generally have the latch up from five o'clock till bed time and we learn more out of books than in.

I'm glad you're reading *Histoire de Ma Vie*, it's pleasant to be enjoying the same book. I'm in the fifteenth volume and think the interest increases; the convent life is wonderfully described. Oswald Charlton, British Secretary of Legation, took me in to dinner on Friday at the Camerons'; he belongs to a Catholic family in Northumberland, says his mother was at the convent in Paris with George Sand. He told me an anecdote worthy of Pepys. In London a year or two ago he went to a drawing-room at Buckingham Palace, wishing to see his wife, who was to be presented, but the Master of Ceremonies refused him admission, saying, "Her Majesty only receives gentlemen without trousers." Aristarchi Bey has at last come back from New York and is full of news and society gossip. He describes New York society as equally torn by Langtry scandal and Mrs. Tom Cushing's last ball dress, which he described to me in detail—an orange velvet waist, untrimmed, a white silk skirt with black lace!

Why don't you come on here with Mr. Sidney Bartlett? He is good company and his son will see that you are cared for. It's dull socially in dogwood time; you shall have a stout meal at eight-thirty and a south room with a good fire all day. *Do. Adiós*, affectionately

M. A.

---

[1] At the November elections, Patterson, a Democrat, was elected Governor of Pennsylvania by a plurality of 40,202 over Beaver, regular Republican, and Stewart, independent Republican. The latter polled 43,743 votes. The Democrats also obtained a majority of eleven in the Legislature on joint ballot.

1607 H STREET,
December 27.

DEAR PATER: Many thanks for what Mr. James would have called your "potential" Christmas present. Having potted away the July present in a smart victoria, double harness, and five new dresses, you encore me! I've no doubt even Jay Gould would enjoy a five-hundred-dollar cheque for monkeys, and if I put this into terrapin and oak logs, it will none the less be amusing. I had a bad head-ache all Christmas day and so put off thanking you. Miss Frelinghuysen sent me a present, and Agatha Schurz a lovely high-art sofa cushion, and Aristarchi Bey a silver hand-bell, so that I didn't feel as old as I am. We had a pleasant party at the Beales' last night again; George, my nephew, had a "bully time" and vows Miss Beale "an honour to her family and Aristarchi Bey a daisy!" Tomorrow both boys are invited to a theatre party and supper after it, which they think very fine. We are in the fifth day of superb weather; roads soft and hard and only man is vile. *Adiós*, affectionately

M. A.

1607 H STREET, WASHINGTON,
Sunday, December 31st, 1882.

DEAR PATER: I wrote you Thursday to thank you for your most amusing Christmas present. Today my morning has gone between a visit to my aurist which has produced much discomfort temporarily and a visit from a cousin of the Frelinghuysens, a Mrs. Van Rensselaer,[1] who came for two hours to see our water colours and drawings. She is the art critic of the *New York World* newspaper, a young woman, and intelligent. She seems to have found Seymour Haden very conceited. We've had a superb run of weather lately, making riding a daily joy. The boys are still here and mean to stay till Tuesday, so I suppose they like it. The Andersons invited them to a theatre party Thursday and Henry took George to a reception Friday. Today, Miss Martin and Mr. Lowndes dine here, and at about ten we go to a little supper at Mr. de Willamov's—Bayards, Lewenhaupts, French Minister, and Andersons—to eat the old year

---

[1] Mrs. Schuyler Van Rensselaer (Marianna Griswold—1851-1934).

out. Tomorrow a dinner party at the Bancroft Davises'—shall send our young fry to the theatre.

Tell Ellen that in a letter just received from Mr. Gaskell, he announces the death of Frank Doyle—Sir Francis's eldest son—a brave young officer just home from Egypt. Typhoid fever carried him off. I think she and Whitman met him at Thornes. How are you getting on with George Sand? To me it grows more and more interesting; volume eighteen is charming and I'm sorry it ends with volume twenty. She must have jostled you daily in the Latin Quarter in 1832 in men's clothes, dining in cheap restaurants. Her account of Marie Dorval, the actress, seems to me a marvelous bit of character painting. Saw Mabel Bayard two or three days ago looking very fragile and sweet. I pity her as much as Ellen does, but it all depends on her temperament; she may be cheerful, though she doesn't seem to me so; has lived in a gay Bohemian household and I fancy has no training at all. She's a *tabula rasa* for Boston "kulchow" to bite into like an etching plate. *Adiós*, affectionately

M. A.

1607 H STREET, WASHINGTON,
Sunday, January 7, 1883.

DEAR PATER: Our fine sunny autumn weather broke on Tuesday night and there is even a thin sheet of snow to prevent safe riding, but you got the cold snap, which we missed, luckily, and now the sun is struggling out again.

Sunday last, when our dinner guests went away at ten o'clock, we went to a New Year's Eve supper at the Russian Secretary Wilamov's, found Swedish, Turkish, French, and Brazilian Ministers,[1] Andersons, and Miss Katy Bayard dressed *à la marquise* with powdered hair and tinted cheeks—very pretty and very theatrical. As the house is very small we sat at a half-dozen little tables for oysters, quail, and punch. I thought Roustan looked out of spirits and fancy he was feeling anxious about Gambetta, who was his personal friend and protector. If his death has the effect of strengthening the Republic, as people here think, it may be less of

---

[1] Felippe Nopes Netto, the Brazilian Minister at Washington from October 1882 to August 1883.

a blow than it seems now.[1] We broke up at one o'clock after Madame Catalano had sung us some Russian songs.

Monday a long ride and a dinner at seven-thirty at the Bancroft Davises'—sent the boys to the theatre with Larz Anderson, a boy of Charley's age; Judge Gray, Mr. Lowndes, Aristarchi Bey, pretty Miss McLane, ugly Miss King, etc., at the dinner. Mr. Davis took me in and on my right I had Mr. John King—Ellen met him in Egypt; he's a great bore and his conversation consists of attenuated puns. He should have a free bed in Dr. Holmes's asylum. Tuesday, big crush at the Beales' for General and Mrs. Grant; we shone by our absence. Wednesday, had Senator Edmunds quietly; he is very much depressed since his young daughter's death. His wife and only remaining child—a dreary lifeless girl—have gone south to fight death on the same line. As he left the house, at ten, Mr. Hewitt came in and regaled us with a funny scene they had had that day in the House. When I went to bed I calculated that, from five to eleven, there had been no let-up except for ten minutes, as the last tea visitor left only at ten minutes before seven. It's amusing, and happens not infrequently, and as we don't like hot parties, it's a good way of keeping the electric current unbroken.

Thursday, a very pleasant and not crowded reception at Secretary of State's. I was talking to de Struve, the Russian Minister, who came back this week only, when up came Kasson of Iowa and remarked with a good deal of temper, "Well, we've passed your *Boston* bill."[2] Never dreaming that the Pendleton bill had got through in one day, I laughed and made some flattering allusion to the wings which were sprouting on Congressional shoulders since November elections. It was not till the next morning that we found Kasson had been routed, horse, foot, and dragoons, and he and his bill, on which he doubtless had visions of floating into the White House in 1884, were as dead as Moses and his bulrushes. No one shares Kasson's belief in himself, and that he warmly supports a

[1] The *Nation*, January 3, 1883: "Léon Gambetta (1838-1882), the foremost of French statesmen, died at Ville d'Avray, near Paris, on Sunday night (December 31), after great suffering. The indirect cause of his death was a wound caused by a shot from a revolver fired, it is said, by his mistress (November 27, 1882)."
[2] The *Nation*, January 11, 1883: "The House of Representatives passed the Pendleton Civil-Service Reform Bill on Thursday, without amendment, by a vote of 144 to 47."

measure tends to bring suspicion on it. Congress is like a pack of whipped boys this winter, and each side sneers and laughs at the other. Friday, cut the Cameron reception; last night, the Agricultural Loring's[1] ditto.

In a pitiless rain, on icy sidewalks, Dr. Bessels popped in to tea and so, to save him a lonely restaurant dinner, we asked him to share ours. He told me more or less about George Sand, whom he knew through his brother, who is married to a relative of Alfred de Musset. He dined with George Sand and Dumas the younger in Paris in 1867 and then passed two days at her château at Nohant—the only other guests, two of her nieces; says it is a charming country house, the dining room opened with folding doors on to a terrace, where Chopin dragged his piano and played to the stars; the Chopin piano still stood there. Dr. Bessels says Madame Sand looked like a sheep, had no conversation, scarcely talked at all, but watched others—like the Tappan babes, as I remember them. Maybe Mary is a novelist *en herbe*.

Tell Polly we had a scare about Marquis last night; towards midnight when we moved to bed only Boojum and Possum could be raised. We called and whistled in vain for Marquis, so decided he must have slipped out the front door early in the evening; of course he was lost forever! Henry went back into the library with his candle for something, when he saw a basket chair and green cushion slowly moving toward him in utter silence; then we remembered that some hours before we had stuffed him under it as a punishment for barking. We shall add to his name Marquis, Casabianca. *Adiós*, affectionately

M. A.

1607 H Street, Washington,
Sunday, January 14, 1883.

Dear Pater: A warm sun in a blue sky is doing its best to clear the streets of snow and I hope in a few days we shall get on to our horses again. The past week has been a gay one for those that go with the stream; as we mostly sit on the bank and only now and then dip our toes in, I can tell you but little of the current.

---

[1] Dr. George B. Loring (1817-1891) was the Commissioner of Agriculture.

Monday, went to a reception at Senator Pendleton's. It was very pleasant, many pretty women and some good singing; Mr. Seymour Haden[1] was introduced to me. The next morning Mr. Field brought him in to see the drawings and water colours, which seemed to delight him. He could at sight put the name to every drawing and knew the collector's initials and all. He said that in forty years he had not found more than ten persons to appreciate or enjoy his collection of drawings. At one o'clock we breakfasted with him at the Fields', the sixth at the table being Miss Clymer; it was not very gay. He did his best, but the hostess, though kind and amiable, is not very interesting and there was nothing to call him out. He came in to tea in a driving snowstorm and seemed to enjoy toasting his feet at the fire, and so after everyone else had gone we asked him to stay and dine without going to his hotel to dress, and then we really saw him at his level best. He seems to be an oculist and surgeon, and had many stories to tell of men and manners gathered from a busy life in London of sixty-four years. Henry and I have found that the very pleasantest Englishmen are those in the "upper middle class," as they call it, whose brains and opinions are not entailed. The "stupidity" of his countrymen weighs on Mr. Haden and he is enchanted with a country which is not hampered by "tradition." My friend Miss Anne Palmer delighted him so much in crossing the ocean in November that he vows he cannot and will not lecture in New York if she is to be here that first week of February. He declares that she is his "inspiration" and the rest of the audience are of no account to him. And finally I yielded to his remonstrances and prayers and put her visit a week earlier. She and Mr. Godkin are to come on the 27th. She wrote me in November that she had found this gentleman pleasant and, as she is very *anti*-British usually, any approval from her goes a long way. She is young still, not over twenty-five, and has a vein of humour which I think will go to Mr. Godkin's heart; I don't think they have ever met and they are not in the same "set," which in New York and Boston means a good deal.

---

[1] Sir Francis Seymour Haden (1818-1910), an English surgeon and etcher, founder of the Royal Society of Painter-Etchers and Engravers, of which he was president until 1880.

I am told in confidence by a friend of the Warren family that Mrs. Warren is immensely elated at the Bayard connection.

Wednesday, Miss Schurz came for a week's visit and goes from here to Judge Aldis's;[1] invited Jenny Hooper[2] and two young men to dine that evening. Thursday, was the Cameron-Rodgers wedding—an evening reception.[3] I gave out but made Henry go, and at ten he took Miss Schurz and Jenny on to the Frelinghuysens' and saw that the latter had a good time and plenty of men introduced. She is with a large party of six at Wormley's and her chaperon, Mrs. Lee,[4] understands the business of running a campaign perfectly. I should think the change would amuse Jenny much. I should offer to take her to a party tomorrow, but I've had to give up the last three nights as Dr. Loring is very anxious that I shall not catch a cold just now—told me yesterday my drums were looking better, getting some colour and less like mother-of-pearl, and the shrieking is better. I'm not going more than once a week to him if the improvement lasts. Miss Schurz takes care of herself; had a dinner given her on Friday; backed out from a party to which I had got her an invite that evening; Henry took her to one last night. Tonight, Senator Edmunds is coming to dine quietly, and, as people are always popping in to tea at five, she is amused in a mild way all the time. When Lent sets in we shall have some small dinners; in this rush it doesn't pay.

Congress bumbles on. Everyone laughs at its assumed spasms of virtue, no one is deceived by any reform pretenses; the augurs laugh when they meet as of old and the public laughs still louder, but when public opinion bosses, in place of Blaine, Conkling, Cameron & Co., we're not likely to go off the track. Anyway, a broad-gauge road is better than a narrow one—goes further and carries more freight.

---

[1] Judge Asa O. Aldis, Commissioner on the part of the United States on the French and American Claims Commission, then in session in Washington.
[2] Jane Greene Hooper (b. 1857), daughter of Nathaniel Hooper, married Edward Gardiner Gardiner.
[3] Wedding of Virginia Cameron, daughter of Senator Cameron, and Lieutenant Alexander Rodgers, U.S.A.
[4] Mrs. Francis W. Lee.

Have read *Mr. Isaacs*[1] this week and like it—it's quite refreshing after the Ann Elizas, Henry James and Howells, etc.—the tiger hunt is very good. *Adiós*

M. A.

1607 H STREET, WASHINGTON,
Sunday, January 21, 1883.

DEAR PATER: A week of dull bad weather makes a bad dull letter, and now we are anxiously watching to see if the threatened cold wave is to break over us or carrom on to the Alleghenies and submerge New England. Friday, we tried the saddle, but the horses not being roughed we couldn't get out of a walk.

Miss Schurz left me Wednesday after a week's visit and went on to Judge Aldis's, but comes in to tea often. The MacVeaghs did not come; they are urgent that we should go over to Philadelphia, as they want to give us a dinner and show us some of their lights. I have asked them to let us wait till April, as a railway journey in winter always gives me a bad cold and Dr. Loring is very anxious that I shall not catch one; he sees improvement; but as far as shrieking goes, there is no special change. Patience is my only resource and I suppose a machine is bound to get rickety after running for thirty-nine years. I earnestly pray that its final fate may be that of the "one horse shay." If I had not been staying by the fireside o'evenings I could tell you much social gossip, as there are parties every evening and often two. I'm sorry not to be able to do more for Jenny, but I hear of her here and fancy she's amused. I've got her an invite to a dance at Mrs. Beale's on Tuesday given to a "sloper," Miss Crocker; if it's a bad night I shall make Henry enact Iphigenia. Last night he had to go to a man's dinner which he found as tough as he feared—one of his neighbours, William C. Reeves, whose ideas and opinions are not paraded to the vulgar. Boston is rampant here. Today the Lewis Stackpoles dine here and Major-General Ronald Mackensie, a gallant young soldier on furlough from Arizona and an old friend of ours. Tomorrow a little

---

[1] *Mr. Isaacs*, a novel by Francis Marion Crawford (1854-1909), appeared in 1882.

dinner for Miss McLane of Baltimore—have tucked in the Cabot Lodges.

There goes our chuckle-headed sovereign on his way from church! He doesn't look as if he fed only on spiritual food.

Tell Ned we shall be charmed to see him after February 5th, as next Saturday we have Miss Palmer and Mr. Godkin coming—shall have no extra room. Here comes the wave! It's hit the trees in the park; no riding today, I fear. *Adiós*, affectionately

M. A.

1607 H Street, Washington,
Sunday, January 28th, 1883.

Dear Pater: A warmish, muggy, foggy day. We missed your zero snap last week; still have no saddle weather. Society has raged all the week; two parties a night if we had cared to go. Sunday, Mr. and Mrs. Lewis Stackpole and General Mackensie dined here. Monday, the James Wadsworths, Cabot Lodges, Miss McLane, and Mr. Charlton. I had got invitations for Jenny and Alice Lee to a dance at the Beales', given to some California millionairesses; it was crowded and the heat intense. Miss Lee soon went home faint; I toughed it out till nearly eleven-thirty and then, as Jenny seemed to be enjoying herself, I put her under Mrs. Stackpole's care, but, as she still wanted more, she transferred herself to Mrs. W. W. Story. Mrs. Lee and her party seem to have found their stay at Wormley's enchanting. Mrs. Lee and Alice are like raging whirlwinds and create a movement wherever they go, I fancy. Friday, the British Legation had a dance for the Marquis of Lorne. We hadn't the energy to turn out even to see the Queen's son-in-law; those who went vow that it was very gay. Yesterday, Miss Palmer and Mr. Godkin came at tea time and found a smart hansom to bring them from the station—the Pennsylvania Railroad Company have instituted this reform for twenty-five cents, or seventy-five an hour. We had Aristarchi Bey and Perry Belmont to post them up, the former was most amusing.

(Here my guests' prattling became so amusing that I broke off.) Three-thirty P.M.—I made a call at Judge Aldis's before lunch; found General Walker, on coming home, who stayed to lunch—a vile meal which is inevitable on the Sabbath to give the cook church privileges. He seemed to have little to say except that his household had had five cases of measles this winter. Politically we hear little. The tariff debate is going on daily and it's believed that something will be changed; one article has been put on the free list which yielded twelve dollars and sixty-two cents to the government and the duty increased on another, which add dollars, five million three hundred and sixty-three thousand, so that the friends of infant industries do not murmur greatly. Must go to walk now before tea. Expect Ned Monday, February 4th, when Richardson is due at the Andersons'. *Adiós*, affectionately

M. A.

1607 H STREET, WASHINGTON,
Sunday, February 4th, 1883.

DEAR PATER: We've had a week of pleasant bright weather and two guests who were amused and amusing. Sunday Mr. Lowndes and Mr. Theodore Dwight dined here. Monday, General Walker; went on at ten to tea to Mrs. Pendleton's,—we four,—leaving Henry at home. Tuesday, couldn't induce my guests to go to Presidential reception so we chatted and drank Russian tea till midnight. Wednesday, took Miss Palmer a long drive in my phaeton—sun very warm. At dinner, Count Lewenhaupt and wife and Mr. and Mrs. Randolph Tucker of Virginia—John Randolph's great-nephew—we had some amusing talk and good stories. We had declined a dinner at Senator Pendleton's that evening and three parties. Thursday, sent Henry and Mr. Godkin to the Secretary of State's reception as Miss Palmer and I didn't care to go. Friday, had two parties on hand and were dressed, when a telegram came telling Miss Palmer her only brother was ill at Tunbridge Wells, England, and her mother would sail on the *Alaska* the next morning. As she idolizes the young brother, she thought she might sail with her mother. So in less than half an hour we got her out of her party dress into a travelling one, packed a huge trunk, and Henry took her to the station, got a section, and off she went half stunned with anxiety. She was very plucky and said nothing. Mr. Godkin tried to get ready to go but couldn't get packed in time. Yesterday morning at ten I got a telegram from her saying her mother and sister had sailed on *Alaska* without her as her father was very ill.

It's a cruel blow as her father and brother are the ones of all her family who are very dear to her. Godkin was charmed with her and we laughed more last week than for many a year.

Yesterday P.M., we took a three hours' ride, the turnpikes good as in June, frost out of the ground, though side lanes have still melted snow in them. Yesterday and today, too warm; a blizzard from Manitoba is promised for tonight! Am skimming a three-volume life of Bishop Wilberforce[1] Mr. Dwight sent over from State Department; it is a strange revelation to an outsider and does not increase one's reverence for established church—Aunt Eunice would find it very readable, I've no doubt. Do you remember one Morse of Louisiana, Class of 1829? His daughter came to tea one day last week—bright and attractive, clerk in the Department of Justice—I liked her. She told me Dr. Holmes was a friend and classmate of her father and wrote a charming tribute to him when he died. Telegram from Ned saying he'll get here tomorrow P.M. No politics here, only tariff discussion—quinine, sumac, cotton ties, etc. Miss Beale has gone to a hospital in New York fairly used up—*not* mentally! *Adiós*, affectionately

M. A.

1607 H STREET, WASHINGTON,
Sunday, February 11, 1883.

DEAR PATER: I'm trying to fold my paper like an Arab and silently steal away, Ned and Mr. and Mrs. MacVeagh being too full of chat to make a weekly bulletin intelligible. Ned and H. H. Richardson have been about enjoying themselves in a quiet fashion. Monday David Wells[2] to dine and Nordhoff to see Ned in the evening; about the other days I've forgotten—have a sleepy impression of many people coming and going. Friday Mr. Truxton Beale drove me out to his father's farm to see the famous Arabian stallion given to General Grant by the Sultan; the pedigree goes back to the time of Mahomet, and such a horse! If the Mahometans say "Blessed be Allah" when they see a handsome woman, they might include their horses. I fed him with corn from my hand, he munching it

---

[1] Samuel Wilberforce (1805-1873).
[2] David Ames Wells (1828-1898), an economist and at that time the leading authority on taxation.

lovingly from the ear, then rubbed his nose up and down with the cob, which charmed him.   Mr. Beale said, "He wouldn't let me treat him so."   Henry rode out in company with Lieutenant Emery and the youth Arthur, the heir apparent, a tall sprig of nineteen. We adjourned from the horses to a wood fire in the farmhouse and had milk punch and Russian tea.   Got home at five, and at seven-thirty to a dinner of fourteen at the Secretary of State's—sat between the host and Kasson of Iowa.   The dinner was given to the widow of Griswold Gray, a stylish, well-dressed New York woman, about forty, not handsome and very deaf, a good sensible honest face.   The flowers were charming, a bunch of tulips or lilies-of-the-valley, daffodils, or lilacs loosely tied with a satin ribbon beside each plate—for the women, that is.   Mine was a bunch of lilacs, still sweet.   Ned and Richardson were dined by Mr. Anderson at a restaurant to meet three or four men.   We had to decline a dinner that same evening at the Bayards'—to my regret—and last night one at Judge Aldis's.

The MacVeaghs sent word they'd like to come over yesterday to stay till Tuesday.   Last night we had General McCook and H. H. Richardson, today we are to have the latter, David Wells, and Senator Vance of North Carolina[1]—he is the man who said, twenty years ago, "We'll fight the North till Hell freezes over and then we'll fight 'em on the ice."   We've never met him, but David Wells wants us to, so he invited him in Henry's name; I think we may have a spicy dinner.

No public news that would interest you here.   A showing-up of the Signal Service lobbying which involves some friends of ours. Tariff is the subject most discussed except by *society*, which is interested in the Blaine, Brewster weddings.[2]   I enclose you a card I received from Mrs. Craik Mulock,[3] the authoress of *John Halifax*

---

[1] Zebulon Baird Vance (1830-1894), Senator from North Carolina.

[2] Miss Alice Blaine, daughter of James G. Blaine, married Colonel John J. Coppinger on February 6, 1883, and Miss Mary Brewster, daughter of the Attorney-General, was married on the evening of the same day to Robert J. W. Koons of Philadelphia.

[3] Dinah Maria Mulock (1826-1894), daughter of Thomas Mulock, married, in 1864, G. L. Craik, a partner in the house of Macmillan & Co.   The article "About Sisterhoods," by the author of *John Halifax, Gentleman*, in *Longman's Magazine* of January 1883, begins:--

and my once beloved *Agatha's Husband.* Seeing her article in *Longman's* a month since, I sent her that loose sheet and one other and gave her the name. Lamar made a great speech on free trade last week; it will be out in the *Record* tomorrow. I'm very sorry not to have heard it. I'm dog tired and sleepy and must take a nap before five P.M. With love, affectionately

M. A.

1607 H STREET, WASHINGTON,
Sunday, February 18, 1883.

DEAR PATER: *Qua* climate we might as well be in Bird Cage Walk again—a sunless, rainy week, though we have managed to get four good rides between showers. This morning a thin sheet of snow, but the wet earth has kicked it off by this noon time. No social items for you. Ned and the MacVeaghs left on Monday, and as we'd been dining people pretty steadily in a mild way we've enjoyed a few quiet evenings for reading and Greek—enough people come to tea to keep us in the current.

Thursday, to the Frelinghuysen reception, very pleasant, new German Minister introduced—Eisendecker—and his Pomeranian blonde bride, young and rather pleasing. Baron Schaeffer, the Austrian Minister, commenting here the other afternoon on the thin attendance at the last White House reception, said, "I made a bet with one of my colleagues that we would go through the large East room and not see one handsome or well-dressed woman, and I won my bet." And what astonished him most, he said, was that such a thing was possible in America. By the way, he told us that the librarian of one of the great libraries in Boston, wishing some public documents from Austria, wrote directly to the Emperor! And no notice was taken of it. As he says, "It is not likely the Emperor ever knew of it even, or I think he would have sent them." "The

---

"I slept, and dreamed that life was Beauty:
I woke, and found that life was Duty.
"This couplet—I know not whence it comes—was the favorite axiom of a dear old friend of mine, etc."

The couplet was from a verse written by Marian Adams's mother, Ellen Sturgis Hooper, who wrote many poems which were privately printed on loose sheets.

king, to carry on the joke, ordered ten pounds to be laid down."
One would think that a public librarian might know enough to apply to the American Minister in Vienna; that's what he's for.

This week Patti comes and we've taken seats with Mrs. Don Cameron for the whole week; we seldom get a chance here for any good music; barring the terror of fire and inevitable draughts, I expect to enjoy it. Had a nice letter from Adie a few days ago; I've written to urge her to make us a visit before plunging into Boston; I think among entire strangers she will feel less conscious. Her mother will set her back, I fear, she is such a rasp to Adie's nerves and conscience. Tell Ellen I'll subscribe to her "Annex" with pleasure, but it's no use to expect anything from "Washington nabobs," bless her innocent heart! No one here cares for higher education—for women or men either; they'd laugh in one's face. I wouldn't even hint at it. Yours affectionately

M. A.

1607 H STREET,
February 22.

DEAR PATER: We're having opera here this week—Albani[1] and Patti. Madame Albani Gye brings me a letter of introduction from Minister Lowell in London; her husband is Mr. Ernest Gye, an Englishman; Mr. Lowell says "I am sure you will thank me for bringing you acquainted with her." Today we gave her a little breakfast—Mrs. Bigelow Lawrence, Mrs. Cameron, Aristarchi Bey, and Mr. John Field. She is modest and simple and nice, and her husband quiet and gentlemanly. The gist of this all is that she sings in Boston next week and knows no one there; she's a lady and would enjoy a little social attention. Won't you call on her and if you feel social give her a lunch perhaps? Nanny Wharton will help you. I've written two notes—one to Mrs. Jack Gardner, the other to Mrs. Pratt—saying that if the spirit moves them I hope they'll call on her. Mrs. Lawrence is going to drum up Mrs. Winthrop. If you get Ellen and Whitman and Richardson and a few pleasant folks, she'd like it, I know. We do our share of social

---

[1] Dame Emma (Lajeunesse) Albani (1852-1930), a celebrated Canadian singer, esteemed for her character as well as her art, married in 1878 Ernest Gye, the operatic impresario.

work here and you may as well toil too. *Patti* is a cat in temper with a damaged reputation, and the distinction ought to be made. Affectionately

M. A.

You can easily find her hotel—I forgot to ask her.

1607 H STREET, WASHINGTON,
Sunday, February 25, 1883.

DEAR PATER: As I wrote you Thursday evening, this week just past has been all opera. Mrs. Cameron and we took seats together, and as her Senator is ill she provided a substitute—Monday her brother-in-law, General Miles. Tuesday Perry Belmont dined with us and went with us; late supper at de Bildt's, Swedish Secretary, about fifteen or so, mostly diplomats. Thursday had Albani to breakfast as I wrote you, and it went off nicely. Miss Palmer appeared at tea time just from New York with her hands full of flowers as usual; her brother out of danger, though the doctors told the boy he must die! She—taking a convalescing father to her sister's orange plantation in Florida—stayed to dinner and took my seat at opera with Henry; I to bed with headache.

Yesterday Patti in matinée as farewell. Of course I've caught a bad cold in consequence which Dr. Loring has been warning me would undo all the work he has been putting into my drums; however, that's inevitable. Life north of the tropics is synonymous for catarrh. Today lovely blue sky and soft air; lunch at one-thirty with Congressman James Wadsworth—wish it were saddle instead, but a *viva voce* invitation is not eludable. Great dog show here last week. Came on a box lined with rose-coloured muslin, five wee puppies in it, over it a large card, "These puppies sired by '*Marcus*,' owned by Professor Henry Adams of Boston"!! I've noticed that Brent always Romanizes *Marquis*; catalog has "Owned by Hon. Chas. Francis Adams; 3 for sale, price $35. each." Such is fame!

Telephone Bell[1] lives here; tells General Miles that he has lately found that one can speak by a ray of light instead of wire;

---

[1] Alexander Graham Bell (1847-1922), the inventor of the telephone.

has been making experiments from top of a large building here to Columbia College on a hill a few miles off; light is flashed from a reflector and the voice rides on the ray.

Hope you'll write me that you find Albani as pleasant and sympathetic as we did. *Adiós*, affectionately

M. A.

1607 H STREET, WASHINGTON,
Monday, March 5, 1883.

DEAR PATER: Yesterday I could not find time to write even a postal card to you, so this goes instead. Last week quiet; nursing a cold of evenings; a few good rides. On Friday, a dinner at Mrs. Lawrence's put off owing to death of a connection of hers. Saturday, Miss Randolph came to pass Sunday; we had a little dinner of ten for Lizzie Boott—her pa, Mr. Von Eisendecker (German Minister), and his little young new wife from Pomerania, Mr. Lowndes, Mrs. Jack Miller,[1] and Dr. Bessels. It was quite pleasant.   Eisendecker, who is about Henry's age, is intelligent and well-bred; his father's place in Pomerania adjoins Bismarck's country place and he is said to be an especial favourite of the Great Prince and to owe his frog-like jumps of fortune to him. His little blonde bride, who speaks English perfectly, is enchanted with her new gay life here, having seen nothing of the world up to this, living in a quiet German village owned by her father. I never fancied von Schlözer, who was here until this winter ever since we came; to me he showed only his noisy buffoon side, though Mrs. Lawrence found him "profound" and delightful! Dr. Bessels brought me a present which he will not hear of my refusing, *one* of two large silver spoons brought back by M'Clintock[2] from the frozen north, found in possession of some Esquimaux; it belonged to Sir John Franklin[3]—has his crest on it. The two were given some

---

[1] Mrs. John Miller (Kate Wise), a cousin of Mr. Adams.
[2] Sir Francis Leopold M'Clintock (1819-1907). He took part in all four expeditions in search of Sir John Franklin's ships, the last two of which he commanded, and the last of which was successful in 1859.
[3] Sir John Franklin (1786-1847) commanded an expedition for the discovery of the Northwest Passage, which sailed from Greenhithe on May 19, 1845, and his ships, the *Erebus* and the *Terror*, were last seen July 26 at the entrance to Lan-

years ago by Lady Franklin to Dr. Bessels; it's a valuable relic to hold. Eisendecker seemed charmed with our round table and even the *food*; Lizzie Boott heard him say to his wife across her, "Oh, Lily! *dass vir immer so essen könnten!*" which I duly repeated to Margery *pour encourager les autres* diners.

Yesterday breakfast at nine, then to see Forty-Seventh Congress die; they were not lovely or pleasant in life and were divided in death. General Francis Walker to lunch, folks to tea, Senator Lamar to dinner. He was charming, full of talk on politics, stories, etc., Miss Randolph delighted with him; he to Mississippi in a few days, she back to her school this A.M. before we were up. Hope to hear that your Albani dinner proved pleasant—you'll get this by Wednesday. *Adiós*, affectionately

M. A.

1607 H STREET, WASHINGTON,
Sunday, March 11th, 1883.

DEAR PATER: I will *take the day by the front hair*, as my Portuguese grammar says, as I was blocked last Sunday. A quiet week just passed; the only new acquaintance, Dr. Weir Mitchell[1] of Philadelphia, whom I've long wished to know. He was brought to tea, and was very bright and full of talk; sends me since his new book of poems with a note in which he advises me to thank him before reading it, as most of his friends have done. Mr. Schurz has been staying with us since Wednesday; he seems to enjoy the rest and quiet. When no one is by, I make him play, and he improvises on the piano and—a good talker—chats.

Saturday, we had a duty dinner here of ten: Mr. and Mrs. Sanford—en route from Florida to Brussels, in both places they have houses; she is a handsome woman, was a Miss du Puy of Philadelphia, is very large, and her emeralds and pearls nearly as large as she; she has a modest distrust of whatever voice and manner Nature may have given her, and is as affected as possible; Senator and Mrs. Pendleton, to whom we owed a dinner; Miss Lucy

---

caster Sound. The ships were ice-beset September 12, 1846, and abandoned April 22, 1848, according to records found by M'Clintock. Meanwhile Sir John had died, on June 11, 1847. Lady Franklin died in 1875.
[1] Dr. Silas Weir Mitchell (1829-1914), physician and author.

Frelinghuysen; Mr. Schurz; Miss Bristed;[1] and Mr. de Struve, the Russian Minister.[2] The French Minister was so ill that he gave out, so I got Miss Bristed to take his place, as I had one man too many. It was not the kind of dinner that Henry and I enjoy, but highly dignified and swell. The fresh shad and tomatoes alleviated it somewhat. Mr. de Struve (*er* pronounced) is son of one famous Russian astronomer and brother of another; he went last night to New York to meet the latter, who has come over to inspect a big lens Alvan Clark[3] is making for the Russian Government. As he is a gentleman, and very nice, and knows no one in Boston, we offered him letters, which he joyfully accepted—I gave him one to you and one to Alex Agassiz, and Henry one to President Eliot. Madame de Struve was here for a few months last spring with her five small chicks; she is nice and well-bred, of distinguished forbears. He goes out to bring her back in April, and is thinking of a house in Beverly for the summer; if you will drive him out to Ellen's for a cup of tea and show him Ellen and Lou and Polly, I've no doubt it would please him; and take him to the club or something kind. When they *do* send us a Russian gentleman we may as well be civil—we've had such riff-raff in that line.

Last night we dined with the Bonapartes, only ten, and very pleasant. The new house is large and handsome, intensely French; low entresol, then several rooms *en suite* on second floor. The host took me in, which was not etiquette I thought, and was very pleasant. Each lady had a palm-leaf fan by her place half covered with flowers—mine, red Jacqueminot roses and a wide crimson ribbon on the handle. Colonel Bonaparte shewed me some charming family miniatures after dinner; one by Isabey of Marie Louise, very young, all white lace and pink rose; one of Joséphine Beauharnais, young and lovely, with white flowers in her hair; one, elderly and scraggy, of her when Empress; one of the little Roi de Rome, fat and blonde. At ten-thirty, we all adjourned to George B. Loring's last Saturday reception. I've not succeeded in getting there before,

---

[1] Miss Cecile Bristed, a daughter of Charles Astor Bristed.

[2] Charles de Struve was Russian Minister at Washington from April 11, 1882, to October 27, 1892; he was a son of the German astronomer, Friedrich Georg Wilhelm Struve (1793-1864).

[3] Alvan Clark (1808-1887), a famous manufacturer of telescopes at Cambridge, Mass.

owing to sniffles and storms. Two nice rides, yesterday and Friday; caught in two showers yesterday—one a hail-storm—it rather improved my cold, acting as a counter-irritant.

Should you like to hear about one of last Christmas "monkeys" from you? A big, big turquoise found by Ned in Boston set in wee brilliants and four pearls; everyone thinks it enchanting who has seen it, it's like a summer sky. The other "monkeys" are coming from Russia in May, I hope, something we want very much—you'll see; Mr. Willamov is negotiating it. *Adiós*, affectionately

MARIAN ADAMS

WASHINGTON,
Sunday, March 18, 1883.

DEAR PATER: A lovely spring Sunday, which means a three-hour ride this P.M. We galloped to Bladensburg on Thursday, frogs singing gaily and maples hanging out spring tassels, the earliest shrub all out in Capitol grounds—sort of yellow star. I get a daily bunch of violets from my garden grown in a cold-bed.

Quiet week socially. On Tuesday, to a somewhat ghastly tea at ex-Secretary McCulloch's[1]—Calvinist divines sleek and smug with their wives, Indiana friends of the hostess, newspaper feminine correspondents whom I've been carefully dodging for six winters, going even so far as to leave their calls unreturned. After a brief struggle, on to Madame Catalano's—informal and gay—where we found old acquaintances. Roustan, the French Minister, poured into my ears the vials of his Gallic wrath, apropos of the late treaty with Madagascar; his French is not classic, no one here can understand more than a quarter of his speech, and as he boiled with wrath he was even more incoherent than ever. Ollendorf is so congenial with its familiar "Have you the coat of the tailor" or the "apricot of my sister?" Vainly I assured him that *we* thought the treaty quite worth of Offenbach and that fifty million Americans were not responsible for the vagaries of one respectable Presbyterian gentleman who happened to take it into his head to recognise

[1] Hugh McCulloch (1808-1895) was Comptroller of the Currency under Secretary Chase, whom he succeeded in 1865 as Secretary of the Treasury, which office he retained until the close of President Johnson's administration; from October 1884 until March 1885, he was again Secretary of the Treasury.

the Queen of Madagascar. Finally I remarked, "Monsieur Roustan, *il y a des fous dans tous le pays*," which profound remark acted as a brake. When I got home I bade Mr. Schurz good-night and good-bye as he was off early the next morning, but Henry quoted to him my conversation with Roustan, who he thought had reason to be angry. Next day came a long leader in the *N. Y. Evening Post* which seems to us calculated to infuriate the Minister still more and is certainly not written in very good taste. Now comes "Chapter III." Last night we went to a big dinner at Mrs. Bigelow Lawrence's; the Russian Minister took me in, Count Lewenhaupt on my left, Aristarchi Bey opposite; they—the last two—began on this editorial, which they suspected to be the outcome of that conversation, part of which Aristarchi had listened to, and they pretended that I had written it. I denounced it as in our opinion impertinent to the French Republic and quite unworthy of the paper, and I hope I made an impression, but anything like a diplomatic scrimmage is nuts to those whose particular ox is not gored and they feel far from sympathy with a republic whose foreign policy is as shadowed as that of France just now. Lewenhaupt says the article in the *Post* was at once translated in full into the French newspaper in New York, so that Roustan will not fail to see it.

Mr. de Struve has postponed his visit to Boston for a week or so, as his brother has not yet come; he is trying to master our lingo, asked me "What is hog? Is it not what beer is made from?" and yet was puzzled why in that case France and Germany should forbid our exporting it to them! Then later on I used the word "fiend," which he was astounded to find only the familiar "devil." As we left the table he said with an expression of intense satisfaction, "Well. I have learned something, *hog* and *fiend*," and was bewildered that we all laughed.

Have you read Josiah Quincy's *Figures of the Past?* If not, you'll find it very entertaining. Mrs. Bancroft denies vigorously that Cora Livingston[1] had any beauty—only charm of manner, she says. Mr. Bancroft told me Friday an amusing story of Daniel

---

[1] Josiah Quincy (1802-1882), in his *Figures of the Past*, describes meeting Miss Cora Livingston at a ball in Washington in 1826: "I was introduced to Miss Cora Livingston; and I must be able to paint the rose to describe a lady who undoubtedly is the greatest belle in the United States."

Webster going to Albany and calling on Mrs. Nat Thayer's mother—the "Patroon's"[1] wife—and asking one of her daughters in marriage whom he had never seen. The mother took the offer upstairs and brought it down again; Webster finally would only take "no" from the young woman in person. His idea was that it would give him a powerful political position in New York State.

Philip Schuyler is to dine with us quietly today, and Count Lippe-Weissenfeld. The Schuylers are kept at Wormley's by the desperate illness of young Miss Langdon, Mrs. Schuyler's second daughter—Mrs. George Chase's niece. Miss Marion Langdon is a perfect beauty and has been the belle of New York this winter; she won't come and dine, being in deep mourning for her grandmother; the young sister fell suddenly on the piazza in Arlington two weeks ago, struck with meningitis, and was given up for some days—a strong, gay, healthy girl who had never had a day's illness before!

Many thanks for your kindness to Albani. Ask Ellen if Ned has given her fifty dollars from me for her "Annex." *Adiós*, affectionately

M. A.

1607 H STREET, WASHINGTON,
Sunday, March 25, 1883.

DEAR PATER: Here comes Easter Sunday when the spirits rise of our good Catholic and Episcopalian friends. For forty days and nights they have rather "slowed up"—only opera, dinners, poker parties, and such penitential sacrifices. Friday, we had a little snow-squall, and cold windy weather for two or three days, checking flowers and leaves; today is turning out well. No social gossip. Sunday, Mr. Schuyler and Count Lippe dined here; the latter showed us a photograph of a dead man's face with a curious story to it. A few years ago, more or less, this same count Lippe was Secretary of Legation in Copenhagen and one night, while playing whist at the British Minister's there, his eye fell on a strange oil painting hanging on the wall. On enquiry he was told that the

---

[1] Stephen Van Rensselaer (1765-1839), called "The Patroon"; he was the eighth Patroon of Rensselaerwick. Mrs. Thayer was a Miss Van Rensselaer.

Marquess of Bute—a descendant of the Earl of Bothwell—had not long before come over to Denmark and asked and obtained permission of the King to hunt for Bothwell's tomb, as it was known that he had escaped from his dukedom in the Orkneys and finally died as a prisoner in Denmark.[1] After a while a clue was found, then the grave—relics proving that it must be Bothwell's; on opening the coffin a plate of glass lay over the face; Bute telegraphed to Copenhagen for a painter, who made a sketch of the corpse's face; the glass got disturbed, a film passed over the features, and they faded away. Lippe insisted that Sir Charles White should let him have a photograph of the painting, after which the plate was broken. It's a card photograph only—a high forehead, large aquiline nose, high cheek bones, the mouth too much fallen in to show what its real expression might have been—a ghostly, fascinating face. Lippe said he would give me one of the copies. I looked up in Froude all he has to say of Bothwell; he says no portrait of him exists, and discredits the story of the finding his grave; so does Burton, a Scotch historian, and says some learned Dane was writing a pamphlet about it which was not out when our edition of the history was published. Anyway, it's a curious riddle and it seems hardly probable that so important a state prisoner should have perished in an unrecorded grave only three hundred years ago. Won't you ask Mr. Cutter[2] if he has or can get that Danish pamphlet? (*History of Scotland*, J. H. Burton, Vol. IV, p. 472, note at foot: "Prof. Schiern etc.") I shall not breathe a doubt to the simpleminded Austrian because I want the photograph. I think I wrote you before that it was in the ancestral potato-patch of this gentleman that Varus lost his legions; it is now the principality of Lippe-Detmold.

I have always wanted to own *Bewick's Birds*, but now I've written to New York for a book I saw advertised in a chance catalogue which sounds even nicer, *Tommy Trip's History of Beasts and Birds, etc.* written by Oliver Goldsmith, illustrated by Thomas

---

[1] James Hepburn, fourth Earl of Bothwell (1536-1578), husband of Mary, Queen of Scots, who divorced him in 1570. "After the downfall of Mary, Bothwell was placed in close and solitary confinement in the castle of Dragsholm or Adelersborg in Zealand. Here he became insane, and died on April 14, 1578."
[2] Charles Ammi Cutter, librarian of the Boston Athenæum from 1869 to 1892.

Bewick in 1779,[1] only two hundred and fifty copies printed, marked "very scarce"; and also I saw catalogued a book you've long wanted—it ought to have come two days ago. I've written a second time—if it comes and is satisfactory I shall send it to you.

Thursday evening, we went to a whist and poker party at Dr. George B. Loring's; last night, dined with the German Minister and his young new wife—Eisendecker—at Wormley's, so that Henry might see and fall a prey to the beauty of Miss Langdon, Phil. Schuyler's stepdaughter, whose seat is near their table; we had a very gay dinner. The little Ministress—barely twenty, fresh from her Pomeranian nursery—is enchanted with everything, especially the *mashed potatoes*, which are new to her, and she insisted on my stirring apple-sauce into my ice-cream. After dinner Henry and I went up to the Schuylers' parlour for a call, and then at ten we went to a small tea at Countess Lewenhaupt's, where the Eisendeckers came, sat round a table with tea and little cakes, and had a nice cosy time. The Belgian Minister[2] nearly convulsed Madame Lewenhaupt by admiring my big turquoise and then telling us they are not precious stones. Have no value, and are made of *bone*! Madame Lewenhaupt is longing to quote it to Aristarchi Bey as the Turks admire turquoises, and value them especially. *Adiós*, affectionately

M. A.

WASHINGTON,
Sunday, April 1st, 1883.

DEAR PATER: Winter is still "lingering like an unloved guest." Yesterday a driving snow-storm all day and even this P.M. the trees are bending with wet snow in Lafayette Square. Five years ago today we went to Mt. Vernon, sat on the lawn in summer heat, both banks of the Potomac rosy with peach trees in full bloom all the way down. Of course this is only an "hors d'œuvre," like Roman punch before asparagus; my spring bonnet is waiting impatiently on the shelf. I divided my morning on Thursday between trimming it and reading a book of the *Iliad*, which now runs as easily as

---

[1] Thomas Bewick (1753-1828), an English wood engraver.
[2] Théodore de Bounder de Melsbroeck, Belgian Minister at Washington from 1881 to 1889.

French, and yet though I'm reading it for the fourth or fifth time I couldn't read a page of *Paradise Lost* to save my head!

We've had no gaiety this last week; only one or two things offered, which did not tempt me. Thursday Aristarchi Bey and Perry Belmont dined here and we sat over the fire till nearly midnight, the former declaring he had had a "lovely time.' He got a dispatch on Monday evening just as he was going to Mrs. Vanderbilt's ball, telling him Tevfik Bey was to succeed him;[1] the latter is a Mussulman, a pure Turk, while our friend is Greek. I fancy politics is at the bottom of it; Outrey was served in the same way, but then Aristarchi is twenty years younger. Of all scrubby trades I think diplomacy the meanest for Europeans and Americans. Henry has gone to Mrs. Turnbull's funeral. Poor woman, a broken hip and perhaps a broken heart have embittered her last years.

Nothing up here. Someone is to get Timothy Howe's place. This administration hasn't many admirers; if it manages to pull through decently it will be a relief. Bill Chandler, of unsavory fame as a lobbyist, is considered the ablest man in the Cabinet; socially he and his wife are not successful. Butler seems to be a thorn in his own State and a laughingstock outside. Why don't the Corporation of Harvard show a little *pluck* and decline to give him a degree? Everyone would respect them for it and they'll be ridiculous if they give it. Ask Ned if they really mean to give that wretched old blatherskite a public endorsement? They'd better not lower the college colours in the mud for such a man.

The book I wrote for has come; it is amusing. I shall send it off in a day or two. You can suppress the last half if you like either by excision or rebinding. Please don't forget to ask Mr. Cutter about that Danish pamphlet on Bothwell. *Adiós*, affectionately

M. A.

---

[1] Apropos of the recall of Aristarchi Bey, Henry Adams writes to Carl Schurz, March 30, 1883: "You have seen that Aristarchi is recalled. I have reason to think that he does not want to go home. His ambition is to utilise his experience and abilities on the press. He would like to take such a position as that of Blowitz on the London *Times*, and of course there is no man either in America or in Europe better fitted for such work."

1607 H STREET, WASHINGTON,
Sunday, April 8, 1883.

DEAR PATER: A quiet week just gone by with no excitements of
any kind; several warm days, today rather cooler; foliage very late,
maples in flower—but so they were a month ago. A few hepaticas
and arbutus out.

Thursday dined at Judge Gray's to meet the John Grays; he
was nice as ever. Mrs. Cameron, Miss Clymer, and Roustan, the
French Minister, made up the eight. If people would give up big
dinners of eighteen and twenty, and never exceed ten, how much
society would gain. We invited the John C. Grays to dine here tomorrow, but they were already engaged to the Bayards, and I've
yielded to a tempting invitation of Anne Palmer's, who is back
from Florida and reigning alone in New York, and am going on
tomorrow to stay till Thursday. Henry can't leave his work and
dogs, but urges me to go; and as I think I'm getting to be worse
than Mrs. Holmes, I'm going to see how single blessedness feels
after eleven years of double. Accepted an invitation to dine with
Mr. Godkin Wednesday, which he telegraphed. Miss Palmer
knows various artists and out-of-the-usual-line people, so we shall
see pictures and studios, and not shops, for two days.

Mimi and Mr. Lyman[1] are going back tomorrow A.M., and have
got my seat with them. Mimi has been shut up in the Riggs House
with a bronchial code she came on to cure. She came in to tea Friday. Mr. de Struve did not get to Boston after all; sailed for Russia
last week to bring back his wife and babies, so returned our letters
of introduction. Alex Agassiz comes on to the Academy Meeting
next Friday, and is to stay with us until Tuesday, 17th. Am glad
Culpeper reached you. Had you already seen it? I hope not. His
account of coffee berries is charming. Am glad Bil Bigelow is so
happy in Japan; Boston is so depressing to him that I doubt if he
can ever live there; and why should he? What is Adie to do?
Surely something pleasant can be found. Best love to her when
you see her. *Adiós*, affectionately

M. A.

---

[1] Mr. and Mrs. Theodore Lyman.

1607 H STREET, WASHINGTON,
Sunday, April 15, 1883.

DEAR PATER: Here I am again after a most amusing four days'
visit to New York. My hostess was charming and devoted, her father—an elderly man, not interesting—was only on hand at dinner
time. Monday evening, Mr. Schurz and Agatha and Mr. Arnold
Hague, a scientific associate of Clarence King, came to dine.
Tuesday early, went to St. Gaudens's studio. He's a friend of Miss
Palmer; unhappily he was out and we had no time to get there
again. His great bas-relief monument to Bob Shaw is very fine,
they say—Anne Palmer has seen the cast or plan. It's to be in-
serted in the wall by the sidewalk in front of the State House and a
seat under it; in low relief an infinite body of soldiers with bayo-
nets pointing up, and in front, in much higher relief, Bob Shaw on
horseback. Let us be grateful that William Story has not got this in
hand; I dislike the man and all his works. Saw the "American Artists" exhibition that same morning—as a whole, very poor, we
thought. One very striking full-length portrait of a Miss Burck-
hardt by John Sargent, a promising Philadelphia artist whom we
fell in with at Seville in 1879. This picture made a sensation in last
year's Salon—a youngish woman, not pretty, in a most severely
fascinating black satin gown; not one touch of colour anywhere,
only a white rose in her left hand. Strolled into an inner room
where Sutton has some exquisite gold lacquer, which he showed
us; suddenly I saw a big five by four picture hanging on his wall—
a Turner from top to bottom,—"Conway Castle,"—found by an
American artist, Moran, in the Island of Jersey in the hands of an
English family some years ago; he holds it at ten thousand dollars.
I wish some good Samaritan would give it to the Art Museum in
Boston. Tell Ned I saw there a superb old Chinese dish, jade colour—tracery under the dull glaze—about two feet in diameter and
turned up at right angles, a brim about three inches, deliciously
modeled, made beyond everything for five lily pads and four white
lilies—one hundred and seventy-five dollars. I don't wish to put
so much money in anything so easily broken, but it is hauntingly
fascinating. Home to lunch; only a little hunchback artist, an intimate friend of Anne Palmer, very intelligent and full of humour; he
had two pictures in the exhibition which I didn't care for. Early

six-thirty dinner, only a Dr. Stimpson—young man. Other men failing, we made the papa go as fourth; saw a roaring farce by an English troupe at the Union Square. Home to a supper of lager beer, cheese, and pretzels.

Wednesday, out early with Agatha Schurz, mousing in shops for two hours; lunched with George W. Curtis[1] at Effie's—she being in Albany watching a bill in the legislature; had an hour or more pleasant talk with Mr. Curtis. Then drove to 52d Street to see Emily Beale; found her in a dreary little hole of a room—about 12 x 7—flat on her back and low in her mind, unable to drive, having daily surgery, and in for it till June at least. Dr. Thomas promises a thorough cure. She would be more than grateful if you'd write to her, though she cannot answer. She'd had a long letter from Attorney-General Brewster the morning I saw her. From there back to Miss Palmer, and then to Mr. Beckwith's[2] studio, whose black poodle walked about on two legs sweetly; then, all three in a coupé to F. D. Millet's[3] whom I'd not seen since he was at Beverly in 1876. He was cordial, and his wife pretty and nice; and an exquisite young girl—infinitely prettier than Langtry—who was sitting as model in Eden-like costume stayed after working hours to let him drape her in many charming Eastern stuffs to amuse us. I've urged Mr. and Mrs. Millet to come on here in dogwood week—and they've half promised to—and stay with us. Dinner that evening at Godkins': Schurz, Henry James, Miss Sands, and Miss C.; the latter is most distasteful to me, a loud voice and a coarse tongue, I think, but she may be better underneath. I knew her twenty-one years ago in Lenox. We were a month together in the same boarding house. She goes this week to Cambridge to stay with her cousin.

---

[1] George William Curtis (1824-1892), an American man of letters, the political editor of *Harper's Weekly*, and president of the National Civil Service Reform League. He married, in 1856, Anna Shaw, a daughter of Robert G. Shaw and Sarah Blake Sturgis; she was an older sister of Josephine Shaw (Effie), the widow of Charles Russell Lowell.

[2] James Carroll Beckwith (1852-1917), an American portrait painter.

[3] Francis Davis Millet (1946-1912), an American artist and writer; he was a trustee of the Metropolitan Museum of Art and Secretary of the American Academy of Rome.

Had bought return tickets for Thursday, but stayed a day longer to see Barnum's Circus. Saw King's mother that morning about a school of art for Charleston, S.C., for which she is most anxious to raise money. For Allston's[1] sake it may be grateful to give them a helping hand; they'll be very glad for some good casts. I wrote to Aunt Anne two weeks ago, and Miss Folsom writes me that she (A. S. H.) will give "a hundred or so," and she thinks will just as readily make it five hundred dollars, "if you tell her it's a good thing." Won't you speak to Carrie Tappan—and perhaps Mrs. William Weld? We must help educate and cultivate a vanquished foe. Allston and Richardson show that there is seed worth forcing in that barren land.

Went to Ned's friend, Feuordant, in P.M., wishing to verify a coin—gold one—of French Minister here, who was depressed on finding that mine was in Smith's Dictionary, and his was not. From my description, Feuordant said it was struck at Panormus in Sicily, about 300 B.C., and the head with earring, that of Proserpine, etc. Then I showed him my Apollo, thinking Ned had bought it of him in 1863, but he sweetly and firmly declared it a forgery, done probably in Smyrna two hundred odd years ago, and made out a strong case, I must say. Tell Ned. It will interest him. The man is very charming, I thought; he said if it were possible that it could be what we thought, its value would be a thousand dollars!

Went that evening to Barnum's, two jolly youths dining and going with us—a Mr. Pryor and Poultney Bigelow, son of our erratic friend Mrs. John Bigelow. The show was very fine, especially the races; came home to beer, cheese, and songs by a wood fire, and many good stories. Home Friday, chatted with Mr. Harry Lee and General McClellan on the train; Henry came to the station in the victoria and we took a long drive with the pair in summer heat and came home with a big bunch of bloodroot. Henry says he's glad I enjoyed *my* week, but that it's *his* last alone, though he had a charming ladies' dinner Wednesday and a party at the British Legation Thursday. Alex came yesterday A.M. early; Philip

---

[1] Washington Allston (1779-1843), historical painter and poet; born in South Carolina; graduated at Harvard College in 1800; lived in Boston or Cambridge from 1818 until the time of his death. He was a friend of the Sturgis family, who admired his work and bought some of his pictures.

Schuyler to dinner last night; eight today. We are off in saddle now and shall find peach blossoms out today. Affectionately

M. A.

WASHINGTON,
Sunday, April 22, 1883.

DEAR PATER: A blessed rain is soaking the roots of trees and grass today and tomorrow will pelt gaily on your head; magnolia, japonica, and forsythia make a fine show opposite our windows and the rides are getting better every day; shall soon let the fire go out under my five o'clock teakettle and say "Good-bye, proud world, I'm going (*away from*) home."

Last Sunday we had to dinner Mr. and Mrs. Eisendecker, Dr. and Mrs. Loring—taking advantage of Alex Agassiz's being here, as he likes the Commissioner of Agriculture—and Miss Bayard, who made up eight; it was very pleasant and Mrs. Loring, the second and new wife, who is a fine musician, gave us some good music. Monday before breakfast we—Alex and I rather—went over Anderson's new house. It does Richardson great credit; if we had thirty thousand a year it would suit us to a *T*. Alex is anxious to buy a lot here and have Richardson build him a really simple cheap house, and I believe he can do it. Such clients as F. L. Higginson and Anderson are not educated as to what is ultimate—don't know their own minds, though the proportions are not excessive in either case—and being highly irritable, they take out their temper in railing at H. H. R., who sets many temptations before them as it's his business to; Dorsheimer and Ned have found it possible to curb his extravagance, though.

Monday Aristarchi Bey dined here quietly and Marsh came in evening. Tuesday Agassiz moved to Justice Gray's; Mr. Pumpelly[1] to tea and stayed on to dine, was charming as ever. His account of the Great Northwest on the line of the Northern Pacific is like a fairy tale. The line at this end is finished as far as Bozeman, near where he has found a great coal field on a mountain; myriads of first-class emigrants are crowding up from California—

---

[1] Raphael Pumpelly (1837-1923), then working for Henry Villard on the Northern Transcontinental Survey.

Germans and Swedes. He goes back again this summer. Among his staff of young scientific men he is most enthusiastic about a man named Eldridge, a Bostonian whose mother is or was a sister of Nathan Matthews, who has treated them ill in some way. I've no desire to go abroad again, but should like to go in a director's car over that line to the Pacific when the country is a little more settled up and to the west coast of Mexico in winter, when that country is a little more settled down. Wednesday dined with the John Fields—Alex, Weir Mitchell, Mrs. Lawrence, Miss Clymer, and Sandy Bliss; had a nice long chat with Dr. Mitchell after dinner. He is very full of fun, always comes in to tea now when he is in town.

Thursday to bed early and made Henry take my regrets to a young dance at Mrs. Bancroft Davis's, where my frisky husband even danced. Friday a dinner here—Mrs. Lawrence, Mrs. Cameron, Miss Dulaney, Marsh, Pumpelly, and Henry James, the latter charmed with Mrs. Lawrence and Mrs. Cameron, whom he had never met before. Yesterday some Britons brought me a letter from Sir John Clark, a young son of the famous Lord Lawrence, late Indian Governor-General.[1] They came to tea and brought Herbert of McCross, owner of the lakes of Killarney. Lawrence and his young wife dine here today; also James and a Mr. Richardson. Gurney's friend James Russell Soley[2] came to tea yesterday; we thought him attractive, never saw him before; also Linzee Amory, just from Florida. Marsh is much pleased at being chosen President of the Academy. President Arthur appears to have overeaten himself in Savannah; as Edwards will succeed him, we should bear his taking off with pagan fortitude. *Adiós*, affectionately

M. A.

---

[1] Herbert Alexander Lawrence (b. 1861), fourth son of the first Lord Lawrence (1811-1879), who was Viceroy of India 1864-1868.
[2] James Russell Soley (1850-1911), a professor at the United States Naval Academy; in 1883, appointed to superintend the publication of the Naval Records of the Civil War.

1607 H Street, Washington,
Sunday, April 29, 1883.

Dear Pater: Again a cool rainy Sunday so you'll probably get in tomorrow. Since Tuesday we have beaten the country far and near in the saddle, finding new paths in the forest, fording streams, and coming home decked out with cherry, peach, and unknown flowers. I found apple blossoms in the market but none quite out in the track of our ride. Have made two wire open troughs in front of lower first-floor windows, mine for plants, Henry's for dogs! Mine gay with roses red, white, and pink—blue daisies, nasturtiums hiding the wire box; Henry's neutral tint with Marquis, Possum, Friday, and Boojum. Friday is Marquis's baby, who is the "sinecure" of all eyes.

Our dissipations of the week have been: Sunday English Lawrences to dine, Henry James and Clifford Richardson; Lowndes in the evening. Tuesday a small ten o'clock toot at Mrs. John Field's; later on to Madame Catalano. Thursday Henry to a man's dinner at Wormley's given by a John A. King of New York—grave and highly respectable; I to Mrs. Pendleton's at tea, where Henry joined me—small talk of sixty or so. Was introduced to a Madame de Iturbide, who lives in Mexico, and her son Don Augustin, grandson of the Emperor Iturbide shot some sixty years ago.[1] The mama was Alice Green of this city, who married a certain Iturbide, diplomate here early in 1860 or 61. John Bigelow, ex-Minister, has an interesting paper in *Harper's* for April worth your looking up. They are well-bred and intelligent—Madame about Ellen Gurney's age—she is staying at the old family place beyond Georgetown and I mean to drive out and call on her some day this week. She goes to Mexico in a few weeks, says it's charming from May to September in that city, so in three or four years when the railway is done we think we'll take a summer there instead of Beverly.

---

[1] Augustine de Iturbide (1783-1824); under his leadership the last of the Spanish Viceroys was forced to recognize the independence of Mexico; he was elected and crowned as Emperor, July 21, 1822; he was forced to abdicate the nineteenth of March following, and was deported to Italy. He returned, however, the following year—not knowing that in the meantime he had been outlawed—and was captured and shot, July 15, 1824.

9:30 P.M. Had to break off there, so, having no guests, I'll finish this for tonight's box. Friday evening a young and very small
dance at the Bancroft Davises' to which we went as lookers-on
with a few other middle-aged folks. Yesterday a long ride over
ground invaded by Early in his raid on Washington in 1864, July.
We forded a stream in a wild valley under the once-frowning forti-
fications of Fort de Russy, the frown smoothed into a senile smile.
The clouds opened on us as we wound up the heights, with pelting
rain and hot sun's rays at the same time producing the sensation of
a Turkish bath. This P.M. consecrated to some calls; one on a
charming Spanish lady, Madame Puy de Lome, newly come—her
husband Secretary of Legation[1] and said to be very intelligent and
given to books; the señora is very handsome. Mrs. Lawrence and
sister, Mr. Field, and Bessels dropped in to tea.

Think we shall go next week for two days to Luray Cave in the
Shenandoah Valley, and the beautiful Miss Langdon is going with
us—several others too, though it's to be no one's party, only a
chance meeting of a few congenial spirits; the early spring in that
valley is enchanting, they say, and the cave a great sight. Have just
finished *The Blockade and the Cruisers* by J. R. Soley, Gurney's
friend. It's deeply interesting and well told. Do get it if you've not
already. Soley, who married a daughter of one of the *nine* Miss
Woolseys, of whom you and I met seven at Conway in 1857, has
come here to live; he came to tea one day not long ago and we
thought him very nice. His wife has a six-weeks baby, but I fancy
will come and dine pretty soon. This place is rapidly drawing
many men other and better than politicians and may have a good
effect on that predatory horde. Our former acquaintance Senator
Fair seems to be a bad lot if the insinuations of today's paper are
correct, even worse than Senator Tabor of Colorado, for whose
disgusting behavior during a term of thirty days the late Senate
blushed. Tabor is said in ordering a carriage from a stable here to
have ordered four horses and "mind you give me a driver with a
tall hat and one of them red bugs on the side of it." I think I ought

---

[1] Señor Don Enrique Dupuy de Lome, First Secretary of the Spanish Legation at
Washington. At the outbreak of the Spanish War, he was the Spanish Minister
there.

to tell Brent to console him for being denied "one of them bugs."
Adiós

CLOVER

1607 H STREET, WASHINGTON,
Sunday, May 6th, 1883.

DEAR PATER: I shall be surprised, if I ever get to Heaven, to find a
better day than this. The park opposite is fully green and my wire
balcony is gay with roses and heliotrope and blue daisies. It rained
up and down yesterday afternoon and evening, and the weather
map has no "low" west of us now, which is a matter of importance
to us, as we start tomorrow for the Cave of Luray in the Shenandoah Valley. We—so far as at present known—being Mr. and
Mrs. Eisendecker, the German Minister and his charming little
twenty-year-old wife, Miss Chapman (Mrs. Lawrence's sister),
Miss Lucy Frelinghuysen, Mr. Lowndes, Henry, and I; I fancy
some more men will join us—Miss Langdon and Miss Mercer
have given out. We start at ten A.M. for Point of Rocks, wait two
hours at Shenandoah Junction for a train—shall lunch *al fresco*—
and go down or rather up the valley, reach Luray by five P.M.,
where a new inn is said to be very good, with wood fires, etc. This
is a picture of it. Tuesday, we shall give to the cave and the country, and some or all go on Wednesday to Natural Bridge and home
via Lexington. We wish much to see all the valley, which at this
season ought to be delightful. How I wish you were going with us;
I know you would enjoy the company and all; it's my invention,
too, so I feel responsible.

We've been riding far and hard this last week, one day to
Rockville beyond Bladensburg and home through that picturesque
old town, the country a mass of colour—pink, red, yellow, and
white. We shall hang on here as long as possible; we miss the
country so at Beverly. We meet no nickel-plated harnesses in our
rides here with stockbrokers behind them—sooner or later they'll
drive us all away, I fear. We have solved the problem here at last
of cheap transportation. The city is now well set up with the best
London hansoms—twenty-five cents a trip—and single herdics—
cabs holding four inside, folding door behind, low step, light inside, two very high wheels—also twenty-five cents each trip. Now

it seems to me that one of these cabs would be very nice for your depot work and taking chicks to the beach—four sliding glass windows and so perfect protection against rain, small striped awnings against hot sun when wanted. Those high express wagons are desperate to get in and out of. If we ever went to town I should set up a herdic, but as it is it would never be used. I'm going to write to Peter Herdic of Philadelphia and ask the price, and also if they cannot have *four* wheels, which are easier on a steep rise. Please read or tell this to Ellen and see if it doesn't fire her young soul.

Miss Beale has come home, most unexpectedly, after three months in hospital—completely cured, the doctor says. She had an internal twist which has been straightened out. I have not seen her yet as she has so many visitors and has to be kept rather quiet. As it had been supposed that she had an incurable malady, the verdict is very cheering to her family and friends. Mrs. Adams writes Henry on May 4th that Hattie Thayer is engaged, but did not give the man's name, so I had to send over to the Beales to learn that it's John F. Andrew. I am so glad she has gone out of the Beacon Street crowd; she's a very nice sensible girl and her money will go to the right spot. I took a fancy to the second sister, who was here this winter, and saw her several times. Also Mrs. Adams speaks of "Mrs. Peabody's sad and touching death"; what Mrs. Peabody— and when? I think you wrote me that both Gertrude and Rosamond Lawrence Peabody were ill. When I go north in summer, I never dare to ask for anyone's wife or husband or child; so give me a marriage and death column, weekly—births, I'm not interested in especially. I cannot write any more, the birds are singing Sunday hymns in their newly furnished choirs omitting neither third nor fourth stanzas—all-day-long hymns. *Adiós*, your affectionate

M. A.

1607 H STREET, WASHINGTON,
Sunday, May 13, 1883.

DEAR PATER: I'm sitting by an open window behind a screen of roses and heliotrope, partly writing to you and keeping my left eye on the "miserable sinners" who are going by to church in very good clothes. I fancy no prayer-book repentance would bring them to confess that their Sunday clothes are bad—those are no matter of heredity, but so very personal.

We went on our expedition on Monday and had a charming three days' outing, not a drop of rain; passed "John Brown's fort" at Harper's Ferry at noon; had two hours to wait at Shenandoah Junction, which we spent in a grove near the station lunching, Mr. Lowndes and I boiling water for tea, which was very good. The party grew to nine: Mr. and Mrs. Eisendecker, Miss Lucy Frelinghuysen, Miss Fanny Chapman, Mr. John Field, Mr. Lowndes, Captain Story, and Henry and I. At three P.M., we took the train up the valley, which was even more beautiful than we expected; the Blue Ridge justifies its name, the Shenandoah River is most picturesque, the banks lined with flowers, while dogwood and red-bud trees fill all the middle distance. Now and then the ruins of a stone house or mill remind us that we were among the old battle fields and in the valley which Sheridan ploughed so deeply. Mr. Lowndes had been up and down that country, even fighting at Bull Run, and could tell us many stories of the enemy's movements—to him it must seem a hideous far-off dream. Got to Luray at five P.M., found a most ideal "early English inn" like a very large and pretty country house, built on a slope in an amphitheatre of mountains. The first story of bluish limestone, wood above, deep wide piazzas, immense fireplaces five and six feet wide for logs, handsome rugs, curtains, and modern furniture; bedrooms with open fireplaces, cherry furniture, spring beds, hot and cold baths; and an excellent table, jet-black negresses in white mob caps flitting about, and in short, as one of the party said, "just like a charming country house without the bore of a hostess." That evening we rested, as it was very warm; I made them Russian tea at ten o'clock in the hall and then we broke up.

Tuesday, after breakfast, drove a mile or so to the cave, which is very large and cool and fascinating, lighted in many places by electricity; that took nearly two hours. When we came out into the light we sat in a row in the sun to be "shined" as to boots. My boy, who looked like a *réduction sauvage* of Scipio Africanus, staggered under the title of "Saint Elmo." Mr. Lowndes told him Brer Rabbit stories which convulsed his saintly features with secular giggles. We went home to dinner at two-thirty; then naps, talk, tea, whist, more tea, and bed.

Back to Manassas Junction on Wednesday, at Front Royal an hour's halt for a train to Alexandria on the Virginia Midland; another lunch under the trees; then a ride of several hours through Thoroughfare Gap, past Bull Run Gap, and so on by Manassas to Alexandria; caught a boat for Washington and cooled off with a half hour just at sunset on the river, and so home for dinner at eight o'clock, everyone agreeing as we parted that it had been a great success from first to last.

Thursday, some thirty of the men of Henry's age and younger gave Aristarchi Bey a farewell dinner at Wormley's, no foreigners, except Charlton and Howard of the British Legation[1] and Willamov (Russian), being let in; those three swore they were *not* foreigners and *would* join. Late in the evening came to me the huge basket of roses from the table with "Mr. Walker Blaine's compliments"! That wise and pleasant young man lets it be understood that he takes up none of his father's quarrels. Perry Belmont spoke at the dinner and extremely well, Henry said, and Jerome Bonaparte told me that Henry made a "lovely speech"; they all said it went off finely. Yesterday, Messrs Saurin, Charlton, and Johnstone,[2] secretaries of the British Legation, gave a small Belshazzar at Wormley's farm and kindly asked us. I gave out, not feeling very smart; Henry dropped in on horseback and found a regular seated dinner of twenty or thirty going on—band of music, etc.—and apologized and slipped off before dark. I supposed it was to be a large informal tea-nic only, so wrote a humble explanation and apology in the evening; Mrs. Cameron, from under the window, tells me they kept it up with dancing till nine-thirty. Today, Madame Catalano dines here, and her brother Willamov; she sails for Russia on Wednesday with three babies, one immense dog, and an alligator. Mr. John Jay happened in to tea yesterday, so I asked him, as his daughter is the wife of the German Ambassador at St. Petersburg; he can send messages by this little Russian lady. Poor Mrs. John Hay will get the sad news of her father's death on land-

---

[1] Henry Howard (1843-1921), then Second Secretary of the British Legation at Washington; he had married in 1867 Cecilia, daughter of George Riggs, the Washington banker.

[2] The Honorable Alan Johnstone, then Third Secretary of the British Legation at Washington.

ing next Saturday—Amasa Stone of Cleveland, who leaves six million dollars and only two daughters. John Hay wrote to ask if we could meet them in New York and have a little fun together. It will come hard to them. *Adiós*

M. A.

1607 H Street, Washington,
Sunday, May 20, 1883.

DEAR PATER: Nothing very new under the burning sun of the week just gone, except trees and flowers. Sunday, Madame Catalano and Mr. de Willamov and Mr. John Jay dined here; the first sailed for Russia on Wednesday to pass the summer on a lake twelve hours from St. Petersburg. Good-bye is being said here daily now. Monday, had to breakfast Madame de Iturbide and her son, Miss Meyer, and Mr. Field. Tuesday, Mrs. Cameron to breakfast. Wednesday evening, a small farewell tea for her—only sixteen in all: we had ice-cream and strawberries and champagne and drank her bon voyage. She stayed till nearly one A.M. and left for New York and Europe early the next morning; we shall miss her much. I fancy "Don" will not come back to the Senate anyway; will perhaps make a trade with some Republican; if he resigned, as he ought, it would bring in a Democrat and so give that party a casting vote. As things are now balanced and as he is a pal of President Arthur, that will not be allowed. He's going into railroading again, it is said. Wednesday, General Walker and Miss Lucy Frelinghuysen breakfasted here.

Your scheme of low *succursale* by Richardson sounds charming, I hope you have it under weigh already; to combine playroom and study is original, to say the least, like grog shop and chapel. I fear you'll find five young ones too much for you, but we can always take two off your hands if you do.

Thursday, Mrs. Lawrence had a large farewell dinner to Aristarchi Bey—speech making, etc. Colonel Bonaparte took me in, had Count Leyden,[1] a new German Secretary of Legation, on left—quite intelligent. Today, we've a duty dinner, Mr. and Mrs. Griswold of Bangor, Maine,—*tout ce qu'il y a de plus* Bangor,—a

---

[1] Count Casimir von Leyden.

former scholar of Henry's, clerk in library here; Dwight of State Department to help us through. Am going to take a photo with my new machine this P.M. at Rock Creek—Brent driving, three dogs, machine, and us. I sent a photo to Adie to your care, not knowing where she is. *Adiós*, affectionately

M. A.

WASHINGTON,
Sunday, 3 P.M., May 17.

DEAR PATER: I've only time to send you a short screed before riding, the day having slipped away. Nothing to tell you. Sunday, Aristarchi Bey came to lunch and say good-bye, and I photographed him as a "dude"—small straw hat on his head; but, alas! It is not a success and I fear will not print; I'm not skilled yet—and Henry, which is so good, is really owing to Richardson. Had our duty dinner Sunday evening and it went off very well. No society this week; now that we take our daily ride late, dining at seven-thirty, we see none of the people who used to drop in to tea. Emily Beale to breakfast Friday—thin and pale and none of her old go, but it may come back with health. Tonight, Mr. Bancroft, Mr. and Mrs. Soley, and a Miss Morse of Louisiana—clerk in the Department of Justice—are to dine here. Mr. Bancroft sent me a superb lot of roses from his garden, so that I sent mine to someone else; I've picked four dozen yesterday and today—red, pink, and yellow—and shall have bushels this next week or two.

The weather is perfect, and we don't fix any time for breaking up, a process we hate. Thanks for your invitation to the dogs, but they go now by sea with Brent and are in his care.

Have you read General Humphreys's *Virginia Campaign*?[1] He has honoured me by sending me a copy as from himself; Henry was already deep in it, and found it most interesting but very hard reading. Humphreys is very attractive; but since his daughter's death four years ago, they are never seen in society and he will not even dine out. I hope that in your next letter I shall hear that you've broken ground for Richardson's annex; I wish you'd have it

---

[1] General Andrew Atkinson Humphreys (1810-1883); after the Civil War he was on duty at Washington as Chief of Engineers until he retired in 1879.

of cobblestones, like Mr. Fred Ames's lodge that is fascinating. Is there no chance that some choice spirits will hire the Fred Dexters'? We want a few middle-aged pals very much—the N——s and we haven't very much in common. Does he improve on acquaintance—develop a few vices, that is? Love to Aunt Eunice; I hope she will be in town till really warm weather. *Adiós*, affectionately

M. A.

EPILOGUE

Clover Adams took her own life on Sunday, December 6, 1885. She was buried in Washington, in the Rock Creek Cemetery, which was then a quiet, unfrequented churchyard. There, thirty-two years later, Henry Adams was buried at her side in accordance with the following direction contained in his will of November 27, 1908:

"I direct my executors to see that my body is buried by the side of my deceased wife, and that no inscription, date, letters or other attempt at memorial, except the monument I have already constructed, shall be placed over or near our graves."

In 1886, a year after the death of Clover Adams, Henry Adams commissioned the noted sculptor Augustus Saint-Gaudens to make the figure for the monument and Stanford White to design its granite setting. The monument was not completed until 1891, a year or more after it had been promised, and Adams was much concerned at the delay as well as anxious as to the success of the sculptor in interpreting his idea.

Saint-Gaudens's name for the monument's hooded and seated bronze figure is "The Mystery of the Hereafter and The Peace of God that Passeth Understanding," but the public commonly called it "Grief," an appellation that Henry Adams heartily disliked.

SELECTED BIBLIOGRAPHY

Adams, Henry. *Democracy: An American Novel*, 1880. Reprinted in the Library of America. See entry below on *Esther*.

—— *The Education of Henry Adams: An Autobiography*. Boston and New York: Houghton Mifflin, 1918. Reprinted many times. Conveniently available in the Library of America edition, cited in the following entry.

—— *Esther* [Frances Snow Compton, pseudo.], 1884. In *Novels, Mont Saint Michel, The Education*, ed. Ernest Samuels and Jayne N. Samuels. New York: Library of America, 1983.

—— *The Letters of Henry Adams*, 6 vols., ed. J. C. Levenson et al. Cambridge, MA: Harvard University Press, 1982-1988.

—— *Supplement to The Letters of Henry Adams*, 2 vols., ed. J. C. Levenson et al. Boston: Massachusetts Historical Society, 1989.

Byrd, Max. *Grant: A Novel*. New York: Bantam Books, 2000.

Friedrich, Otto. *Clover: The Tragic Love Story of Clover and Henry Adams and Their Brilliant Life in America's Gilded Age*. New York: Simon and Schuster, 1979.

Kaledin, Eugenia. *The Education of Mrs. Henry Adams*, 2nd ed. Amherst, MA: University of Massachusetts Press, 1994.

Nagel, Paul C. *Descent from Glory: Four Generations of the John Adams Family*. New York: Oxford University Press, 1983.

—— *The Adams Women: Abigail and Louisa Adams, Their Sisters and Daughters*. New York: Oxford University Press, 1987.

O'Toole, Patricia. *The Five of Hearts: An Intimate Portrait of Henry Adams and His Friends*, 1880-1918. New York: Clarkson Potter, 1990.

Roberts, Cokie. *Founding Mothers: The Women Who Raised Our Nation*. New York: HarperCollins, 2004.

Samuels, Ernest. *Henry Adams*, 3 vols. Cambridge, MA: Harvard University Press, 1947-1964. Abridged in 1 vol., 1989.

Vidal, Gore. *Empire: A Novel*. New York: Random House, 1987.

NOTE: The edition of *The Letters of Henry Adams* used in Ward Thoron's notes is that edited by Worthington C. Ford, New York, 1930. The edition of *The Education of Henry Adams* used is the first edition, New York, 1918.